Missed, Liquid Firm: An Essay on Risk, Finance, and Firm

Hun Seog

Tonekey

eBook: ISBN-13: 979-8-9946545-0-7
Paperback: ISBN-13: 979-8-9946545-1-4

Cover design by: TNC

To Nha

ABOUT THE BOOK

Hun Seog is a professor of insurance and finance at the Seoul National University Business School. He has authored books and articles on capitalism, firm, insurance and finance.

This book is an essay-style writing by an economist that challenges the fundamental epistemes and axioms of modern economics and business studies. It employs imagination—grounded in anthropology, philosophy, and sociology—to reveal the mythological and magical dimensions of capitalism. The discussion intersects with economics and finance while drawing on the ideas of Mauss, Polanyi, Foucault, Deleuze, Marx, and Weber, among others. At its core, the book examines essential components of the capitalist system, such as risk, money, and trade, along with the institutions that embody them, including insurance, finance, markets, and firms. It also addresses recent global events, such as the 2008 financial crisis and the COVID-19 pandemic.

MISSED, LIQUID FIRM

AN ESSAY ON RISK, FINANCE, AND FIRM

HUN SEOG

CONTENTS

PREFACE

Modern economics and business studies discuss individuals, markets, and corporations within the framework of capitalism, and also explore the nature and role of governments and institutions. This book is an essay-like writing that questions the fundamental episteme and axioms of economics and business studies, re-examining their meanings.

The core themes of this book are the essential components of the capitalist system, such as risk, money, and trade, as well as the institutions that embody them, including insurance, finance, markets, and firms. It also addresses recent global events, such as the 2008 financial crisis and the COVID-19 pandemic.

To understand the modern economy, what we need is imagination. Imagination is needed not for absurd fantasy, but to recognize that the rationality and scientific rigor upon which economics and business studies are presumed to rest may not be as solid as they appear. Thus, we seek to depict capitalism through the lens of mythology, ritual, magic, and alchemy.

Moreover, risk, finance, and firm can be understood through the three states of matter—gas, liquid, and solid. Such metaphors are already embedded in our language and thought. These states transform, move, and interact, reviving the forgotten medieval alchemy in modern times. While capitalism may be partially explained through science and rational calculation, it can only be fully understood through the eyes of myth, ritual, and alchemy.

1. MYTH

When the heavenly gods looked down under the clouds, they saw beautiful rivers and mountains. There were green trees and beautiful flowers, and various animals and insects were running around. Yet, a lament echoed among the gods, for there existed no beings akin to them, endowed with intellect and reason. Thus, they shaped figures from clay, laying them upon the earth and calling them "humans."

Contrary to the gods' hopes, these humans did not rise above their bestial companions. They lived in harmony with the creatures around them, often behaving and thinking in ways reminiscent of their wild counterparts. Disappointed, the deities sought to create a being more akin to themselves. However, their plans were met with opposition from the god of the underworld, who feared such a creation would disrupt the delicate balance between the divine and mortal realms.

Despite these objections, gods took mortal spouses and begot offspring—beings known as demigods, half divine and half human. These demigods possessed abilities far beyond ordinary mortals: they could peer into the future, navigate through darkness and fog as if it were daylight, and wield powers akin to immortality, commanding the elements at their whim. Thus, they could move and manipulate everything in the world as they wished.

Yet, unlike the gods whose powers seemed boundless, demigods harbored a singular vulnerability: they were mortal in the face of blazing fire. Fire, the wrathful domain of the underworld deity, wielded power over them, capable of melting their bodies and bringing about their demise. Demigods could not evade the retribution of the underworld god, a reminder of their dual nature and the precarious balance they embodied between mortal fragility and divine prowess.

Demigods found solace in the cool embrace of running water, delighting in its gentle currents as they bathed and played within its depths. The constant flow enveloped their divine forms, a protective barrier against the searing threat of fire. Beneath the shimmering surface, they nurtured dreams of eternal life, untouched by the mortal dangers that lurked beyond.

If they kept away from burning fire, they could enjoy eternal life. Based on their superior abilities, these demigods divided and ruled the world as superior god-like beings. The world gradually became richer.

Yet, as their reign continued, they grew indifferent to the welfare of the humans they ruled. The demigod rulers erected temples adorned with their images and idols across the land, compelling human beings to worship and obey them. Those who defied them faced severe punishment. The happiness of humans no longer mattered; what counted was the number of temples built in honor of the rulers. Domination of the world turned into a game, a competition among the demigods to control more territory. The human beings who once welcomed the demigods' rule now cursed them and fought among themselves.

As jealousy and strife among the demigods intensified, they eventually did not shy away from deadly competition with one another. One day, they heard a story about a mountain with the highest peak on Earth, from which hot red liquid was flowing down. They decided to make a wager: whoever could endure the red liquid the longest would rule all the land. That red liquid was lava flowing from a volcano. The lava, possessing the qualities of both flowing water and burning fire, posed a deadly risk even to the demigods. Yet, blinded by jealousy and rivalry, they forced themselves into the molten lava. The ability to foresee the future, once possessed by the demigods, failed to function in the face of this grave crisis, and they were unable to grasp the danger ahead. Those who leaped into the lava fell victim to the curse of the underground god and lost their lives. Their bodies, engulfed by the lava, disintegrated, dissolved, and flowed away, disappearing without a trace.

The humans, mere spectators from a distance, stood paralyzed by indecision. They despised the demigods who had ruled over them with brutality. Yet, now faced with the sudden absence of their rulers, a profound unease gripped their hearts. They had never dared to conceive a world free from divine dominion, and the uncertainty of what lay ahead filled them with dread. Before their eyes, the air shimmered and quivered under the relentless assault of molten lava's searing heat.

**

The modern economy and society in which we live are full of myths. In those myths, firms, markets, and finance appear as heroes, creating adventure stories. What makes myths interesting and meaningful is the adversity that befalls them, or the connections and flows, such as chance and fate. In modern myths, these connections are made by risk, money, and trade. In fact, what makes a myth a true myth is the adversity and fate that the hero faces rather than the hero himself, the visible protagonist. The journey to understand modern myths must start with risk, money, and trade.

2. RISK

Risk And Variability

When confronted with the question of what is a risk, many will answer simply with the possibility or concern that something bad will happen. These answers also represent our feelings of danger in our daily life. These answers can also be found in dictionaries. The Merriam-Webster dictionary defines risk as "the possibility of loss or injury." The Oxford English dictionary similarly describes risk as "the possibility of loss, injury, or other adverse or unwelcome circumstance; a chance or situation involving such a possibility."

On the other hand, economics textbooks often define risk as the uncertainty of the future, which is often likened to variability. Reading the textbooks, we tend to accept this notion: "Yes. There's a risk because you don't know what's going to happen." At first glance, this definition seems similar to the everyday feeling mentioned above.

However, this is an illusion. A little further thought reveals that the uncertainty in the future is not only different, and sometimes contradictory, to the common sense feeling that something bad will happen. If we passed by a building that would almost certainly collapse due to poor construction, we would feel very risky and anxious. We will all say that the risk is great. If you are a true economist, however, you have to say that risk is low because there is little variability or uncertainty.

In reality, we do not even think of the word 'uncertainty' as separate from the words 'fear' and 'adversity'. If uncertainty is referred to as risk, then uncertainty refers to the possibility of loss or suffering, not simple variability. That is, uncertainty does not isomorphically correspond to variability. Uncertainty becomes variability only in certain circumstances, such as in economics textbooks or when calculating profits.

In this way, the common-sense notion of risk is twisted in economics. "Risk is something that can have both good and bad consequences. Risk is not all bad." say. Economics develops cold-hearted formulas for variability as if observing the worries of the world from a far distance.

Presumably, this bias toward risk in economics stems from mathematical convenience. Even when actuarial science first introduced risk to mathematics in the 17th century, risk meant gambling to make money. After all, isn't gambling a game that focuses on winning money rather than losing money? When focusing on returns, risk is read as variability.

Or look at a pendulum swinging from side to side, or a spring swinging up and down. The movement of such an object is not fixed, so it must be uncertain. Whether the pendulum is on the left or on the right, what is good or bad? It is just moving without heart. Mathematics and physics would have had to come up with a name for the degree of deviation from the mean, the central point. And scientists in the plight of language just took the expedient of calling it a risk. And as a result of that very expedient, the term risk confuses us. Both the potential for harm and the heartless variability have come to be called risk.

In the modern age of scientists and economists who want to be like scientists, they dominate the language of society. Thus, their prejudices and delusions are also placed on language and press on our consciousness. They say, " I will enlighten you on your ignorance and prejudice. Risk is not bad, just variability."

But they also shout that it is risky next to a collapsing building. What they truly do not know are their own prejudices and oblivion. The only time risk becomes variability is when they scribble mathematical formulas on paper.

And here comes linguistics. Risk, as the possibility of misfortune, is the risk that is with us. Such risks are those that the speaker actually feels and perceives. That is, risk exists as a subject. This risk exists alongside or next to the subject. In contrast, in economics, risk exists as variability. Risk exists as an object in the distance. The difference between the subject and the object is the difference between the risk perceived by ordinary people and the risk found in economics textbooks. Nevertheless, economics tries to put the object in the place of the subject, not in its original place. This is a gesture aimed at returning the position that has been repositioned since Kant back to the time of Plato. That's why it becomes awkward.

Economics emphasizes variability because we are living in an era of capitalism. In the era of capitalism, all of us we have to focus on profit and success. Therefore, risk should be interpreted as variability despite our feeling. Just as the interest in gambling attempted to calculate the risk in the seventeenth century, the risk calculation in modern economics is always interpreted with an emphasis on profit. That is, in our time risk should be read as variability rather than dangerous. This is because risk should always be connected to the opportunity for profit.

This is the perception and language that capitalism requires. But is it because the pace of development of capitalism is too fast? It seems that the perceptions and linguistic habits in most of us have not yet evolved to fit capitalism.

Risk And Pollution

But risk doesn't just mean that something bad will possibly happen. People have attached meaning and emotion to risk beyond mere possibility. After all, isn't life a process of going through countless risks? How can life be replaced by simple possibilities? It is precisely at this point that the difficulty in understanding risk lies. Each person may perceive risks differently. For some it might be a matter of self-esteem, for others it might be a fiercely blazing flame. In this way, risk is not something that can be grasped, nor does it take on a certain form.

For some people, risk becomes pollution (Mary Douglas, 2001). We often have an obsession with purity and cleanliness. Pure blood, pure love, clean body and mind, purification rituals... Purity is beautiful, clean and unpolluted. People are attached to purity. However, this excessive attachment with purity manifests as a pathological obsession throughout human history. The history of human struggle may be the history of the long struggle between those who want to preserve the pure lineage and those who deny it.

To the pure, therefore, the risk is pollution and infection. See the taboos listed in the Christian Bible. In Leviticus, animals that do not have split hoofs or do not ruminate, and fish without fins and scales are forbidden to be eaten. What about the taboos in the Islamic Qur'an, Hindu and Buddhist scriptures? Such taboos are merely the result of mythical imagination and lack the precision of logic to rationalize them. Some have tried to justify them. Hygiene purpose, tools for cleanliness, philosophical meanings, etc. Perhaps some of such rationales might apply at first. But even in an era when such grounds no longer existed, taboos have been observed. It is because in their imagination and narratives those taboos are already established as opposites to divinity and purity. So what further justification is needed? Besides saying that those taboos are just a product of myth.

Risk is something that contaminates purity. What are contaminants? Contaminants are not just given, but are determined by where they are located and how they are summoned (Douglas, 2001). Shoes are pure when they are outside the house, but even the cleanest shoes become contaminants when placed on the sofa. Food is pure when it is on the table, but becomes contaminants when it is on the bed. Something becomes contaminants not because it is dirty, but because it is decoded as contamination.

Above all else, those who harm the reproduction of the species and the well-being of the ruling group become contaminants. So historically, the resistance of slaves or the protest of the weak have been treated as contaminants and have been purified. It is in the same vein that strangers and other tribes who have committed minor intrusions also degenerate into objects to be purified. Strangers and others fall victim to violence without the perpetrator's awareness (Rene Girard, 2007). Purity is maintained only by disinfection or removal before contamination spreads. There are no weak or victimized contaminants. Contaminants are objects of purification that must be thoroughly disinfected and cannot be victims. Thus, the scapegoat is sacrificed without people being aware of it. Herein lies the cruelty of history.

Ultimately, what is decoded as pollution and how to deal with it will depend on the perception and mindset of a society or group (Douglas and Wildavsky, 1983). An authoritarian society will promise to take swift and decisive action against pollution that can harm society, while an individualistic society will emphasize a relatively autonomous response as each person's interests are intertwined. In this way, a risk is interpreted differently depending on the perception and way of thinking of society. The same source of pollution is a risk in some societies but is ignored or just read as an opportunity for profit in others. In this sense, a risk becomes something chosen, not something that exists.

Risk And Trauma

Even when we limit risk to the likelihood of something bad happening, our emotions are quite different from mathematical calculations (Paul Slovic, 1987; Slovic et al., 2004). People do not apply strict mathematical standards to risks that are unfamiliar to them or rare risks that could cause significant harm. People are known to be excessively afraid of the risk of low probability - high severity.

Mathematical calculations are precise only for simple risks, such as a game of dice. In the case of complex risks, simple experience and probability calculations become meaningless. Risk is something that feels too complex and multidimensional to be expressed as a one-dimensional number stuck between 0 and 1. People project their desires and emotions/affects onto the object of risk.

Experts familiar with mathematical calculations tend to think that only numbers should represent risk. Experts always try to reduce to a formula, even where that is not possible. Even though mathematical probability is just a closed and cramped compact space on a one-dimensional line, it tries to squeeze all the risks in the world into that narrow space. People often ignore probability sometimes because they are not familiar with mathematics, and other times because they feel cramped in a small space. At this point, the conversation between experts and the general public is cut off. The misunderstanding of probability calculation and the misunderstandings about the multidimensionality of risk reproach each other.

A drastic shock that cannot be handled remains as a trauma. When does a shock become a trauma? Sigmund Freud makes a distinction between the shock that I caused myself and the shock that others caused to me. The latter shock that penetrates my defense mechanism remains traumatic when I am helpless: "It happened to me." The way to overcome this trauma is to transform it into something I can control and handle. That is, it should be changed to "I made it happen."

Risk can also become trauma. While the possibility of future harm that I create and accept can be simply called a risk, the possibility of harm that I will suffer helplessly goes beyond a simple risk and becomes a trauma. Sociologist Niklas Luhmann (1993) called this trauma a "danger" to distinguish it from a risk. If Freud's prescription is correct, the solution to this trauma would be to involve myself in the harm. When harm is placed within my control, trauma is reduced to the category of everyday risk. If I can participate in decisions that can possibly harm me, a danger can turn into a risk.

Then who creates the trauma? Who are the persons who inflict the harm that I will suffer helplessly? It is, after all, powerful persons with power. The public powers of government and judicial institutions neutralize the power of ordinary citizens and disarm us in the name of the public good. See the conflict between the local community and the central government over the construction of garbage dumps, power plants, etc. The government blames the ignorance of local residents, but it is the government officials who are truly ignorant. They do not know the direction in which the local residents are looking, something they can tell right away just by looking at their eyes. Local residents are talking about the trauma caused by the government's unilateral decision and notification. Government officials pretend not to know that mathematical probability values are not a cure for the trauma.

Another trauma trigger in the capitalist era is the wealthy and their businesses. Firms take the pursuit of profit as their calling, and remove any obstacles to the fulfillment of that calling. Trauma occurs to those who are removed and abandoned in that way: urban planning, development projects, stock price manipulation, the collusion between politics and business, etc. Firms rush to fulfill their calling in various fields and sow trauma as a by-product. Nuclear accidents in Three Mile Island (1979), Chernobyl (1986), and Fukushima (2011), Union Carbide 's Bhopal gas accident in India (1984), Samsung Heavy Industries Taean oil spill (2007), BP oil in the Gulf of Mexico The spill (2010), the sinking of the Sewol ferry (2014), the global financial crisis (1997, 2008)... Firms and governments produce trauma, sometimes independently and sometimes jointly.

And there are so-called experts between the government and firms. Those in power often leverage the aura of science. Experts such as scientists, engineers, and economists work hard in their respective roles, advising the government and participating in corporate decision-making. They may play their role faithfully in their respective fields. Nevertheless, or precisely because of it, they help produce trauma.

And those in power not only use the power of science, but also hide the trauma they have caused by choosing and forcing an appropriate scapegoat. Now the risk is shifted away from the powerful and passed on to the scapegoat in the name of science.

Pure Blood

On the other hand, aren't governments and firms just part of the enveloping system? Ultimately, those who control the system will become the perpetrators. At this point, the pure bloodline might still be important. The systems of government, politics, firms, and management are influenced by a large number of people. However, in the meantime, the pure-blood hordes control and manipulate the system through various channels to prevent contamination and preserve their purity and symbolism.

So what does pure bloodline mean? Pure blood refers to blood lineage being continuously maintained and passed down through offspring. The lineage in the capitalist society of the 21st century is somewhat different from that of a tribal state or dynasty. Of course, pedigree is still important to the parties involved. But the most important lineage in capitalism is not a person's lineage. It is money or capital (Deleuze and Guattari, 2014). Blood capital, the money that runs through blood line, constitutes the most important pure blood. Offspring are not only born to humans or living things. Capital also gives birth to offspring called interest and profit. It is this bloodline of capital that constitutes the most important pure lineage. The pure blood of capitalism that must be constantly multiplied and maintained is capital and money.

Nevertheless, the essence of blood ties in the past and blood capital in the capitalist era is the same. The same analogy holds for the tracing of genealogy and the stages of succession. Here we see that the appearance of modern society has not changed much from that of the mythical society. The symbols of purity and authority have simply changed from blood and gold to capital and banknotes.

Even at the moment when we ridicule the class-based lineageism of the past as pre-modern, we do not feel suspicious about the lineageism of capital. Efforts to earn even a penny more in interest from investment do not feel much different from the gesture of trying to have more offspring for the prosperity of the family. It was probably so in the past too. In the past, it would have been difficult for people to realize the problems about the world they lived in. Our way of thinking can also become a laughing stock for our descendants. We still haven't escaped from lineageism. We are still unable to wake up from the world of myth.

Risk And Gas

Above all, risk is the future. Accidents or damage that have already occurred are no longer a risk. Before the accident occurred, it must have been someone's risk. However, if an accident had occurred, the accident may have already scarred the victim or possibly swallowed him up. Wounds are no longer a risk, but pain and suffering. Wounds and damage are only the realization of risk and are not the risk itself. No, it may be more accurate to say that it is a trace of realization rather than a realization. In any case, a risk can exist only on the premise that it has not yet occurred. It is a contradiction that risk exists only on the premise of non-existence. The irony is that risk disappears at the very moment it reveals its existence.

The pain of risk exists not only because it is realized and leaves scars, but also because it is feared from the fact that it has not been realized. Is the pain of hurt greater or the pain of fear greater?

The risk exists there or over there rather than here. The moment we feel risk, the risk is not here, but there. And the risk is only coming towards us, here. Risk is constantly moving from there to here, or from that side to this direction. Maybe it exists in multiple places at the same time. And yet its sharp tip always points towards us. But exactly the moment it gets here, the risk disappears and only pain remains. Risk exists only until it reaches us and is realized as suffering.

As such, risk is a ghost. Risk exists as fear and dread, and changes into a different form the moment its identity is revealed. The ghosts that haunt cemeteries and haunted houses reveal themselves in a variety of horrors. Nevertheless, the fear lies in the mind of the viewer, not the ghost itself. So a ghost resembles risk.

Then, the risk is rather the gas. A gas is invisible and undetectable, but exists everywhere and lives in various forms in our consciousness. A gas that exists over there but also right next to it. And the moment it collides with us, a chemical reaction occurs and its properties change. A gas can change into another gas, liquefy into a liquid, or sublimate into a solid. Thus, risk is a gas, a ghost, and the future.

Risk And Profit

Firms rush to achieve the ultimate goal of profit. The inanimate object called a firm reigns over and commands the living entity. Frank Knight once stressed that corporate profits come from coping with uncertainty (Frank Knight, 2009). Since everything in this world is uncertain, it does not seem to be wrong.

But what is the profit of a firm, especially a stock company? Doesn't the vague expression "firm" actually claim that the firm belongs to shareholders? The idea that firms belong to shareholders is both naive and provocative. This is because such equations have already become a relic of the past the moment personality is given to a firm. Those who have been embracing faded relics, as if reminiscing about the glorious past, would be considered naive. Being provocative can be said to be the insidious intention of those who claim that it belongs to shareholders. These are people who covet what belongs to others because they do not want to admit that it is no longer theirs. But let’s postpone this discussion for a moment. For the time being, let's assume that corporate profits are as meaningful as they say. Let us only focus on risk and profit here.

If risk is a gas, a ghost, and the future, what should the profit be? Profit is a liquid, not a gas. Firms surrounded by the invisible gas of risk are pursuing the slightest opportunity for profit. Thus, profit is finally collected from the air. Profits are embodied in dividends and stock prices and flow like a river to shareholders. So we call it liquidity. The flowing river will find new opportunities, turn new streams, and create new flows. A stream of water has meaning only when it flows, otherwise it will rot. Profit is the liquidity that results from the liquefaction of risk. And we call that liquefaction process the management of a firm.

Profit is also the present. Profit is a metaphorical expression representing risks and opportunities, which are ghosts and mirages, in the present. To identify risks and opportunities, corporate executives constantly replace the future with the present and rise into the air. For that they have to defy gravity and reverse time. This is the essence of profit. Transforming gas into liquid requires going against the laws of nature and time.

Consequently, profit becomes unnatural and burdensome. And perhaps what is more unnatural than the profit itself is the process of obtaining it. If a firm's pursuit of profit is burdensome and causes pain to someone, it is because of the unnatural and burdensome process.

In order to transform a gas into a liquid, the cold energy must be condensed and preserved. Thus, profit must be cold and cold-hearted. This is why firms must make cold-hearted decisions and take sharp, dagger-like actions in order to increase profits. The process of liquefaction is inevitably cold. Knowing the coldness of this process, many corporate managers have no choice but to remain silent about the suffering of the victims.

In addition, corporate managers should not blame themselves for the pain they inflict on victims. For that they have to keep hypnotizing themselves. "This process is simply a process of liquefaction and there are no personal grudges or malice. It happens only because they do their best for the profit of the firm. Competition is like a game; if there are winners, there are also losers." As market competition is praised as the driving force of economic development, the pain of losers is gradually being forgotten.

The pain will remain as a trauma to the loser, but the trauma of guilt lurks for the winner and observers as well. The most surprising fact about capitalism is that it has succeeded in preventing the winner's guilty feelings from turning into trauma, by constantly producing modern myths of the market, competition, and efficiency, and by repositioning the winner of the competition as a mythical hero. What played that role, in the early capitalist era, may have been Calvinist Protestantism (as mentioned by Weber) or the intoxication with violence and exploitation (as observed by Marx). And in modern times, the shiny packaging of efficiency and economic growth or idolized stories of heroism have played that role. Even today, a new myth is born, and within the myth, guilt disappears and is replaced by the intoxication of victory and heroism.

3. MONEY

Money And Trade

Money is something that cannot be left out of modern economic life. In modern capitalism, nothing is more important than money. In the market, goods are traded at prices expressed in money, and corporate profits, stock prices, or a country's economic growth are also expressed in money. The fact that prices play a central role in capitalism also means that money plays that role. It is true that money plays the most important role in our lives, but perhaps nothing is more difficult to understand than money.

Above all, there is a starting point that is often misunderstood. The question is whether market trade precedes money or vice versa. We generally believe that trade first existed in the form of barter, and that money was created to solve the inconvenience of barter. This viewpoint stems from equating the exchange of goods with trade. It is natural that humans live together in society and exchange goods accordingly. Also, if we accept the exchange as the same as market trade, there would already have been trade before money was invented. Isn't trade before the invention of money called barter? Barter is the exchange of goods for goods without money. Given that money did not exist, the quantities of goods would have been exchanged in proportion to their relative prices. Since exchanging goods without money is inconvenient to, it seems natural to infer that money was created to solve this problem.

Of course, there is an aspect where money alleviates the inconvenience of barter. This is because carrying the goods yourself and exchanging them can be inconvenient in many ways. However, if we understand that market trade is premised on prices, and that it is the role of money to set those prices, then money should come before trade, not the other way around (David Graeber, 2011). The fundamental role of money lies in serving as a common measure that determines the exchange rate between various goods. If barter refers to not simply the exchange of goods for goods, but the exchange of goods for goods according to prices (it is usually interpreted in this sense), then barter could not have come before money.

The functions of money include not only serving as a medium of exchange but also as a unit of account (or a measure of value) and a store of value. As a unit of account, money has the magic of allowing disparate goods to be measured in a common unit. The role of money as a unit of account is similar to the role in mathematics of making different numbers divisible by a common divisor. Two disparate goods, apples and shoes, can be divided through a common measure called the monetary unit. Money makes the incommensurable commensurable.

Goods can become objects of market trade only when their values are calculated and priced. Goods can be traded only if price tags are attached. Price is an exchange value determined by a common measure. That common measure is what money does. Money must exist for price tags to be attached, and only with price tags can the market reveal itself. Furthermore, the necessity to calculate the value of goods existed long before the goods were traded, indicating that the emergence of money predates market trade.

When money was created and incommensurable goods began to be commensurable, the possibility of trade would have already sprouted. However, the mere possibility does not guarantee its realization. Trade can be rather inconvenient because it requires money as a medium of exchange. Trade can be inconvenient because exchange rates must be calculated in money. Unnecessary medium and calculations can be more of a hindrance than a convenience. The reason why the exchange of goods without money seems inconvenient is due to the belief that the exchange of goods must be a trade. Under this belief, trade requires price tags, and money is needed to make price calculations efficient. Then a world without money is bound to be inconvenient. However, because the exchange of goods does not necessarily have to take the form of trade, the meaning of money is, in fact, distorted in the direction toward the market. We will take a closer look at this issue later.

Liquid Called Money

But it's strange. Why is money called liquid? Money was originally solid in nature. Aren't all things called commodity money, such as rice or silk, or metal money, such as gold, silver, and copper, all solid? Isn't the money that forms the basis of modern capitalism also metal or a solid called paper attached to it? Did things that were originally solids meet the market and move quickly, becoming called liquids instead of their original properties? Was the distinction between solids and liquids a matter of mobility rather than the properties of the substances? In any case, some solids that monopolized humanity's love lost their nature and acquired the status of liquids.

In the era of information technology since the late 20th century, the development of information technology eventually began to shift the form of money from a solid to a gas. Online, money is transformed into digital numbers. The fact that money is transferred and traded online is a declaration that money has now acquired gaseous properties as an intangible entity. Yes, there is no reason for money to be solid. Money only needs to be a measure of value, like a ruler, and a memory to store the value. Although it takes people a long time to realize it, money can fulfill its role as long as it is a social promise.

The reason money had to be solid was to establish ownership by placing it in someone's hand, not merely because of the shine of the metal itself. The era of information technology means that information and technology also become objects of ownership. As information and technology were gases, not solids, they could not be grasped, so they were not an object of ownership for a long time. However, the world of owning gas has finally arrived, and this is the era of information technology. As long as it becomes an object of ownership and can be stored, there is no need to insist that money wear an unwieldy solid suit. However, the gas cannot be possessed by holding it in the hand, but must be kept in a sealed bag or container. When you can put it in your container, ownership can become confirmed and remembered. As information technology has shown us the role of sealed containers in the form of electronic wallets and online accounts, we have finally declared that we can own gases.

In the age of information, let us consider the most important terms for computers or online environments. Above all, information is a measurement expressed in numbers; and it is memory and storage that gives meaning to information. Information is remembered as data in folders and the cloud, and stored as files. The stored information is retrieved again, calculated, decoded, and transformed. Storage goes beyond simply storing content and leads to classification that distinguishes it from others. Through classification, one piece of information is distinguished from other information, thereby securing its own identity and producing discrimination and difference. The storage of differentiated information is given a unique identifying name, and as a result, the information becomes an object of ownership. In other words, storage produces discrimination, and discrimination determines the scope of ownership.

Meanwhile, the performance of information technology depends on the speed of calculation and transformation. The true nature of information may be binary numbers, but the ability to calculate and transform is the energy that breathes life into information. Therefore, the speed of information transformation is a yardstick for measuring the effectiveness of information.

At the points of memory, storage, and speed, information and money have similarities, like vectors with their heads pointing in the same direction. Let us again recall the original function of money. Money is, above all else, a measure that indicates value. In addition, money is a device that stores and remembers value, that is, a memory bank (Keith Hart, 2000). Memory implies that it contains content and value. Thanks to its memory of value, money can be exchanged for other values. As with the storage of information, the storage of money implies classification and discrimination and determines the scope of ownership. Being able to "save" implies that it can be held in someone's hand and transferred. The function of storage is to be open to the very right of ownership.

Furthermore, money performs another fundamental function by being exchanged and circulated in the market. The exchange of money is another name for calculation and transformation. The exchange rate is determined through the calculation of value, and through exchange, money is transformed into goods while changing its owner. The function of money as a medium of exchange depends on the speed at which it is transformed. As the speed of transformation slows, money gradually loses its function as a medium of exchange and markets gradually lose their meaning. As a result, wealth may stagnate or decrease. Conversely, when the speed of exchange increases, markets become more vibrant and wealth is produced. However, too fast a speed is also undesirable. Excessively fast speeds create wealth bubbles.

The speed of money transformation serves as a gauge measuring the vitality of the capitalist system. If money is compared to the blood of a capitalist economy, the transformation speed of money is like an oximeter that measures the amount of oxygen in the blood. Just as both insufficient and excessive oxygen are harmful to the human body, an appropriate rate of money transformation is necessary for a healthy economy.

Money exists by measuring value as a symbol and remembering it, and creates wealth by being transformed.

In addition, storage of money establishes ownership. This precisely reflects the existence and function of information. Information and money, with their common language of measurement, memory, storage and transformation, find themselves in each other. In this way, information becomes money and money also becomes information. Just as money has produced wealth, information now produces wealth. Therefore, contrary to what many people think, it is not as though cryptocurrencies like Bitcoin, defined in virtual space, have transformed information into money. Information itself is already money.

Strangely enough, liquid does not actually become money. When solids and gases claimed to be money and thus liquids, true liquids never actually achieved the status of money. If so, the essence of money may not be liquid. Just as a parasite cannot survive on its own and needs a host, it may be the case that money also needs liquid as a host for its survival. Thus, an object that is liquid itself may not be able to exist as money.

On the other hand, the fact that a gas becomes money does not mean that money is no longer a liquid. Money is a liquid even when it is solid, so it is a liquid even when it is a gas. Solid, liquid, and gas are names assigned according to their roles and meanings, not according to the material properties themselves. Money is always a liquid, whether its material is a solid or a gas. Money, which transforms and moves between life and death, is therefore always perceived as liquid. When money is a liquid that does not move, it no longer maintains its role as a liquid. It hardens into a solid or disappears into a gas. Or it may just be rotting away like stagnant water. As long as it moves between people, a gas becomes a liquid. Perhaps the gas is a light volatile liquid.

The reason why the true liquid did not become money may be due to the restrictions that it has to flow among people. A liquid that flows at its will cannot become a liquid called money for that very reason. It should not flow on its own. Only by flowing among people through the process of ownership transfer does it qualify to be called money. Solids have been playing that role for a long time. Solids became the first form of money simply because they could be grasped in one's hand and exchanged directly with another person. In the age of information, information could also be collected and stored so that its ownership could be established. By flowing between virtual wallets, it is now possible to aim for the status of money that only solids have enjoyed in the past. However, true liquids cannot be held in the hand like solids, nor can they move between virtual wallets like the gas called information. As a result, only true liquids could not become money, and had no choice but to watch as solids and gases called themselves liquids.

The liquid called money should not simply flow continuously; it needs to move and pause, alternating between movement and stillness. Therefore, a true liquid that continuously flows and constantly seeks transformation cannot become money. If money cannot pause and is continuously exchanged and transformed, it negates the very essence of its existence. If the market continues to transform money at the speed of light, the market ceases to be a market for trading in money and instead becomes a market for barter. It is as important for money to be stored and stopped as it is to flow. Money must be stopped to get a new name, wealth. Money produces wealth when it flows and becomes wealth itself when it stops.

Desire For Money: Bitcoin

Just like DOTORI (acorns) coins of Cyworld of Korea in memories and the Bitcoin based on the myth of decentralization, so too do digital currencies diligently serve as a medium of trade. So many people think of them as money. When there was a debate about the moneyness of Bitcoin, some saw it as a decentralized money system that would replace the centralized money system, thus not questioning Bitcoin's status as money. Isn't it already possible to transact with Bitcoin online or at coffee shops? Bitcoin is a resistance money against state control. Meanwhile, for others, Bitcoin is just an object of speculation with no intrinsic value. Although it is used as if money among some people, it is a risky object of speculation whose value can evaporate at any time.

It is true that Bitcoin and similar digital currencies and cryptocurrencies operate as a medium of trade and function as money. On the other hand, it is also true that they have no intrinsic value. But something is being overlooked here. The true moneyness is not determined by such facts. In other words, the fact that something is used in trades does not automatically make it money, and the lack of intrinsic value does not disqualify it from being money.

The Korean won or US dollar, which we now recognize as money, also have no intrinsic value. While the government's guarantee may be treated as intrinsic value, it cannot be true intrinsic value. Modern money is a promise. When that promise is trusted, it becomes its intrinsic value. In this sense, Bitcoin, too, can be considered to have intrinsic value as long as its promise is trusted. The intrinsic value of modern money is determined by promises, and those promises come from outside the money. In that sense, modern money has no truly intrinsic value.

Then, is it the volatility of intrinsic value rather than the existence of intrinsic value itself that is the problem? However, this is just a difference in perspective. The US dollar value compared to the Korean won also changes frequently. However, the fluctuation of dollar value does not directly deny that dollar is money. While volatility can pose challenges to the stability of the money, it does not necessarily invalidate the money itself.

On the other hand, the mere fact that Bitcoin is used as a medium for trades does not make Bitcoin money itself. Look at the gift card. Gift cards are used as a medium for trades, but they do not qualify as money themselves. Misunderstandings about money lead to misunderstandings about Bitcoin, which only confuses us.

Then, is Bitcoin money or not? The answer is that Bitcoin

is not money, at least not for now. It is not for the reasons commonly cited, but for other reasons. Earlier, we discussed the unit of account as a more significant function of money than a medium of exchange. The main reason why Bitcoin is not money is because it fails to serve as a unit of account.

A unit of account or a measure of value is the ability to put price tags on things. The ability to put price tags on others with one's own power is none other than the unit of account. Money must acquire the ability of a unit of account before serving as a medium of exchange.

Look at Bitcoin. The gaze of people who exchange Bitcoin is not directed at the Bitcoin attached to goods. What their eyes focus on is the price tag attached to Bitcoin. Bitcoin does not have the ability to put price tags on others with its own power. Instead, it serves as a medium of exchange with a price tag attached to itself in the name of others. Those who transact with Bitcoin do not base their transactions on the price tags set by Bitcoin itself. When transacting with Bitcoin, they are comparing the price of a good with the price of Bitcoin. This is why Bitcoin is not money even for those who transact with Bitcoin.

The Korean won (or the US dollar) attaches price tags to both goods and Bitcoin. Even at the moment of making a transaction with Bitcoin, the money is not Bitcoin, but Korean won. Even for those who treat Bitcoin as money and trade with it, the money is not Bitcoin but the Korean won. Bitcoin is not money. Bitcoin is just a kind of gift card. Gift card is a medium of exchange, but is not money itself. The reason is that a transaction with a gift card involves comparing the prices of goods with the price of the gift card. Gift card has no ability to put the price tags for goods on its own.

The price volatility of Bitcoin exists because its price is set in terms of Korean won or other currencies. Bitcoin, an empty promise that has not achieved money status, is bound to have high price volatility. However, contrary to what many people think, it is important to recognize that Bitcoin's inability to become money is not due to its price volatility or its nature as a speculative asset. The very moment we talk about the volatility of Bitcoin price, we are already acknowledging that Bitcoin is not money. True money is one that has the ability to put a price tag on Bitcoin. No one is saying that the volatility of the Korean won is high by pricing it in Bitcoin. If a price tag is attached to the won with Bitcoin, the won will also be highly volatile. If the volatility is so high that it is not money, the won should not be money either.

At this very point, there is a reason why the Korean won is money but Bitcoin is not. This is due to the very fact that the won can put a price tag on Bitcoin, but Bitcoin cannot put a price tag on the won. Not because the price of Bitcoin is highly volatile, but because of the price attached to Bitcoin itself, Bitcoin cannot become money. Money is something that puts price tags on others in its own name, not something with a price tag attached in other's name.

The price volatility does not prevent Bitcoin from becoming money. Conversely, because Bitcoin is not money, price volatility exists. Meanwhile, the idea that it cannot become money due to price volatility causes another error. The error is the perception that once price volatility disappears, Bitcoin will be able to function as money. In principle, it is true that if price volatility is zero, it can be used the same as money. But that's where a serious problem arises. If something manufactured privately can be used with the same value as authorized money, it becomes a counterfeit money.

Governments of each country have made every effort to maintain their monopolies on money by using public authority to ban counterfeit money. In light of the government's arduous efforts, the fact that counterfeit money was manufactured using digital technology does not seem to be a reason to tolerate it. If Bitcoin's price volatility truly disappears, Bitcoin will now be judged as counterfeit money before becoming money. It may be highly unlikely, but if the country allows this, Bitcoin could truly gain the status of money. However, this acceptance will come at the cost of accepting other counterfeit money. If Bitcoin cannot withstand criticism for being counterfeit money, it must continually demonstrate volatility to prove that it is not a counterfeit currency. Finally, the volatility of Bitcoin's price becomes the reason for Bitcoin's existence. Price volatility is a reason to tolerate Bitcoin's existence and thus becomes a prerequisite for Bitcoin to function as a medium of exchange. Paradoxically, Bitcoin is allowed to function as money precisely because it is not money.

Still, if you want to call Bitcoin money, we may call it other's money. This is because foreign money is ultimately not our money. Measuring the dollar in terms of won is done because the dollar is a foreign currency in Korea. In other words, Bitcoin is foreign money in the same way as the dollar is. However, even if Bitcoin is interpreted as foreign money, Bitcoin is just foreign money in every country. In no country can it become entirely its own money.

Nevertheless, there are cases where Bitcoin could become closer to true money. It is as if foreign money is sometimes more reliable than domestic money. Just as the dollar is more preferred in countries where the domestic currency is highly unstable, there is a possibility that Bitcoin can replace the domestic currency in such countries. When the centralized national money fails to fulfill its roles, foreign money is what is needed. It is precisely at that point where Bitcoin's role as foreign money can take off. However, the more Bitcoin's role is emphasized, the more it will reveal a situation that is neither desirable nor beautiful.

Lastly, let us think about the meaning of money decentralization. Modern money is managed by the state under a centralized system. Since Bitcoin is money issued arbitrarily by individuals or groups, it would not be wrong to say that it is decentralized. However, it cannot be said that centralization is bad and decentralization is good. Maybe this is a bad effect of economics. This is because economics constantly preaches that decentralization and markets are good and that centralization and government are bad. Of course, if you look a little closer, you can easily see that centralized money is more efficient economically.

Apart from the perspective of economic efficiency, states hold significant importance in modern money. The reason modern money needs a state, as mentioned above, lies in the fact that it has no intrinsic value. In the first place, money is an empty promise with no intrinsic value. What makes such a promise money is trust. To instill a strong vitality in currency, what is needed is the trust that is as broad and strong as possible. That is why the scope of trust has expanded to encompass the borders of the state. If the state is a space of legitimate violence, the space where the trust can be enforced also extends to the borders of the state.

The reason Bitcoin claims to be a decentralized money is neither because it is highly efficient nor because it represents freedom. The fundamental reason why Bitcoin must emphasize decentralization is because Bitcoin has not yet become money. Bitcoin positions itself as an antithesis by demonstrating that it is different from state money. As a result, it seeks to instill trust as money through the myth of decentralization and freedom.

This is a clever strategy. Normally, it would first have to gain trust before becoming money, but in the face of the impregnable state money, a different strategy had to be used. Under this strategy, the order of trust and money is reversed. Rather than becoming money through trust, it aims to become money first and thereby compelling trust.

Number And Law

Money calculates, measures, and stores value. By becoming a unit of account, money can also serve as a general medium of exchange. If calculation and market trade are central features of capitalism, it cannot be denied that money is both the core and the origin of capitalism.

Money is inseparable from numbers from the perspective of

calculation. The Korean character for number, "(so)", comes from the Chinese character "數" which originally depicted the image of counting or calculating with stacked rods. In other words, the number itself contains the meaning of calculation. In the sense of stacking rods, it also conveys the meanings of repetition and density. Interestingly, numbers also contain the meaning of rules or laws. Just as calculating is a rational action, rules and laws may also be the result of rational judgment that runs society. Similarly, another Korean word for number, "(sem)", means counting, and is also connected to rational judgment.

Meanwhile, the English and French expressions for number are number and nombre, respectively, which are said to have their etymology from the Latin "numerus." Numerus has meanings such as number, quantity, and collection. However, it is said that numerus is more fundamentally derived from "nem," which means to distribute or share. The meaning is conveyed from nem to numerus in that it must be calculated and counted before being distributed. On the other hand, even before that, in the era of ancient Greece, nem was connected to "nomos," which meant rules, laws, and customs. In the West, the concept of number and nombre come from numerus, which is related to nem and to nomos. In the West, as in the East, numbers are closely related not only to counting and calculation, but also to rules and laws.

In ancient Greece, nomos was opposed to physis. Physis is nature, while nomos is a custom or law created by humans. Physis is something essential or given, while nomos is something that is created and changed by humans. On the other hand, physis is a raw or rough thing, while nomos is a rationally refined order.

In this way, money is connected to nomos. Money is a product of reason that expresses the counting of numbers and represents a refined order. Therefore, the market is not a place that exists in a rough state of nature, but a place where laws and rules imposed by humans are applied. The market is a space that operates only within the framework of laws and rules.

What this means is that the market is an artificial creation, which seems to contrast with the economic view. In economics since Adam Smith, the market has been described as something that exists naturally. Since humans have the propensity to trade and exchange goods, the existence of a market is inevitable and natural. Such beliefs have sometimes been expressed as laissez-faire, and in modern times, they are expressed as resistance to state intervention in the market. Government intervention is often portrayed as a harmful hand that disrupts the order of the market and causes inefficiency.

This perspective may be partially or fragmentarily correct, but when you take a step back and look at the bigger picture, it does not seem to be the case. This is because a market based on money may be a representation of nomos, but it is not a representation of physis. If money is a product of reason that serves as a unit of counting and calculation, then that reason operates only on the basis of laws and rules. The entity that can set and enforce the laws and rules is political power and the state. In modern times, only the state has the power to legitimately enforce and impose laws. The market cannot exist without the public power of the state. The ability to impose trust on money is also thanks to the power of the state. The state presents itself as a guardian who establishes and maintains market order before becoming an obstacle to the order of the market.

The relationship between the market and power is closer than one might think. This is why political power puts its own face on the obverse of the coin. The findings of Marx, Weber, and Polanyi regarding the relationship between capitalism and power ultimately confirm that the market is indeed a manifestation of nomos.

4. TRADE AND GIFT

Trade

Before the era of capitalism, markets accounted for only a small portion of economic activity (Karl Polanyi, 2001). Since markets were often associated with violence or war, it may have been better for people if there were no markets.

Adam Smith said that humans have the propensity to trade and exchange [truck, barter and exchange] goods (Adam Smith, 2001). Adam Smith, later economics scholars, and most people living today, consciously or unconsciously, equate the exchange of goods with market trade. However, upon reflection, market trade is just one method of exchanging goods. Trade is not the only way goods are exchanged.

A non-trading, but still important, method of exchanging goods is the gift. Many people think of gifts as exceptional, but in fact, gifts, as an exchange of goods, can still be more important than trade. For example, someone in the family may buy food ingredients through trading at the market. But when the family cooks with the ingredients and then gathers to eat together, foods are exchanged between family members in the form of gifts rather than trade. Another important example can be found in organizations including firms. When people within a firm cooperate to produce and sell products, goods are exchanged between them in the form of a gift rather than a trade. As can be seen from the above, the term "gift" here is used in a broader sense than the typical meaning of a present. It can be seen as including most exchanges of goods which is not trade.

If we understand that a trade is an exchange in which certain conditions are met, we can make a clearer comparison between trade and gift. Fundamentally, trading in the market means exchange of equivalent values. Exchange occurs on the premise that the prices of giving and receiving are the same. Therefore, market trade presupposes a measure of price. If you know the price of apples and pears, you can exchange them according to their prices. Generally, a trade goes through a process in which a good is exchanged for money corresponding to its price. Trade in which money is not directly involved is called barter. In barter, goods are directly exchanged according to their prices.

Another characteristic of market trade is that it is a spot or immediate exchange, where the exchange occurs simultaneously. Goods or money of the same value must be exchanged at the same time. Of course, there are cases where the price is paid later, such as through credit or installment payments. However, even in this case, it does not stray too far from the category of immediate exchange. The reason is that credit payment is not a vague delay in payment, but merely an intangible good called a debt contract taking its place. Including compulsory debt contracts, credit or installment contracts are also equivalent exchanges and immediate exchanges.

Gift

According to Marcel Mauss (2000), human exchange of goods begins not in the form of a trade but in the form of a gift. Consider the exchange of goods between family members. There are no price tags attached to goods that are exchanged between a couple or between parents and children. Parents do not get paid to cook dinners for their children. The exchange at this time is not an exchange of equivalents, but an exchange of possibly "unequal" values. Exchange is often one-sided, or even if it is mutual, the exchange is not necessarily equivalent. Not only is there an inequality in values, but there may also be a time difference in the exchange itself. The repayment for many things parents do for their children is postponed until later and is not explicit. The repayment is neither a directly calculated price nor a delayed payment of that price. This unequal and time-lagged exchange is what Morse referred to as a gift.

In this way, gifts are distinguished from trades. Trades are equivalent and are immediate exchanges, whereas gifts are non-equivalent and time-delayed exchanges. Humans have been exchanging goods in the form of gifts for a long time since the beginning. Market trades do not reveal themselves until much later.

But gifts are not free. This is because the person receiving the gift has an obligation to repay it someday. Since it is a non-equivalent exchange anyway, it may be possible not to repay. However, the person who does not repay the gift is admitting that his status is inferior. If he does not want it, he should repay it with something better if possible. Thus, the gift is not free.

Mauss also emphasizes: Gifts come with an obligation to give and an obligation to receive. These obligations are inherent in the meaning of non-equivalent exchange and time-lagged exchange. This is because non-equivalent and time-lagged exchanges assume that the parties to the exchange will continue to maintain social relationships and live in community in the future. Because the social relationship between the parties will be maintained, the exchange can be non-equivalent or delayed. The exchange of goods takes place within social relationships. In order for such social relationships to be maintained, gifts must be given, received, and repaid. To stop this process is to cut off social ties or to admit inferiority with no ability to repay.

Karl Polanyi (2001) goes further. Polanyi distinguishes between individual gift exchanges among people of similar status and collective gift exchanges mediated by the tribe's leader. Exchanges between people of similar status are conducted under the principle of reciprocity. Mauss' gift story is more clearly understood in the case of reciprocity. In contrast, collective gift exchange is carried out under the principle of redistribution, in which members collect goods in a community storehouse and the leader redistributes the collected goods among members. If reciprocity is the principle of exchange of goods between individuals, redistribution is the principle of exchange of goods that distributes the accumulated goods of a tribe or community among its members.

Polanyi emphasizes that the current era, where markets are ubiquitous, is not a longstanding feature in human history. It was not until after capitalism or the industrial revolution that markets became widespread. And, the state stands at the pivotal turning point where the market begins to dominate society. Such a great transformation would not have been possible without the violent coercion of the state. In the age of gifts, the exchange of goods functioned as part of social relationships. However, in the era of trades, the market separated the exchange of goods from social relationships and subordinated the social system to the market.

Since the trade is an equivalent and immediate exchange, it does not presuppose an ongoing relationship with the other party to the trade. No, rather, when a relationship becomes ongoing, it becomes difficult to receive the exact price. Market trades, by their very nature, are carried out on the premise of severance of social relationships. Trades are conducted between strangers.

This may be the reason why the market was unable to show itself for a long time even after the creation of money. From the time money came into the world as a common measure, the possibility of equivalent exchange of heterogeneous goods was already open. But that was just one possibility. Just like receiving no gift, making an immediate equivalent exchange at the exact price meant severing a social relationship. Therefore, it was difficult for trades to completely replace gifts without the will to sever social relationships.

The obligation regarding gifts pointed out by Mauss is also connected to the obligation not to trade. In order for market trades to flourish, it must be possible for social ties to be severed. In the era of market trades, the social system must be reorganized to operate with social relationships severed.

Therefore, rather than the market being incorporated as part of social relationships, social relationships must be greatly transformed to match the conditions required by the market (Polanyi, 2001). The current era of capitalism is one in which market and social relationships have been reversed.

Equivalent Or Nonequivalent Exchange

In the previous discussion, gift was placed in opposition to trade, but in reality, gift and trade may not be as different as one thinks. In fact, this is also the point that Mauss emphasized. The fact that gifts are not free, and that receiving a gift entails an obligation to reciprocate, ultimately implies that gifts are somewhat similar to trades. Of course, there is still a significant difference between gifts and trades, as trades involve equivalent and immediate exchange.

In a way, gifts might be viewed as a form of equivalent exchange. In trades, equivalent exchange considers only the equal prices of the goods themselves. In gifts, however, equivalent exchange encompasses not only the prices of the goods but also the social value exchanged between the parties involved. Here, social value, loosely defined, means value in social status or power relations. If there is a difference in the prices of goods exchanged, the difference can be made up in social value. Thus, the value of goods does not need to be converted into precise prices. Any shortfall or excess can be adjusted through social value. In this sense, gifts could be considered a form of equivalent exchange in a holistic sense. However, this holistic value is difficult to quantify, making it less clear-cut than market prices.

In contrast, trades consider only the equivalence of prices of goods, not the overall social value. Trades assume there are no social relationships exchanged between the parties. When the social value exchanged is zero, only the equivalence of prices guarantees overall equivalence. In this sense, trades can be seen as an extreme example of gifts—essentially, gifts where the exchanged social value is zero.

While gifts can be interpreted as a total equivalent exchange, conversely, trades can also be interpreted as a nonequivalent exchange. When trades are described as equivalent exchanges, this actually means that the same price is exchanged rather than the same value. Even if an apple and a pear are exchanged at the same price, it does not mean that the value of the apple is equivalent to the value of the pear for both parties involved in the trade. The value at this time is what is called use value or utility value in economics, and is distinguished from exchange value known as price. If goods have different use values, but have the same price, they are traded as equals. Ultimately, from the perspective of use value, trades are not truly equivalent exchanges.

In trade, exchanges are made based on a promised exchange value known, but this does not mean that truly equal values are being exchanged. In the end, true value lies in each individual's mind, so the concept of a truly equivalent exchange cannot be established, whether in trade or in gift. Therefore, it might be more accurate to say that both gifts and trades are forms of nonequivalent exchanges, rather than considering only gifts as equivalent exchanges.

Ignoring social values in trade may not necessarily be a bad thing. In reality, the exchange of social value tends to be unfair. Of course, there are also exchanges between neighbors in similar circumstances. But what is much more problematic is the exchange between people of different social statuses. The exchange of social values between them would have often been unfair. If the nonequivalent exchange of goods were complemented by the exchange of social values, the social relationship would have been exchanged in a relationship of domination and subordination. So, if a gift was a nonequivalent exchange, it would have been a form of nonequivalent exchange that often favored the socially powerful. The exchange would have been one that demanded absolute subordination to the socially underprivileged. Thus, a gift becomes poison as in the

German language.

Therefore, the fact that market trades are premised on severing social relationships may have been advantageous to the weak. This may be why the market and capitalism likely offered more opportunities to break free from existing social oppression. The development of capitalism and individualism could not help but go hand in hand, precisely because of the severance of these social relationships. The reason why capitalism is imprinted on us in the name of freedom is probably related to this. In the era when gifts ruled, the market may have been a companion of war and violence, but under capitalism, the market inevitably became a symbol of freedom and individuality.

What the severance of social relationships resulting from trade means is that success or failure in the market is directly linked to social success or failure. This is undoubtedly the dark side of capitalism. In the era of gifts, success and failure were not entirely determined by the market, so failure in the market was a story limited to only a few. Moreover, even if one failed in the market, there was a society that would accept him. So, some may miss the era of gifts.

Overall, however, a capitalist economy based on trade may have given individuals more freedom and mitigated social subordination compared to a pre-modern economy centered on gift. This was because the majority of population were in socially subordinate positions in the era of gifts. For them, gifts meant violence and subordination, while trades represented freedom and independence.

Although humans may be social animals, they do not wish to be bound in relationships of social subordination. In that sense, humans are both social and individual beings. The market would have aligned with modernization because it dismantled social subordination. However, when excessive individualization caused market losers to immediately become social outcasts, sociality would revive and challenge the market. Communism and socialism, which emerged as a reaction to capitalism, were the very challenge, and the modern welfare state would have been created as a response and compromise to this challenge. Both sociality and individuality are important and necessary for a healthy society.

Social relationships that are unregulated and unchecked are likely to transform into relationships of domination and subordination between the strong and the weak in any era. Only the patterns differ. In the age of gifts, the never-ending exchange of gifts is carried out on the premise of continuous social relationships. As a result, social relationships lead to direct domination and subordination between the parties, with the weak becoming subordinate to the strong.

In contrast, in the era of capitalism, social relationships are severed through discontinuous trades. Thus, domination and subordination become neither direct nor explicit. If he can regain his strength in the meantime, he can live a life of freedom. However, for the weak who have lost their resilience, these severed social relationships only become an even bigger shackle. Thus, the weak will again subordinate themselves to the strong. But this subordination will be indirect or epistemological through wealth, rather than in a direct person-to-person relationship. If polarization worsens under capitalism, it only means that indirect subordination is expanding.

A Modern Gift: Social Safety Nets And Firms

Modern capitalism appears to be an era dominated by trades. Considering that GDP and its growth rate, which only record trades, are elevated to a position of absolute power, and that stock prices, bond prices, and risk prices are regarded as absolute indicators for managerial decisions, it seems difficult to deny the dominance of trades. Not only that, but gifts have gradually become synonymous with bribes, while transactions have come to be used as a basis for ethical judgment.

However, gifts have not diminished in importance even today.

First of all, gifts exchanged between individuals have become more diverse and frequent than in the past. In order to give a gift, you must purchase goods from the market, so the expansion of the market is also required for the expansion of gifts. That's why firms continue to create and stimulate anniversaries and events where gifts are exchanged. The fact that a significant portion of sales in the consumer goods market occurs during Thanksgiving holidays and the year-end holidays highlights the importance of gifts.

The exchange of gifts mentioned above is, in itself, a self-explanatory gift mechanism. However, in many places, gift mechanisms, called by other names, take precedence over trade. Among them are, paradoxically, those that could even be considered the pillars that support modern capitalist society. One is the social safety net system and the other is firms.

The social safety net system generally includes the social welfare system, social insurance system, and other similar programs. It encompasses various mechanisms through which the state collects goods or resources from the socially strong in the form of compulsory taxes or social insurance premiums and provides support to the weak. The weak receive benefits either for free or by paying a small amount. This is a gift mechanism designed to remedy the social disruption caused by capitalist trades and to aid the resulting victims. Or, it is also a modern mechanism of redistribution mentioned by Polanyi. Most people living in modern times, though with varying degrees, do not deny the significance and necessity of the social safety net system. This is because it is not a return to the era of gifts, but a solution to the problems caused by trade in the era of trade.

Social insurance is the embodiment of the fundamental spirit of insurance. The spirit of insurance is originally about mutual aid which means helping people who are in trouble. Therefore, mutual aid cannot essentially be an equivalent exchange or an immediate exchange. Helping someone in need must (at least at that point) be one-sided, so it must be a gift. The reward is later paid back by helping others when they are in trouble. The insurance spirit of mutual aid is linked to a gift in which goods are exchanged between people in a group, rather than a gift between individual parties.

Paradoxically, due to the fundamental nature of insurance, the modern private insurance market becomes a place where capitalist conflicts are reproduced. This is because the spirit of insurance, which is at the opposite end of market trade, and the market mechanism through which goods must be traded cannot fundamentally avoid the conflict.

While the social safety net is an easily recognizable gift mechanism, it is not easy to perceive that the exchange of goods within a firm also operates on a gift mechanism. Although Coase had a vague idea of this point when discussing the nature of the firm, half a century had to pass before it was accepted in economics. Of course, Coase also did not view firms from the perspective of the fundamental conflict between gift and trade. Coase may not have been able to face the fundamental problem because he took the existence of trade for granted according to the tradition of economics. We will revisit Coase's theory of the firm later, but for now, let us discuss the firm from the perspective of gift.

Coase observed that the transfer of goods within a firm does not follow the trade mechanism. He attributed this to the fact that trades involve costs—what he called transaction costs. In his view, the exchange of goods, which starts as a trade, transforms into a different transfer mechanism when transaction costs become significant. While the market relies on free will in trades, the transfer of goods within a firm is governed by authority and command.

A firm is a community that operates under division of labor and collaboration with a common goal. The transfer of goods within a firm is not determined by the interests of each department, but by whether it meets the common goal. Within a firm, goods are transferred not by trade but by authority and command. In other words, goods are transferred through the gift mechanism.

However, the gift mechanism within a firm is not something that has resulted from the internalization of trades, unlike economics might suggest. Rather, it may be that the gift retains its primitive form before it was transformed into a trade. From the perspective of community, the corporate communities might not be so different from the tribes or village communities that existed in ancient times. The transfer of goods within a firm follows the gift mechanism, much like the transfer of goods within a tribe in the past.

When the exchange that was initially a gift gradually degenerates into a market trade under capitalism, the gift continues to take its place inside the firm, which is the heart of capitalism. It symbolically shows that trade can never completely overcome gift.

Just as a community disintegrates, a corporate community can also disintegrate. When the transfer price of goods between departments is calculated as a market trade in the name of incentives, the sense of community between those departments begins to disappear. As information processing and technology advance, making connections with external networks more accessible, the sense of belonging to a corporate community will naturally decrease. The size of a firm will then be determined by its presence as a community.

In this way, a firm is both a main player at the forefront of market trades and, at the same time, a participant in internal gift exchange, inherently embodying contradiction. A firm emerges as a symbol of paradox, as it is the leading player in the market, active at the forefront of capitalism, but at the same time, it has no choice but to internally reject the market.

Island

The era of gifts is similar to a scene where people are lined up holding hands. The height of the earth's surface can be different, so some people will be in high places and others will be in low places. Nevertheless, people are connected from hand to hand, and the exchange of goods passes from hand to hand. The exchange of goods passing from hand to hand is nothing other than a gift. And holding hands means insurance of mutual aid that will provide help when needed. Thus, a gift becomes insurance.

Soon, the liquid called money spread over the surface of the earth. Initially, a small amount of liquid merely dampened the surface slightly, so it wasn't a major issue. Some people might find it unpleasant to wet their pants with muddy water, but for most people, it didn't cause any major problems in their relationships. Then, as the liquid continued to increase, it came to form a river and even an ocean. People could no longer stand holding hands in the swirling current. Eventually, the people had to let go of their joined hands and move to a slightly higher place, while the relentless current flowed between them.

The flowing liquid separates and isolates people. Thus, people have now become islands. Islands can only be connected to other islands through waterways called money. The exchange of goods that occurs between isolated islands is precisely trade. Capitalism is a world where isolated individuals are connected only through the liquidity called money.

When Coase (1937), following D. H. Robertson, described firms as "islands of conscious power in this ocean of unconscious co-operation," it contained an important truth. However, what has been overlooked is the fact that not only firms but also individuals in the market are islands, regardless of whether they are consumers, intermediaries, or producers. Money and markets have turned everyone, not just firms, into islands. If an individual is a lonely island, a firm is just an island where several people gather together.

Meanwhile, it is people rather than firms that are conscious. So, a firm is not an island of conscious power, but rather an island of people with conscious power. Because they were gathered on one island, they were able to hold hands inside. As a result, the exchange of goods within the island becomes a gift, not a trade. Rather than defining a firm within the dichotomy of consciousness and unconsciousness, it might be better to define it within the dichotomy of isolation and connection.

If individuals and firms are islands, then what is the social safety net in the sea of markets? It is perhaps the light of a lighthouse. It is the light that allows lonely islands to endure and not give up. Although each is an isolated island surrounded by waves, the lighthouse provides the hope and assurance that one is not alone. Although it does not allow people to hold hands directly, the lighthouse light illuminates and connects everywhere. Because it has become such a lighthouse, the social safety net must be a gift, not a trade.

5. INSURANCE

Oblivion

Humans, and humanity cannot escape the swamp of risk. Humanity has struggled to cope with risk. Isn't the history of humanity ultimately a record of efforts to respond to and overcome risks? On the one hand, humanity created religion and confronted each other; on the other hand, it continuously worked on aiding the poor and freeing slaves through mutual aid and protection of the weak. All these efforts are ultimately different forms of insurance, aimed at protecting themselves from risk.

Nietzsche says, the risk to humans is produced by memory (Friedrich Nietzsche, 2002). Humanity needed speech and writing to constantly remember, which eventually created conflict and risk. Speech and writing are often depicted as great distinguishing features that set humans apart from animals, but on the other hand, they are also distinguishing features that lead humans to misery.

Thus, oblivion may be the best insurance. The reason we need insurance is actually to forget. What should we forget? We should forget the fear and pain of the impending risk. It would be even better if we could forget the very existence of risk. We should live as if risk is a distant matter concerning others. Pain should only happen to others. Thus, insurance must be about oblivion. True insurance should be able to make us forget to the extent that even the meaning of insurance itself is erased.

Insurance Market

That is why it is difficult for the insurance market to provide true insurance. The insurance market constantly tries to impress upon insurance consumers the existence and meaning of insurance. In this way, insurance firms must summon consumers' memories of risk and reveal their existence. This defines the behavior pattern of capitalist firms. Only by doing so can firms reap profits. It is precisely in this aspect that the inherent contradiction of the insurance market exists.

People are feeling uncomfortable about the insurance market. Insurance premiums are paid regularly, but it is difficult to receive the insurance benefit when an accident occurs. If there is no accident, you don't get a penny, which can be even more frustrating.

The insurance industry says: Insurance consumers' negative perceptions stem from misunderstanding and ignorance about insurance. Consumers do not realize that with insurance, you only receive the insurance benefit when an accident occurs, and that they are still benefiting from insurance even if no accident occur. These complaints from the insurance industry have some truth. Ultimately, insurance products are different from financial products that are a form of savings and investment. It is difficult for the general public to understand that insurance is a consumption goods that is consumed continuously. Unlike what many people mistakenly believe, insurance products are not financial products like savings, but rather consumption goods like apples. However, few people would consider insurance to be closer to apples than to savings.

But will dissatisfaction go away if we eliminate such misunderstandings? If insurance is about oblivion, then insurance firms must ask themselves whether they have faithfully fulfilled the role for oblivion. Instead of helping to forget risk, do insurance firms not continually evoke risk and create another risk for consumers regarding insurance benefits? They should question themselves about this."

Insurance firms entice customers with various flattering promises while selling insurance. They claim that once you sign the contract and pay the premiums, they will be there as a friend when you are in difficulty and need help. However, when an accident occurs, they hesitate to provide help. It is only then that people realize the true purpose of insurance firms is their own profit. They profit by receiving more and paying out less. Thus, the risk is not forgotten through the trade of insurance products.

However, if we look beyond insurance products and consider insurance itself, is insurance inherently as negative as it seems? The way insurance operates in the market is an unavoidable negative aspect of capitalism. The insurance market diminishes the true meaning of insurance. Insurance may inherently be incompatible with the market. Originally, insurance is an expression of mutual aid. Mutual aid is manifested by willingly sacrificing oneself for the benefit of others. However, insurance products in the market are designed to achieve profit, taking advantage of the spirit of mutual aid as a mechanism to that end. Can the pursuit of individual profit coexist with the spirit of mutual aid?

In this way, the insurance market is a space where insurance, and thus risk, is traded while denying the spirit of insurance. There, the desire for profit conflicts with the spirit of mutual aid to share suffering. Consequently, a gloomy atmosphere always surrounds the insurance market. Consumers who have purchased insurance constantly watch the insurers with a furrowed brow, monitoring their behavior. Initially, consumers likely wanted to forget, but now they must continuously monitor the insurer. Watchers must no longer forget. This is the fateful contradiction of the insurance market: the two inherently contradictory spirits of profit and mutual aid clash directly in the market.

However, it is unavoidable. Capitalism seeks to trade not only goods but also memories, experiences, and empty promises in the market. The market operates only within memories and records. Contracts must constantly be recorded and tracked. Trades that are not recorded or tracked are denied their existence.

Therefore, the essence of the capitalist market is probably memory and records rather than trades. The reason money can serve as a medium of exchange is precisely its ability to record and remember value. Now, the insurance market becomes the greatest irony of capitalism. This is because, from the moment insurance is traded for oblivion, the trade must no longer be forgotten. If humanity's misfortune began with the memory of things that should be forgotten, then the conflict in the insurance market is a representation and a microcosm of that misfortune.

Insurance Spirit

True insurance does not exist in the market. Originally, insurance was extremely anti-market. This is because insurance exists not as a market commodity contracted and traded for individual interests, but as a community mechanism to embrace and comfort each other. Who would call it mutual aid imbued with community spirit if monetary payments are made only after calculating one's own interests? Original insurance is fundamentally a mechanism of gift. Only when insurance is exchanged in the form of a gift, not as a trade, does the spirit of insurance remain alive. Thus, the spirit of insurance becomes "hau" (Mauss, 2000). Like hau, the Maori spirit embedded and transferred in gifts, the spirit of insurance is embedded in the mutual aid gift and transferred along with the gift.

Insurance, as a community mechanism, embodies the spirit of insurance, which is the spirit of mutual aid or solidarity. The Korean word for solidarity, "yeondae", comes from the Chinese characters "連帶" which imply being linked and connected like a belt. Solidum, the Latin origin of the English word 'solidarity' and the French 'solidarité,' means complete union. 'Solid,' which implies firmness and strength, shares the same origin. Solidarity means that members of the community rely on each other and form a stable, unshakeable union. Thus, the spirit of insurance takes on the form of a solid.

In contrast, market trades require a liquid called money, and this liquid is a calculating machine. Sellers must calculate costs and prices, and buyers must calculate utility and compare various prices. The driving force of trading is calculation. According to Weber, isn't capitalism a mechanism founded on rational calculation?

The insurance market is no exception. Insurance products can only be traded once they have been calculated, but the spirit of insurance evaporates at the moment profit and loss are calculated. This is because profits and losses are strictly based on personal calculations, which are only possible when the interconnected hands are let go. No one should think of insurance products as pure expressions of the spirit of solidarity. This is the fate of the insurance market. Herein lies the limitation and tragedy of the insurance market. The insurance market cosplays as a community spirit, but ultimately it can only serve the higher goal of profit. Consumers, realizing this belatedly, suffer doubly from the gap between reality and expectation.

Even though modern communities cannot be free from interests, true insurance originally lies in the community, not in the market. Because the spirit of insurance wants to be solid, while the trades in the market want to be liquid, the market cannot implement true insurance. The insurance market is a space where contradictions between solids and liquids collide. This is precisely why mutual insurance associations or cooperatives are formed among people in the same industries. Those people compete for profit but also form a community through a sense of camaraderie. This community spirit inevitably manifests as insurance. Although insurance markets are everywhere, they cannot foster a sense of community, which is why such cooperatives are created.

Above all, however, the most meaningful and significant community is the state. A global community would be even better, but that still seems like a distant future. Humanity chose the state, a large community, at the cost of giving up many smaller communities, and now demands a community spirit suited to the state. After many twists and turns, the state has taken on the mission of protecting its citizens from risk on behalf of smaller communities. Thus, public or social insurance was born, and modern society can be described as being in the era of social insurance. In modern capitalism, where the market dominates society, the expansion of social insurance is another expression of the longing for the sense of community that capitalism has gradually erased.

Of course, the expression of longing for community is a separate matter from whether the state has fulfilled its role. The state is managed by bureaucrats and politicians, who are influenced by various stakeholders. These actors constantly conflict, negotiate, and compromise over the scope of social insurance. Those who disdain the community spirit of social insurance seek to reduce community involvement, while those who wish to rely on the community try to expand it. Many who are in between, without a clear awareness of what they truly want, are left with no choice but to take one side or the other.

Whether one likes or dislikes the role of the state, it remains true that the genuine implementation of insurance is only possible through the state. Even the functioning of private insurance markets cannot exist without state intervention. We often forget the importance of the state, and mistakenly consider the market as a self-sustaining perpetual motion machine. However, perpetual motion machines that disregard the fundamental laws of physics cannot exist. Similarly, we forget that capitalist markets cannot exist without the state as a guardian. This is even more true for insurance markets, as insurance, by its very nature, is anti-market. Ultimately, the insurance market is an institution that operates only within the scope permitted by the state.

However, this does not mean the current state rules over the market. As Michel Foucault suggested, the neoliberal state might be an apparatus existing for the market (Foucault, 2012b).

After all, those in power running the state find it difficult to escape their own interests and perceptions of the times. Thus, there is no need to complain about the insurance market being interfered with and regulated by the state. Even if it is partially inconvenient interference, the state will ultimately make every effort for the well-being of the insurance market.

Insurance And Risk Calculation

In modern insurance, risk is represented by actuaries as numbers and symbols—probability, probability distribution, statistics, variance, etc. However, risk is something that cannot be calculated. The probability I feel is different from the probability you feel, and even my own perception of probability changes each time I think about it. Do not assume that the probability calculations used in dice games can be applied to the risks of life. Mathematicians try to express risk with common calculation formulas and objective numbers, but risk is inherently multidimensional and subjective. Moreover, given that risk is accompanied by fear and anxiety, how can any actuarial calculation measure the fear and anxiety? Can my fear and your fear be quantified into a single number?

This may be why mathematics of risk didn't emerge for so long. Risk has always existed, but it has always been coupled with fear. While Pascal and Fermat are said to have calculated risk, this is not accurate. Mathematicians' probabilities did not truly calculate risk because risk cannot be inherently reduced to mathematics. Only after ignoring all fear, sorrow, anxiety about the future, and morality could the number called probability emerge. Mathematical probability was revealed only after reducing multiple dimensions to one dimension. With so many omitted and ignored blank spaces, mathematical probability remains incomplete and unstable.

On the one hand, the birth of actuarial science allowed for the calculation of risk, leading to a leap in human civilization and intellectual capacity. On the other hand, it confined our understanding of risk to formulas governed by physical laws and basic arithmetic operations. Now, as time has passed, many believe that risk can be represented only by numbers neatly lined up in a cramped space.

Insurance already existed long before the calculation of risk, because the calculation of risk could only emerge after shedding all its complexities and simplifying it. While accurate risk calculation may be crucial in the market where risk is traded, it is not so important within the community spirit of solidarity. In fact, the history of insurance shows that even in the market, accurate risk calculation has not always been paramount. Recall that the essence of the market is the pursuit of profit, not mutual aid. The insurance market can exist as long as it pursues profit by dealing with risk, even though risk calculation is not accurate.

Market insurance is difficult to distinguish from gambling in that it seeks profit by targeting risk. The moment insurance is traded in the market, it changes from mutual aid to gambling. In gambling, accurate calculation of risk is not a primary concern. This is because in gambling, people do not participate by calculating relative profits and losses; instead, they jump in with the hope of achieving the highest possible gain.

Textbooks teach us that insurance and gambling are opposites. However, this is true only when insurance retains its original spirit. The moment insurance enters the arena of the market, it often reveals itself as a fraternal twin of gambling. The insurance market has tried hard to draw a line between itself and gambling, but it has not always been successful.

The idea that insurance and gambling are often indistinguishable is not merely a conceptual theory. Look at the financial product Credit Default Swap (CDS) during the 2008 financial crisis. CDS was marketed as an insurance product and sold to investors as such. However, after the financial crisis hit, it became clear that CDS was gambling rather than risk-reducing insurance. Later, critics emphasize that this product was not insurance in the first place. Or, some say it was misused insurance. The more accurate truth, however, is that insurance itself is not fundamentally different from gambling. The moment insurance is traded in the market, the line between insurance and gambling becomes blurred and destined to gradually disappear.

However, let us not dismiss all the efforts of the insurance industry. Many are still diligently working to prevent insurance from becoming gambling. After all, CDS was traded speculatively not in the insurance market, but in the financial market that is unable to properly understand the nature of insurance.

Gifts And Insurance

It was observed earlier that the true spirit of insurance cannot be realized in the market. True insurance is meaningful only if it is exchanged in the form of a gift, not a trade. Here, let us consider the converse of the proposition that insurance is a gift: a gift is insurance.

What does a gift do? Above all, the exchange of gifts involves giving and receiving goods, and it is based on the division of labor. Division of labor refers to a form in which individuals rely on each other rather than obtaining or producing things on their own. The same applies to trades in that they are based on the division of labor. When different goods held by people are exchanged with price tags, it is a trade. When these goods are exchanged holistically within the context of social relationships, it becomes a gift.

Holistic exchange of goods in social relationships implies that gifts are an insurance mechanism. The reason why people do not live alone but live in groups and societies is because society is an insurance mechanism for sharing and dispersing risks. Whether gifts are based on reciprocity or on larger-scale redistribution, they embody the spirit of insurance. The larger the group, the better the risks can be shared, which is supported by the mathematical finding known as the law of large numbers.

On the other hand, since market trades are equivalent exchanges based on cold calculation, social relationships are severed, and as a result, society's insurance mechanism is also severed. The severance of social relationships due to market trades means the severance of the insurance spirit. This is because the spirit of insurance cannot remain independently within an individual but must always be connected to others within society to be realized. Therefore, whether it is a gift imbued with spirit, poor relief laws of the past, or modern social welfare systems, all these are representations of the insurance spirit and are only possible with the premise of connections among people in society.

Therefore, the converse of the proposition that true insurance is exchanged in the form of a gift also holds true. The mechanism of gift exchange itself is insurance and replicates the true spirit of insurance. The fact that market trades sever or damage social relationships means that trades sever or damage the spirit of insurance. Social relationships are another name for insurance. Insurance is a gift, and a gift is insurance.

If capitalism is an economic system that replaces gifts with trades, then it must also establish a mechanism to substitute the insurance function in a disconnected society. This is where the insurance market comes into play. The insurance market emerges as a capitalist device that absorbs the insurance function of society into the market. This is precisely what gives the insurance market its unique status in capitalism. The insurance market is not just another market similar to others. It is a symbol that fully represents the capitalist notion that it is okay to sever social relationships, and thus becomes a market that declares the beginning and triumph of capitalism. The insurance market is both the beginning and the end of capitalism.

Émile Durkheim (2014) saw the organic solidarity of society within the division of labor system of capitalism. The division of labor achieves social solidarity by making each person's life interconnected and reliant on others. This view reproduces the capitalist view that individual selfish behavior becomes a social virtue.

The idea that selfishness can lead to a social virtue and that capitalism can foster social solidarity holds some degree of truth, but the link is weak and unstable. The idea holds true only when everything functions properly. However, when the contradictions within society are amplified or when internal and external shocks occur, that link is bound to break.

The idea that selfishness becomes a social virtue and that capitalism realizes social solidarity exists not as an identity but as a hopeful solution to an equation that holds true only at certain moments and under specific conditions. Social solidarity based on selfishness and market trades may mimic superficially the spirit of insurance, but it cannot resolve fundamental contradictions. That is why it is inherently fragile and prone to collapse. When the economy or society faces a crisis, the social solidarity based on selfishness loses its luster.

Social Insurance And Insurance Market

As the true spirit of insurance cannot exist in the insurance market and must manifest within the community, the duty falls upon social insurance. Although social insurance is perceived differently across societies and operates within various systems, it fundamentally holds an important role as a mechanism for sharing communal risks and providing a social safety net.

On the surface, social insurance and insurance markets appear to perform similar functions and utilize the same operating principles. Thus, at times, social insurance and the insurance market attempt to replace each other, leading to conflicts. Let us outline the fundamental differences between social insurance and the insurance market below.

Above all, social insurance is where the spirit of insurance can be genuinely represented. If the spirit of insurance represents community solidarity, it cannot be manifested in the market. Since the spirit of insurance involves the strong and the healthy extending a helping hand to the weak and the sick, the market, where individual interests intersect, fundamentally has its limits. Although Durkheim indirectly observed a sense of solidarity in the market, it is merely superficial and consequential solidarity. The spirit of insurance should be found in the motivation, not in the consequence. Hence, the representation of the spirit of insurance is entrusted to social insurance rather than the insurance market. Of course, the mere name of social insurance does not guarantee it fulfilling this role. Perspectives on social insurance can vary depending on the state and society. Social insurance will be able to properly represent the spirit of insurance when it is operated from the perspective of solidarity.

In addition, social insurance serves as a gift mechanism because it represents the spirit of insurance. On the other hand, since the insurance market operates as a trade mechanism, social insurance and the insurance market are again differentiated. The differences between gifts and trades observed earlier are directly reflected in the differences between social insurance and the insurance market.

The distinction between social insurance and the insurance market may be understood as a difference in their direction of movement. Social insurance is an institution that helps oneself by helping others, whereas the insurance market is an institution that helps others by satisfying one's own self-interest. While social insurance is a vector directed from others to oneself, the insurance market is a vector directed from oneself to others. When observed superficially or statically, both vectors may be indistinguishable because they span oneself and others. However, the difference in direction will become apparent when society as a whole is truly in trouble.

The difference in direction also affects how to read the law of large numbers. The law of large numbers is a fundamental principle widely used in both social insurance and the insurance market. However, social insurance and the insurance market are differentiated in the direction of viewing the law. The law of large numbers is a hopeful mathematical discovery that as the number of risks increases, the risk per unit decreases and can ultimately disappear. Thus, whether in social insurance or insurance markets, pooling more risks results in higher efficacy of reducing average risk per unit.

For social insurance, this reduction in risk occurs because the better-off provide help to the worse-off. This perspective on the law of large numbers involves viewing it as a tool for helping those in worse-off positions (on the left side of the distribution) to move towards the mean, which is achieved by shifting those in better-off positions (on the right side of the distribution) towards the left.

In contrast, the way the insurance market utilizes the law of large numbers is by aiming to move away from the average point, looking towards the right side of the distribution, which increases the insurer's profit as it moves further from the average. Thus, while social insurance looks to the law of large numbers to bring things back to the mean, the insurance market views it as a tool to deviate from the mean. The law of large numbers traditionally suggests regression to the mean, but in the insurance market, it becomes a means to move away from the mean.

6. INSURANCE AND THE STATE

Insurance: The Mission Of The State

The spirit of insurance is manifested in the community. In modern society, it is the state that is required to carry out that mission. The state, after all, can be seen as a clear, large-scale community delineated by various laws, rules, and violence. While the government, which is responsible for running the state, governs its citizens, the most important job of the government is to act as an insurer.

Consider the universally agreed-upon duties of the state. Above all, the state is a community for public safety and national defense. Public safety and national defense involve protecting citizens from risks. What about the state's role in welfare? The economic and administrative functions of every state are ultimately directed towards the welfare of its citizens. These functions aim at ensuring the safety, security, and comfort of citizens' lives, which is essentially insurance.

When the state faithfully fulfills its role as an insurer, including risk management, society becomes stable and healthy. However, if something goes wrong even for a moment, society falls into confusion and pain, and the government also faces a crisis. Just as an insolvent insurer is shunned by consumers, a modern state that identifies itself as an insurer will be abandoned by its citizens if it neglects its role as an insurer.

Nevertheless, the concept of the state as an insurer is not historically self-evident and, in some sense, is a modern construct. Since ancient times, groups and societies have always played the role of an insurer to some extent. If the saying "humans are social animals" means that people rely on society rather than merely living together, then society has always fulfilled the role of an insurer. Throughout most of history, however, the insurer function of rulers was limited, and even then, it was merely a benefaction of monarchs or kings, not an obligation.

However, with the advent of modernity, as the state began to replace society and rulers transformed from sovereigns or kings into administrators, the insurance function started to shift from a ruler's right to an obligation. Alongside the advancements in science and economics, as the focus of governance shifted from individual citizens to the population as a whole, the state's role as an insurer became more clearly revealed.

Market And The State

As argued by Marx and Polanyi, the era of capitalism was inaugurated through the violent forces of capitalists and the state, with society succumbing to the demands of the market. What is the relationship between the state and the market today? According to Foucault's observations, the subordination of the state to the market has deepened in the modern capitalist era (Foucault, 2012b). The market has not only expanded its domain across the entire economy, but has also ultimately managed to subjugate state administration and governance to its control. Since the 20th century, the rise of neoliberalism and the expansion of economics have led to a scenario where the market governs the state and sets the goals of governance. The modern market has evolved beyond the laissez-faire principles advocated by classical economics, transforming into a market where the state must actively manage efficient competition. Even when the state exercises control over the market, it must do so under the pretext of ensuring the market functions smoothly. It has become no longer possible to say that the market is merely a part of the state.

Rather, the state has been reduced to the role of supporting the market. Furthermore, the logic of the market and competition has spread throughout society. The principles of the market are no longer confined to the market itself but become applied to each individual in society. Consequently, individuals are now expected to actively manage and invest in themselves to increase their values in the market. In this way, individuals themselves have become firms.

The term, "human resources," which treats people as mere tools or materials for production, is widely accepted without hesitation. We live in an era where people see themselves as investments and commodities. Our behavior is now driven by how we are evaluated in the market. Individuals have become firms and commodities, and society and the state have been absorbed by the market.

This observation highlights an important truth. However, it is also true that the state does not always act as a subordinate to the market. The state is not a fixed entity; its role changes based on the political powers that govern it. The market's dominance over the state is only possible to the extent that the state permits it. Political powers have the ability to curb the market whenever it oversteps its bounds, while they often yield to the market's influence. The relationship between the state and the market is inevitably variable. The conflict between the liberalism represented by the market and the socialism represented by the state community remains ever-changing.

Governmentality And Insurance

The concept of the state is neither tangible nor real. It is merely a fictional creation of human imagination. Whether it is the Leviathan meant to overcome the chaos of the natural state, a shield to protect one's natural rights, or a contract among people, the narratives that justify the state are as fictitious as the concept of the state itself. This fictional entity has evolved from tribal territories to kingdoms or cities, and then to the modern notion of the state. With the advancements in technology and science, the state has become more capable of intricately managing and regulating its people than ever before.

However, ultimately, the state does not think and act on its own, but rather, it is decided and operated by some people. In a democratic republic, administrative tasks are carried out by the heads of administration elected by the people and the bureaucratic system that supports them. Politicians, who are periodically chosen by the people, are at the center of this system. Politicians create laws and rules, the executive branch enforces them, and the judiciary monitors for any violations of the law. The state is often equated with the government or the executive branch that executes administrative tasks.

From the perspective of governmentality, Foucault compares the monarchy and the modern state (Foucault 1991, 2012b). Before the formation of the modern state, the monarch managed the state for the prestige and sovereignty of the monarch. The sovereignty of the monarch is quite personal. The monarch rules the people by seizing their products and through death and corporal punishment. In contrast, the modern state is a society of so-called governmentality. In a society of governmentality, the state organizes and encourages production and manages the lives of its citizens. In other words, unlike the monarchy which seizes production and manages death, the modern state encourages production and manages life. The governmentality of the modern state began in Europe in the 17th and 18th centuries and reached its peak through the 20th century.

The central task of governmentality in the modern state is not in the personal rule of the monarch as in the past, but rather in the principles and direction of state management. Of course, the direction of state management will be influenced by the prevailing knowledge of the era, that is, the episteme (Foucault, 2012a).

From the Middle Ages to modern times, European states

financed their wars and extravagance by extracting funds from the populace. Sometimes this was done under the guise of taxation, and other times through the issuance of government debt or bonds. Repayment of these loans often took the form of annuities. As a result, the state needed to manage the births and deaths of its citizens. Actuarial science and statistics developed, and data on urban and rural populations were collected and analyzed.

Finally, insurance and statistics joined hands with the rulers of the state and came into prominence. After all, isn't statistics literally the science of the state? An era has arrived where the state manages the lives, illnesses, accidents, and deaths of its citizens. Actuarial science and statistics are based on data and numbers. Therefore, through statistics, the state's interest in its citizens is not in individuals per se, but in citizens as data and as a collective population. When modern insurance and statistics met governmentality, citizens became data.

If the modern state presupposes the seizure of territory and citizens, then the role of the state is to manage the lives of the citizens within its territory. This is governmentality. Furthermore, understanding that the era of the modern state coincides with the era of capitalism, it is not surprising that the spirit dominating modern governmentality is rooted in capitalist economic thought and economics.

In the late 18th century, when Adam Smith opened the door to modern economics, he argued that the market driven by self-interest could benefit both the parties involved in trades and the market as a whole. This marked a departure from mercantilism, which had a zero-sum competitive strategy and a state-first mentality (Foucault, 2012b). Smith claimed that there was a way for fair competition to benefit everyone. The same applied to trade, which involved market trades between countries. Free trade was beneficial to merchants from both nations, so state interference was unnecessary. The state's role was to refrain from unnecessary interventions and ensure free competition, allowing the market to function effectively.

Although Smith seemed to implicitly assume that moral conscience should support this system, his arguments were nevertheless interpreted as advocating for the manifestation of self-interest. It was also understood as endorsing a laissez-faire market and minimizing government intervention. Consequently, the era of laissez-faire began, where state non-interference in the market was considered a virtue. However, the liberal economic system produced many poor and proletarians. By the late 19th century, when the so-called neoclassical economics preached the virtues of the free market and competition through physics and mathematics, the specter of socialism was already haunting Europe.

However, liberal economics did not retreat. Neoclassical economics expanded and became more sophisticated, eventually evolving into neoliberal economics. Centered around the Chicago School, neoliberal economics transformed neoclassical economics into a tool for explaining and understanding not only markets but also human behavior and social phenomena. Moreover, neoliberal economics provided a theoretical foundation that further focused the role of the state on facilitating free markets and free competition. Thus, liberal economics has persisted, intertwining with Marxism, Bismarckian and Beveridge-style social welfare, and Keynesian state interventionism. It has at times been constrained and at other times expanded, but it has steadfastly maintained and strengthened its position to the present day.

Foucault named the modern era as the era of discipline. In this context, the state disciplines and trains its citizens through various institutions like schools, the military, hospitals, and factories. Modern society constantly molds its citizens in the direction desired by the state. As people move through different disciplinary units, they become accustomed to each discipline and adapt to new disciplines, gradually becoming the types of human beings that the state and organizations wish them to be. Just as molten metal is molded and adapted to the shape of a mold... (Gilles Deleuze, 1992)

Discipline, as a form of modern governance, dictates the division of risk. It specifies which risks and to what extent these risks will be shared between the state and individuals. If modern governmentality involves managing the lives of citizens, its development inevitably leads to social insurance (in a broad sense, including social welfare). This is because the lives, illnesses, and accidents of citizens are all subjects of insurance. Social insurance is therefore the epitome of life governmentality. If the 20th century represents the peak of disciplinary governmentality, it is also the era when social insurance reached its zenith. As a result, many states expanded their social safety nets in the 20th century, including health insurance, unemployment insurance, and public pensions for their citizens.

However, the extent of the division of risk does not always remain constant. Socialism, captured by capitalism, has vitality and continuously adapts and regenerates itself. Similarly, liberal economics does the same. When one force overpowers another due to circumstances or contingencies, the balance of power tends to shift in that direction. This is why the state's role as insurer is sometimes expanded and sometimes contracted.

In the 21st century, as the discourse of the risk society suggests, an increasing number of risks are being produced by governments, firms, and science. Normally, the state will eventually have to bear a greater share of socially constructed and produced risks. However, another implication of the risk society discourse is that the responsibility for managing these risks may be increasingly shifted onto individuals. Here too, the movement of the counterweight becomes important.

It is no coincidence that social welfare and social insurance are expanded in countries where capitalism has developed. Upon reflection, social insurance is essentially socialist in nature and therefore anti-capitalist. From this perspective, it might seem contradictory that social insurance is well-developed in advanced capitalist countries. However, capitalism has evolved in tandem with a form of governmentality where the state manages and governs the lives of its citizens. In this way, the development of social insurance aligns with the governance practices of modern capitalist states.

The reason capitalism has remained resilient despite numerous contradictions and conflicts is not necessarily that it is superior to socialism, but rather that capitalism has expanded by incorporating and internalizing elements of socialism. Similarly, the failure of past socialist systems may be attributed to their attempt to isolate rather than integrate aspects of capitalism. By internalizing socialism, capitalism gained an advantage in the fight against socialism which sought to expel capitalism from its framework.

Discipline And Neoliberalism

But there need not be only one method of governmentality. Moreover, the content of governmentality changes according to the perception of each era, and more specifically, in modern times, according to the votes of voters. In the neoliberal ideology that characterized the latter half of the 20th century, the emphasis on individual responsibility challenged the role of the state in individuals' lives. Under neoliberalism, discipline changed indirectly rather than directly (François Ewald, 1991). The government sets milestones and announces standards, leaving individuals responsible for transforming the abnormal into the normal and the non-standard into the standard.

However, there need not be only one method of governmentality. Moreover, depending on the prevailing understanding of each era, and more specifically in the modern context, depending on the preferences of voters, the content of governmentality changes. As individual responsibility was emphasized in the late 20th century, represented by neoliberalism, the established role of the state in the lives of individuals was challenged. Under neoliberalism, discipline shifted from direct to indirect forms (François Ewald, 1991). Now, the government sets benchmarks and publishes standards.

Then, it is left to each individual's responsibility to change what is abnormal into normal and what is non-standard into standard.

Since the late 20th century, the weight of the division of risk between the state and the individual has shifted toward the individual. Under the banner of neoliberalism, individuals were forced to choose the path of self-reliance rather than depending on the state. The UK under the Thatcher administration and the US under the Reagan administration became the vanguards of neoliberalism, steering the direction of global politics and economy. Looking narrowly into economics, it is also a period in which neoliberal economics, represented by the Austrian School and the Chicago School that followed it, is gaining hegemony as a reaction to Keynesian economics.

They sought to limit the role of the state to the creation of systems and infrastructure necessary for the efficient operation of the market, and to prohibit unnecessary market intervention. What they wanted from the government was not mere non-interference in the market, as previous liberals had sought, but rather a more proactive creation of market infrastructure and the expansion of market logic (Foucault, 2012b). Individuals were also expected to behave similarly to firms competing in the market. Just like firms, individuals needed to enhance their market value by investing in their human capital and utilizing human resources. Individuals became rational decision-makers who plan, invest, and manage their own consumption, health, labor, and education.

Since the neoclassical economics of the late 19th century, economics has been separated from politics and history and combined with physics and mathematics. As a result, economic agents had to develop a habit of basing their actions on rational calculations. Within neoliberal economics, everyone eventually became a calculating machine, or homo economicus, who constantly needs to compute prices, costs and profits.

In this way, the 20th century was a time when, on the one hand, the state's role in risk sharing expanded, while on the other hand, the concept of homo economicus—individuals compelled to make rational calculations—was developing. These two aspects were destined to clash with each other. In the process of this conflict, many people found it difficult to bear the weight of individual responsibility. Many individuals had not yet transformed themselves into rational calculators. Even in countries where the state failed to properly share risks, the global trend has been used as a justification to shift more responsibility onto individuals in disadvantaged environments.

This period of neoliberal expansion overlaps with the era of discipline. The state sets standards and benchmarks, and individuals are required to calculate and bear responsibility on their own. While the state does share some of the risks, individuals must handle risks beyond that. As neoliberalism expands, the responsibility for risk sharing increasingly shifts from the state to individuals. Indirect regulation through individual responsibility, rather than direct regulation by the state, has increasingly taken hold.

And then, with the outbreak of the global financial crisis in 2008, the weaknesses of neoliberalism were revealed. However, the underlying neoliberal mindset and the emphasis on indirect regulation remained largely unchanged. The government, exhausted by the financial crisis and, more fundamentally, by capitalist development, has become too weak to exercise direct discipline. The weakened power of the state has no choice but to leave risk sharing to individuals. Meanwhile, individuals who were skilled at calculation still appeared to enjoy prosperous lives. Ironically, despite the contradictions and social costs associated with neoliberalism, individuals have increasingly been willing to act in accordance with neoliberal principles, and there has been an increasing emphasis on individual risk sharing.

The unchecked expansion of neoliberalism brought about social chaos, yet those who shone amidst the chaos were the coldly rational homo economicus who adhered faithfully to neoliberal principles. As homo economicus emerged as the hero amid the chaos, economic contradictions remained unresolved and new contradictions accumulated. The lessons from the financial crisis were soon forgotten. The unresolved contradictions were once again thrust upon the world as a fatal pain with the advent of the COVID-19 pandemic in 2020.

Control And Manipulation

The new era we are entering, often referred to as the Information Age, presents both opportunities and challenges for governments. On the one hand, advancements in information and data technology have equipped governments with greater capabilities to control and monitor the daily lives of their citizens. Consider the prevalence of crime dramas featuring forensic science teams or the countless surveillance cameras scattered throughout public spaces. These developments inevitably evoke images of Big Brother from George Orwell's novel.

However, on the other hand, government authority is increasingly being challenged by individuals. With the advancement of information technology and media, it has become more difficult for the government to maintain an information advantage over the private sector in many areas. The emergence of various cryptocurrencies, for instance, tests the government's monopoly over money. This Information Age inevitably brings changes to governmentality.

Deleuze posited that we are transitioning from the era of discipline to the era of control (Deleuze, 1992). In the era of control, everything is continuously connected, with unceasing oversight. Education no longer ends with school but continues throughout one's life. In corporations, numerous incentives perpetually expose workers to instability. Hospitals are not merely places for admissions and discharges but institutions where ongoing health management and check-ups occur. In the era of discipline, individuals experienced intermittent regulation within distinct institutions, with each new institution marking a fresh start. However, in the era of control, everything continues without ending and beginning. Furthermore, individuals are subdivided into masses, samples, and data and decomposed into "dividuals," surfing the vast ocean of information.

Perhaps the era of control is one in which the neoliberal thinking pushes indirect discipline even further. After all, aren't information and computing technology essential for maximizing individuals' capacity for calculation? The shift in discipline that we witnessed in the late 20th century was the transition from the state assuming individuals' risks to individuals having to bear those risks themselves. In an era of such indirect discipline and control, individuals are continuously exposed to the sharing and classification of risks.

However, the era of control should rather be called the era of manipulation. Or perhaps we should say that the era of control has given way to the era of manipulation. Governments can no longer overtly control or discipline their citizens. Just as the government watches the citizens, the citizens also watch the government. As much as the government tries to discipline the citizens, the citizens strive to control the government. This mutual discipline and control lead to policies that seek to press the buttons of operation while concealing intentions. To steer actions in the desired direction, manipulation must occur at an earlier stage, considering more variables and calculating further in advance. Thus, an input made today passes through multiple functions to produce a new output tomorrow or the day after.

Not only must actions be taken in advance, but the complexity of interconnected networks must also be considered. Predicting the direction and extent of spread and transformation is difficult, yet it remains essential. However, it is impossible to control all the variables, networks, and operations of multi-step functions precisely. Consequently, no one can guarantee what the output will be.

Thus, continuity and uncertainty are not so much the results of control but rather of manipulation and skillful operation. Since decisions must be made several steps ahead, continuity must be considered and their results are uncertain. Manipulation must avoid the eyes of numerous watchers, making it indirect. Continuity, uncertainty, and indirectness characterize the era of manipulation, which replaces the era of discipline and control. The era of manipulation emerges when the era of control meets information and networks.

Thus, individuals become more and more dividuals. They hide behind their data, revealing their true selves only when desired. The state collects and analyzes individuals as data, breaking them down into even smaller segments. In this matrix, sliced finely by Descartes' grid, people live with fragmented selves, embodying multiple personas. Imagining people leisurely surfing the sea of information like snakes is far from reality (Deleuze, 1992). People's typical hobby is not leisurely surfing, but rather the frantic masquerade of transformation and transforming robots. The animal representing our era shifts from the snake to the chameleon.

Manipulation, Information, And Insurance

When we speak of the Fourth Industrial Revolution or the Information Revolution, it seems to suggest an era of high accuracy and certainty because information is readily available at our fingertips. However, the Information Age is, in reality, an era of heightened uncertainty. Continuity and networks produce the uncertainty of interactions, and it is precisely this uncertainty that defines the Information Age. Information is increasing and readily available, but for that very reason, uncertainty and risk become greater.

If I want to obtain information and certainty that are beneficial to me, the information must be exclusive to me and others must not know about it. However, when abundant information is available to everyone and it is unclear how each individual will interpret and use that information, the spread of information only amplifies uncertainty. This uncertainty is a high level of unpredictability that cannot be calculated. This uncertainty creates the volatility and madness of the stock market, which Isaac Newton once lamented was more difficult to calculate than the movements of planets. Connections and interactions only produce greater uncertainty as more information becomes available. Uncertainty and risk arise from connections and interactions, characterized by mutual responsiveness. This mutual responsiveness produces incalculable uncertainty.

In the era of manipulation, on the one hand, the accumulation of data allows for more precise calculation of risks, provided those risks are independent and given. In this sense, insurance becomes more sophisticated and expansive. However, the era of manipulation is ultimately an era of incessant uncertainty and fragmented multiple personas, making it impossible to express all risks mathematically. Connections amplify risks in an incalculable manner, and individuals possess different risk calculations for each persona they project. In the era of manipulation, precise actuarial calculations must be abandoned.

However, this does not signify the decline of the commodification of insurance. On the contrary, it expands insurance. Who says insurance must be based on mathematical calculations? As risks, fears, and uncertainties are produced, and as solutions to these become elusive, the demand for insurance increases. Another important fact is that insurance might not necessarily reduce risks. As will be discussed later, insurance is a mechanism that produces risk before reducing it.

7. INSURANCE AND INFORMATION PROBLEM

Information Asymmetry

In reality, insurance is a mechanism for managing and transferring risk. For those who dislike risk, insurance is a good thing. However, insurance also comes with potentially serious side effects, primarily related to information. (Much of this section draws from Seog, 2020c). In modern society, information is crucial, and its significance seems to be growing. Typically, when we think of information, we might think of scientific and technological information, as referenced in discussions about the Information Age. While such information is indeed important and addressed elsewhere in this book, the focus of this chapter is slightly different. Here, we are concerned with the information problems that arise as a side effect of risk transfer through insurance. This information problem is often referred to as the problem of information asymmetry in economics.

The information problem associated with insurance can be illustrated as follows. Suppose my risk is transferred to others through insurance. For instance, imagine I have taken out theft insurance on a certain item. If that item is stolen, the insurance company compensates me with an amount equal to its value. In this scenario, the event of the item being stolen does not cause me any actual loss. As a result, selfishly, I may no longer feel the need to exercise the same level of caution to prevent theft as I did before. This lack of diligence can lead to an increased risk of the item actually being stolen. This adverse effect, where the risk increases due to the absence of normal precautions, is the information problem, a negative side effect of insurance.

This situation is referred to as an information problem because the insurance company can only speculate about the policyholder's decreased diligence but cannot verify or prove it accurately. In other words, this issue arises because the insurance company lacks proper (verifiable) information about the policyholder's behavior. Hence, it is called an information problem or information asymmetry. Another familiar term for this phenomenon is moral hazard. Moral hazard is a term that became familiar with financial crises. At those times, the media used this term to describe the reckless management practices of the executives of firms and large shareholders.

In fact, the problem of information is not limited to moral hazard. In insurance, information problems are often categorized into moral hazard and adverse selection. Adverse selection refers to situations where individuals lie about their abilities or risk levels. Simply put, moral hazard involves secretly engaging in bad behavior, while adverse selection involves lying about one's state or type. Both problems constitute information asymmetry.

Adverse selection is a term that arises from the perspective of the insurer. For instance, consider a situation where an insurer sells life insurance to a consumer and asks about their health status. Suppose the consumer, despite having a serious illness, lies and claims to be in good health, and the insurer believes this false information and charges a lower premium accordingly. The result, of course, would be a loss for the insurer. Adverse selection refers to this poor choice made by the insurer due to misleading information from the consumer. Essentially, the insurer should aim to sell insurance to healthy individuals, but if they are deceived into selling it to someone with poor health, this represents a poor selection, hence the term adverse selection.

In some contexts, the term "information asymmetry" is

used more narrowly to refer specifically to adverse selection. While moral hazard pertains to negative outcomes resulting from active behaviors, adverse selection can be seen as a passive consequence of misrepresenting one's own condition. In practice, distinguishing clearly between adverse selection and moral hazard can be challenging and may not always be straightforward.

Moral Hazard And Morality

Does moral hazard have anything to do with morality? At first glance, this question seems quite strange. Given that "moral" is part of the term, it might seem natural to assume there's a connection. Yes, the question is indeed odd. But this question becomes meaningful precisely because of modern economics.

In economics, moral hazard is preached as being unrelated to morality. As a result, some naive people may come to believe this. When moral hazard began to be seriously addressed in economics by Kenneth Arrow (1963, 1968), Mark Pauly (1968) made a statement that had a profound impact on subsequent economics thought. He argued that moral hazard is not a result of a lack of morality, but rather a problem arising from rational decision-making. Since the behavior is the outcome of rational calculation for one's own interests, economics simply needs to analyze this rational calculation.

Did Pauly's text simply suggest that moral hazard could be the subject of economic analysis rather than being limited to a matter of individual morality? Or did it truly mean that moral hazard is unrelated to morality? In any case, moral hazard began to sever its ties with morality thereafter. Under the banner that economics does not make moral judgments, economics started to analyze moral hazard from a distance. And more and more people are beginning to believe that moral hazard is genuinely unrelated to morality.

Even when embezzling corporate funds, manipulating stock prices and accounting numbers, or appropriating public funds for management bonuses, they insisted that these actions were rational decisions. Despite being criticized in the media and news as moral hazard and morally problematic, they defended themselves by saying that this is how capitalism works. This is how a businessman makes money. Moral hazard is merely the result of rational behavior and not something to be condemned. They claimed that all of this is just part of competition, and that self-interested behavior ultimately benefits society. This is what economics says.

Thus, we have to ask this strange question. Is moral hazard not related to morality? Moral hazard is a coined term formed by combining “moral” and “hazard.” The term "moral hazard" appears to have originated in the insurance market in the mid-19th century. Tom Baker describes the situation at the time as follows (Tom Baker, 1996). The insurance industry desperately needed moral legitimacy and had to demonstrate that it dealt with risk scientifically. The combination of "moral" and "hazard" occurred at the intersection of these two needs. "Moral" signified not only morality but also something related to humans, while "hazard" referred to gambling and risk, like playing dice (Baker, 1996; Rowell and Connelly, 2012).

The insurance industry is an industry that deals with risk, and actuarial science is a moral science that studies human risk as a science of humanity. Thus, "moral hazard" was a complex term that intertwined morality, humanity, risk, and science. By guarding against moral hazard, the insurance industry sought to differentiate itself from gambling and to secure moral legitimacy. Moral hazard, therefore, was a term coined with profoundly moral motivations.

The economic perspective on moral hazard is closely related to the trends of modern economics, which extend from the neoclassical school to neoliberalism. Modern economics focuses on the rational and self-interested Homo Economicus. By nature, this Homo Economicus is less a human and more a calculating machine. Thus, Homo Economicus should be aptly called Machina Economicus, or economic machine (Parkes and Wellman, 2015). There is no need to demand morality from calculating machines. Originally, moral hazard was about morality and thus about humanity. However, as economics is a discipline that studies calculating machines rather than humans, morality is naturally excluded within its framework.

Therefore, when attempts are made to apply research results on machines to human societies, discord inevitably arises. Those who have enchanted themselves into viewing calculating machines as human nature can easily assert that moral hazard is unrelated to morality, having already equated humans with calculating machines. However, in the real world, where humans—not machines—live, it is evident that moral hazard cannot be divorced from morality and, consequently, cannot be separated from human relationships.

Resolving Moral Hazard

Although economics has made efforts to liberate moral hazard from morality, ordinary people have not thought of it that way. Instead, they have increasingly discussed moral hazard in close connection with morality. Look at how the media and news cover moral hazard; the emphasis is always on the lack of morality, not on rationality. Economists may blame the ignorance of the public for this.

However, there is a shared belief between economists and the general public: moral hazard must be resolved. Economics argues that moral hazard should be resolved to eliminate inefficiencies. On the other hand, the general public believes that it should be resolved to restore morality. Neither of these perspectives can be said to be wrong, as moral hazard is undoubtedly a negative phenomenon.

However, we are often silent about the side effects of resolving moral hazard. It is often overlooked that resolving moral hazard can create another moral problem. We often forget that it may be neither possible nor desirable to completely eliminate moral hazard.

There is a schizophrenic overreaction to moral hazard in economics and media news. Perhaps to conceal their own moral shortcomings, people loudly denounce the moral hazard of others. Or is it a classic double standard, justifying one's own moral hazard as a rational choice while condemning others' as moral corruption? We are lenient with our own moral hazard while exaggerating the minor one of others. We oscillate like a schizophrenic between our own moral hazard and others' moral hazard. Maybe this is a meta-issue of moral hazard.

Let us take a look at the incentive system. Incentive systems are a means to prevent moral hazard and provide motivation to improve efficiency. Don't be misled by the term "motivation." Motivation is just another expression for moral hazard. Under the pretext of resolving moral hazard, countless performance-based pay systems are implemented in firms. Differentiated incentives are provided based on performance. If performance is poor, appropriate penalties must be applied. Proper incentives can mitigate moral hazard and increase efficiency. However, this concept of efficiency does not account for the discomfort, anxiety, and conflict experienced by individual workers. The performance-based pay system in firms fosters competition among those being evaluated, thereby eroding the sense of community. This eroded sense of community will gradually undermine the firm value. The solution of incentives for moral hazard incurs the costs of conflict and the disintegration of community spirit.

Let us also consider the concept of "gapjil," the Korean term for bullying and the abuse of power. Although people do not associate gapjil with moral hazard, isn't it a form of moral hazard? Probably, it's not a typical moral hazard. It refers to the cases in which the powerful teach lessons to the powerless. What are these lessons about? They are lessons on the boundaries of moral hazard, on proper work ethics, and on respect for superiors. No one in a position of power who engages in gapjil believes they are fundamentally doing bad to the victim, although excessive teaching and discipline methods may be problematic. However, they justify their actions as necessary for protecting their rights, benefiting the firm or organization, or resolving moral hazard. How different, then, is the incentive system, known as a solution to moral hazard, from gapjil? Verbal and physical violence are not the only forms of gapjil. It comes to us along with a schizophrenic obsession with moral hazard.

How about corporate governance? Discussions on corporate governance focus on ensuring that firms contribute to shareholder value. Actions that go against the interests of shareholders are defined as moral hazard. From the shareholders' perspective, whether it is beneficial to shareholders becomes the criterion for judging moral hazard. Here, efficiency is defined as what benefits the shareholders. Therefore, the argument in corporate governance discussions is that moral hazard should be appropriately controlled to increase efficiency. This means that other stakeholders must be properly controlled in a manner that benefits the shareholders.

However, there is disagreement about whether a firm should belong to its shareholders. Rather, strictly speaking, a firm granted legal personality should not consider shareholders' interests as its ultimate goal. Can it really be called moral to regard a firm, which does not belong to shareholders in the first place, as the shareholder's and to regard anything that hinders shareholders' interests as moral hazard? How different is this from gapjil or bullying?

In fact, all solutions to moral hazard inherently involve a form of gapjil. How is moral hazard addressed? It involves either punishing the behavior when discovered or using incentives. Both methods are ways for those in power to impose their will on those with less power. It's akin to a master evaluating, monitoring, and rewarding or punishing his slaves. Whether it's punishment or incentives, it involves coercive measures. At this point, solutions to moral hazard intersect with gapjil.

If solutions to moral hazard are gapjil, is it better to resolve moral hazard or to leave it unaddressed? What should be the criterion for that judgment? The solutions proposed in economics are judged from the perspective of the powerful, based on serving their interests. In the equations they solve, the objective function always represents the profit and utility of the powerful. Consequently, gapjil should naturally be ignored. This is why, in economics discussions, the perspective of the weak is ignored. The position of the weak exists only as a constraint of inequality.

Furthermore, in business studies, the term "agency problem" is often preferred over "moral hazard." It is not easy to recognize the perception that this shift in terminology imposes upon us. It subtly enforces the perception that moral hazard arises not from the powerful principal but from the powerless slaves, i.e. agents. When moral hazard is relabeled as an agency problem, gapjil can no longer occur.

Sometimes this may cause a pang of conscience. When it does, the powerful are portrayed as the powerless. This is why, in discussions of corporate governance, shareholders are depicted as the most vulnerable and disadvantaged. It is why they portray themselves as nothing more than powerless masters, with their powers and information being taken over by their slaves. They argue that, although they are the masters, they are essentially powerless, only getting what is left over. Therefore, maximizing their interests should be social justice.

But do you see the contradiction here? A contradiction so large it cannot be hidden, no matter how hard one tries. The powerless cannot place their utility as the objective function and bind others as constraints in the maximization problem. The existence of power is not about one's position but about one's ability to impose their solutions on others. Being the last to take what remains is not a sign of weakness but of being at the top of the food chain. In corporate governance discussions, shareholders are astute enough to place their utility at the pinnacle while simultaneously cosplaying as the most vulnerable.

When you try to solve moral hazard from a narrow perspective and from the perspective of the powerful, it inevitably becomes gapjil. However, once morality is removed from moral hazard, the problem of gapjil only becomes vaguely visible. If moral hazard is not judged from a moral standpoint, its resolution will always bring about another moral hazard. This new moral hazard is that of the powerful. Yet, the powerful are reluctant to label their own actions as moral hazard. It is because the term should be applied only when it harms the interests of the powerful.

Therefore, we must once again question the morality of moral hazard. Not just the relationship between moral hazard and morality, but the intrinsic morality of moral hazard itself. Just as Nietzsche did, we should explore the genealogy of moral hazard. We must ask who defines and determines moral hazard. Wouldn't it be considered good to follow the evaluations and rules imposed on slaves by their masters? We must question whether this supposed virtue is nothing more than the master's morality instilled in the slave. Without this question, slaves try to uphold their own virtue and guard against moral deviation, but remain silent about their master's moral hazard. Moral hazard is pervasive and constantly observed, yet the master's gapjil is only occasionally exposed by the media. Even then, only the perceptive few may sense that such gapjil is, in fact, a form of moral hazard.

Public Insurance And Moral Hazard

To accurately understand the relationship between public/social insurance and moral hazard, we must first overcome two common misunderstandings. The first is the belief that private sector, or market, is inherently more efficient than public sector. The second is the tendency to evaluate public insurance primarily from the perspective of resolving moral hazard.

Let us first address the first misunderstanding. This is a widespread misunderstanding. In principle, either the private or public sector can be more efficient depending on the environment and situation. Here, however, we will go beyond this principle. The root of this misunderstanding likely stems from economics. Throughout our economics classrooms, we have been continually given such an impression. Interestingly, the introductory economics textbooks do not explicitly and logically demonstrate that the private sector is superior to the public one. Nevertheless, we perceive it as if this has been proven in the economics textbooks. This perception, achieved without proof but through a few implications, might be the result of collective hypnosis, illusion, or a simply bias in memory.

In general, economics textbooks simply talk about the market. When government intervention is mentioned, it is usually under the assumption that the market was already functioning well. Even when discussing market failures, it is often stated that the government can also fail. As Foucault pointed out, in neoliberal economics, the role of the government is merely to move towards the market and orbit around it. Economics textbooks reflect and describe this kind of thinking. However, this does not prove that the market is always superior to the public.

Insurance is a domain where the private market is completely inferior. Insurance stands at the very point where the market fails. Economics textbooks explain why markets fail. Above all, the insurance market fails due to information problems. The moral hazard and adverse selection we've seen so far lead to market failure. If one cannot discern the actions and lies of the other party, thus cannot penalize him when he acts contrary to the contract, then a proper contract cannot be made. If a contract cannot be enforced properly, the autonomy of the market will lose its meaning. This decline in market efficacy is what is referred to as market failure. Market success and autonomy are only possible when enforcement is assured.

However, there is another important reason for the failure of the insurance market. It is related to the highly mathematical law of large numbers. The more subjects of risk that insurance covers, the more accurately the risk can be calculated and the lower the cost per unit of risk. If the cost per unit decreases, producing more becomes advantageous in competition. This is another factor of market failure known as natural monopoly in economics.

This explains why there is so much dissatisfaction and conflict in the insurance market. Insurers blame consumers' ignorance and moral hazard, while consumers accuse insurers of deceit and incompetence. The market failure arising from the mutual lack of information ultimately manifests as conflict.

Thus, there exists insurance that, after the market fails, ends up in the hands of the state. That is public or social insurance. Public insurance is insurance that citizens have agreed to manage publicly because the damage caused by market failure is too great. The fact that public health insurance is more efficient than private health insurance is not a coincidence. Above all, the law of large numbers tells us that the larger the pool of risks, the more efficiently it can be managed. Considering that the state can manage a risk pool much larger than both competing insurance companies or even private monopolistic insurers, it is not a coincidence that public insurance is more efficient than the insurance market.

What about moral hazard? Pauly argues that public insurance does not necessarily solve moral hazard any better. Therefore, market failure does not automatically justify public intervention. This is true. Moral hazard does not vanish simply because private insurance is replaced by public insurance. However, there is something Pauly did not consider. Pauly's premise is that information asymmetry itself remains unchanged. Yet public insurance can, if it chooses, obtain more information. This is the advantage of public insurance. The power to enforce regulations and obtain information under the name of public authority and the public good—that is the violence granted exclusively to the state. If resolving moral hazard is necessary, the state has the ability to acquire and use consumer information more efficiently than the market. Pauly's argument may be valid within his framework, but when viewed from outside that framework, it appears differently.

Now let us address the second misunderstanding. The efficiency with which moral hazard is controlled is an important evaluation criterion for public health insurance. In fact, the same logic applies not only to insurance but also to the general management of firms. However, let us focus solely on insurance here. The perspective of the media often links moral hazard with public health insurance, such as the National Health Insurance. Of course, this media perspective is not limited to health insurance alone. It also laments the prevalence of insurance fraud and moral hazard in automobile insurance, private health insurance, and accident insurance. Due to moral hazard, innocent people end up paying higher premiums and receiving lower benefits.

Moral hazard indeed exists, and it is challenging to resolve. As Pauly insightfully noted, moral hazard does not discriminate between private and public insurance. However, we should not treat public insurance as if its fate depends on controlling moral hazard. The reason is that public insurance exists not to solve moral hazard but despite it. Public insurance is there to embrace and manage moral hazard, not to eliminate it. If moral hazard were the primary issue, there might be no need for public insurance in the first place.

Sometimes, people argue that private insurance can handle moral hazard better. They claim this is the strength of the market, suggesting that private insurance is superior to public insurance and that public insurance should be privatized.

However, they overlook something. If private insurance appears to manage moral hazard better than public insurance, it is because public insurance is not intended to resolve moral hazard. They fail to realize that the very fact that private insurance focuses on addressing moral hazard is the reason why public insurance needs to exist.

Moral hazard causes harm to honest consumers, but the process of resolving moral hazard also harms them. The solutions to moral hazard proposed by the insurance market include increasing the burden on consumers, refusing or delaying insurance payouts, and subjecting consumers to suspicion and investigation. In either case, honest consumers become victims. Thus, addressing moral hazard often leads to gapjil, or the abuse of power. Powerless consumers become victims of these practices, committed in the name of resolving moral hazard.

Public insurance exists precisely because of the problems that arise from the market's solutions to moral hazard. In principle, public insurance can address moral hazard much more effectively than the market, with the help of governmental authority. However, public insurance must restrain its capabilities as much as possible. This is because using this ability undermines the very reason for the existence of public insurance. Public health insurance exists to guarantee access to healthcare for even the most vulnerable people, not to make them victims of efforts to resolve moral hazard. Strong measures to address moral hazard always result in the greatest harm to the weakest links and those on the borderline. This concern is precisely why public insurance is reluctant to fully resolve moral hazard. It is why, despite worries about moral hazard, there is still a push to increase the coverage rate of medical expenses. More important than resolving moral hazard is the need to embody social solidarity and community spirit, which requires tolerating and embracing moral hazard.

Therefore, public insurance should not be measured solely by the metric of moral hazard. It is undeniable that moral hazard undermines efficiency and causes innocent victims. While moral hazard is a serious and important issue, it is not a top priority. Although the problem of moral hazard does not differentiate between private and public insurance, the priority and willingness to resolve it differ. The busyness and fatigue of modern society related to moral hazard may possibly stem more from its solutions than from the moral hazard itself.

Public Insurance And Adverse Selection

Adverse selection, like moral hazard, presents a similar issue. While adverse selection itself is a problem, its solutions can also become problematic. Economics presents these solutions as if they are the best and ultimate solutions, but the reality is more complex. This is not because reality is irrational, but because economic solutions often represent only partial equilibrium rather than true general equilibrium. This distinction becomes particularly evident in public insurance.

The issue of adverse selection originally emerged in contexts such as health and life insurance. When the term "moral hazard" was first introduced in the late 19th century in Western contexts, it included the concept of adverse selection. From the perspective of morality, there was not much difference between the adverse selection of lying about one's health status, and the moral hazard (in the current sense) of neglecting one's responsibilities.

Let us take a look at health insurance to see why resolving adverse selection is not everything. In health insurance, the issue of adverse selection arises in the following situation: Insurance firms often do not have complete information about the health status of potential policyholders. As a result, it is challenging for insurers to differentiate between low-risk individuals (who are healthy) and high-risk individuals (who are not healthy) when setting premiums. High-risk individuals are more likely to perceive a greater need for insurance compared to low-risk individuals. As a result, if the insurer sells the insurance at the same premium with the expectation that both risk types will purchase it, the insurer will suffer a loss.

Now economics intervenes to solve this adverse selection. A typical economic solution involves insurance firms offering a menu of contracts with different combinations of premiums and coverage. This approach allows policyholders to select a contract that matches their risk types. As a result, high-risk individuals and low-risk individuals choose different contracts, which exposes their individual risks more clearly. Consequently, premiums can be adjusted to better reflect each individual's risk type. While this economic solution is not perfect, it is generally considered to improve efficiency to some extent.

Can public health insurance solve the problem of adverse selection better than private health insurance? The answer is, in principle, "yes." This is because, at the very least, public insurance can also implement the solutions presented in economics. In other words, public insurance cannot be worse than private insurance because it can do what private insurance can do. Moreover, public insurance has capabilities that private insurance cannot replicate, similarly to the case of moral hazard.

Above all, public insurance has compulsory power. In private insurance, insurers cannot force someone to buy insurance. But with public insurance, that is possible. Thus, public insurance can create a menu in more diverse ways or force it to be better for everyone through mutual aid. In addition to being compulsory, public insurance can have access to extensive medical data on insured individuals. This reduces the information asymmetry and allows for more effective risk pooling. In contrast, private insurance often struggles with adverse selection because it cannot enforce mandatory participation and has limited access to comprehensive data. Therefore, public insurance is in a much superior position to resolve adverse selection compared to private insurance.

However, there is something even more important than that. Public insurance does not exist to resolve adverse selection. No, rather, it may be correct to say that public insurance exists to avoid solving adverse selection. The reason is that public health insurance exists to uphold the basic right to health care for all citizens. And this right must be maintained based on social solidarity. Social solidarity involves mutual aid, where low-risk and strong individuals support high-risk and vulnerable individuals, rather than relying solely on individual survival strategies.

Just as with moral hazard, the economic solution to adverse selection aims for each individual to secure contracts suited to his own risk, targeting individual survival. However, this individual survival approach is precisely what social solidarity rejects. Therefore, even though public insurance has the ability to resolve adverse selection, it should not exercise this ability. As long as resolving adverse selection conflicts with social solidarity and the basic rights of citizens, adverse selection should be accommodated rather than resolved. The relative superiority between private insurance and public insurance cannot be judged solely from the narrow perspective of economic efficiency. This would be no different from attempting to evaluate a curved three-dimensional space from the perspective of a one-dimensional straight line.

8. INFORMATION REVOLUTION

Information Revolution

We are currently living in an era commonly referred to as the information revolution. Some call it the Fourth Industrial Revolution, while others consider it part of the Third Industrial Revolution. Regardless of what it is called, this revolution refers to the changes brought about by the rapid development of computers, the internet, mobile phones, and the information and communication technologies since the mid-to-late 20th century. Recently, particular attention has been paid to the advancements in information and communication technologies represented by artificial intelligence (AI), big data, the Internet of Things (IoT), cloud computing, and blockchain.

What is the relationship between the information revolution and insurance? Just as the relationship between finance and the information revolution is exemplified by Fintech, the relationship between insurance and the information revolution is discussed focusing on Insurtech. Insurtech describes the impact of technological changes brought about by the information revolution on the insurance industry and related sectors. It encompasses the various effects of information technology on insurance market practices, products, and the measurement and evaluation of risks.

However, is the impact of the information revolution limited to the technological and commercial changes epitomized by Insurtech? Previously, we examined the relationship between governmentality and insurance. If the information revolution influences insurance, what changes might occur in its relationship with governmentality? Can the information revolution be reduced to a trend encapsulated by the term Insurtech?

The relationship between the information revolution and insurance is more profound and historically significant than what is immediately visible or apparent. Yet, there seems to be a lack of awareness about this deeper connection. To truly understand the current interplay between the information revolution and insurance, we need to embark on a journey through time once again.

Risk Calculation

When Weber sought to trace the origins of capitalism to Calvinism, his narrative was confusing. Rational and calculating Calvinists had to be born from the irrational and magical Calvin, and capitalist greed had to be created from their ascetic behavior. Weber could only escape this confusion by labeling the extremely irrational religious zeal as rational.

An entrepreneur must know how to calculate profit. While calculating profit in business can appear to be a mark of rationality, viewing it as a means of salvation is a facet of irrationality. Since merchants of Gaesung, Korea and Islamic merchants had already calculated profits and kept double-entry bookkeeping, the rationality of Calvinists would not have been particularly unique.

In rational calculation, the emphasis should be on "calculation" rather than "rational." Weren't they particularly preoccupied with calculation rather than being particularly rational? They became merchants themselves and thought and calculated like merchants.

What was it that distinguished European methods of calculation from those in the East when capitalism began? Above all, Europeans tried to calculate risk. In both East and West, risk was originally more than a simple subject of calculation or estimation. Risk was not something that could be accurately calculated. It was invisible and ultimately never fully revealed itself. Risk was something to be avoided, and sometimes it was seen as the workings of heaven or the divine providence and as punishment for sins from the past, including those from past lives.

Thus, even merchants did not calculate risk. They sensed risk and managed it collaboratively with their partners. It was gamblers, not merchants, who needed to calculate risk. In a gambling environment where money exchanged hands based solely on risk, calculating risk was essential. For those for whom gambling was not a pastime but a profession, the calculation of risk became absolutely essential. In societies where gambling was socially accepted, a method of calculating risk finally appeared, which spread to merchants, eventually permeating the entire society. We, in later generations, call the dominance of such gambling thinking in society "capitalism."

Weber identified rational calculation as one of the cores of capitalism. This is undoubtedly a meaningful reference to a key axis of capitalism. However, what is often overlooked is the content of the calculation. The calculation of profit under the double-entry bookkeeping system, while it must recognize the expectation of future values, is essentially a reflection of past profits. Weber's capitalist could calculate their profit through accounting records, but that profit is past profit, and therefore, it is profit without risk.

However, for capitalists, it is essential not only to calculate past, certain profits but also to calculate future risks for new investments. This is precisely where risk calculation becomes crucial. Entrepreneurs of the new era need risk calculations not just for past profits but for unrealized future profits. And it was through this risk calculation that the perspective and methods of calculating risk, which were originally important only to gamblers, became grafted. When the gambling mindset met the capitalist business practice, capitalism was born.

The essence of capitalist calculation lies in risk calculation. By the mid-17th century, when Pascal and Fermat sought to mathematically calculate probabilities, or even earlier when gamblers began trading in risk, capitalism was already taking shape. The recognition of trading in risk led to the creation of the insurance market. The insurance market is a space where risk is traded. Policyholders engage in transactions to reduce or transfer their risks, while insurers profit through gambling on risk. The practice of treating risk as a tradable commodity and a tool for profit represents the "capitalistic insurance ethos" (Seog, 2020b). This new spirit of insurance transformed the spirit of insurance, which originated from the spirit of solidarity of mutual aid in the past, into an object of profit generation.

The idea that risk can be traded created the insurance market and also the financial market. The trading of risk has become a symbol of capitalism. Regardless of the claimed justification for the insurance and financial markets, the essence of these markets is that they are arenas where gambling has been expanded and legitimized in a capitalist manner. The expansion of the capitalistic insurance ethos is not limited to the financial market. In the age of capitalism, the insurance ethos has permeated all markets, providing a foundation for generating profit through the trading of risk.

Episteme And The Capitalistic Insurance Ethos

Each era is characterized by épistémè, the knowledge of its time, says Foucault (2012a). The episteme of the classical era in the late 17th and 18th centuries was defined by identity and difference. This replaced the Renaissance era's focus on similarity. Instead of superficial resemblances, knowledge was organized around fundamental identities and differences in function. Under this episteme, natural history and general grammar were born, and the concern on money was formed. As we moved from the classical era to the modern era in the late 18th century, the episteme shifted towards the study of life and human. The problems of finite life and resources began to emerge. Biology and philology emerged, and modern economics, known as political economy, was born.

In the classical era, which was also the time when capitalism began to take root, where does the episteme of identity and difference come from? If the risk calculation and the capitalistic insurance ethos were crucial insights that opened the door to capitalism, shouldn't they be related to the episteme of the classical era?

What is risk? Risk refers to difference and variation. Calculating risk presupposes the existence of differences. Producing differences and labeling them is the essence of risk calculation. Thus, risk calculation draws out differences, which generates a differential risk classification table. Even today, the insurance industry focuses intently on creating risk classification tables. These tables categorize who is healthier, which buildings have higher fire risks, who or which cars are more likely to be involved in accidents, and so on. These classification tables are the results of risk calculation. Without precise differentiation and classification, an insurer's profit can be neither ensured nor calculated.

Risk calculation and the capitalistic insurance ethos thus produce and classify differences. This reflects the episteme of identity and difference observed by Foucault in the classical era. Whether the capitalistic insurance ethos or the era's episteme came first is not important. What matters is that risk calculation and the capitalistic insurance ethos embodied qualities representative of the classical era's episteme. The knowledge and perception embedded in risk calculation and the capitalistic insurance ethos permeated society alongside the expansion of capitalist thinking, ultimately becoming observed as the era's episteme.

The episteme of similarity in the Renaissance era involves analogy and metaphor. While similarity is still related to classification, it is a vague and imprecise classification. Before the rigorous calculation of risk, a vague classification of risk resembled the notion of similarity. The era of vague estimations of risk was an era of similarity, not one of identity and difference. It was only after the serious commencement of mathematical risk calculation that risk classification became more precise and rigorous. Then, similarity became transformed into identity and difference.

The modern era, which follows the classical era, is a time when life comes into focus and the insurance market significantly expands. For life and human to become central in the discourse of insurance, insurance had to struggle for hegemony against religion. The hegemony over life and human had to be transferred from God to humans. This shift coincided with the period when the insurance market was expanding and had to confront and compromise with religion. To achieve this, insurers had to transform their image from those who defied divine providence to those who conformed to it (Baker, 1997). In addition, it was necessary to spread the belief that insurance was not gambling but produced morally and religiously superior values. It was only in the 20th century, thanks to these efforts, that insurance could be separated from gambling in the minds of the general public.

The concern for life and human, alongside the expansion of the insurance market, also reflects the Zeitgeist, the spirit of the time, found in social insurance. Economics, which deals with decision-making under finite resources, is ultimately a response to the survival risks. Social insurance represents the era's episteme, in that the responsibility for human life is transferred from divine or religious authority to secular governments and the state. The concern for humans and their lives, coping with the risks associated with finite resources, has been represented in the expansion of insurance markets and the development of social insurance. This trend, as we have already observed, is also closely linked to changes in governmentality.

Foucault's episteme can be understood and organized through the lens of risk calculation and the capitalistic insurance ethos. The development and transformation of risk calculation and the capitalistic insurance ethos are closely linked to the evolution of capitalism. In this way, risk and insurance serve as the intersection and pivot axis where the episteme and capitalism meet.

Thus, the insurance market should not be regarded as just one of the diverse markets of capitalism. The insurance market is the very essence of capitalism, and the capitalistic insurance ethos gives birth to capitalistic markets. The era's episteme in the age of capitalism cannot function without intersecting with risk and insurance in some way. This intersection may be a thorough passage like crossing at an intersection, or it might be a subtle contact like a tangent.

As a reward, the insurance market has enjoyed privileges that other markets do not possess. This is because the capitalistic insurance ethos is predicated on the privilege of discrimination. Insurers classify consumers into the same category based on identity and discriminate based on differences. Therefore, the insurance market becomes a market where the contradictory words “fair discrimination” is used. The insurance market is a place where the paradoxical slogan "fair through discrimination" does not seem awkward. The insurance market has come to regard fairness as distribution of shares appropriate for each individual's risk, rather than uniform equity. In this way, the insurance market has positioned itself as a place where Aristotle's distributive justice is realized.

In this context, there is a fundamental conflict between public insurance and the insurance market. Public insurance is based on the principle of indiscriminate fairness, rather than discriminatory distributive justice. Public insurance upholds equity, while the insurance market upholds differentiation as its principle of justice. Thus, while the fundamental conflict between public insurance and the insurance market may superficially appear as a clash between social solidarity and capitalist profit, it can also be understood internally as a conflict between equity and discrimination, or between identity and difference.

Information Revolution And Insurance

It was argued earlier that the era of the information revolution should be appropriately described as an era of manipulation. The information revolution is an era of dividuals, multiple personalities, and chameleonic change. Rather than reducing uncertainty, the information revolution produces more risks and creates higher levels of risk. The combination of information and networks, which is the essence of the information revolution, has made the world more complex, characterized by continuity, connectivity, and uncertainty.

The information revolution is a technological revolution that involves acquiring and processing information more quickly and extensively. Businesses, leveraging revolutionary information processing technologies, enhance their competitiveness and pursue profit by offering their products and services to more consumers and more diverse markets. The information revolution reaches the general public primarily through these new or diverse products and services.

What are those firms ultimately pursuing by relying on the information revolution? They claim to share resources, provide personalized services and conveniences, or reduce resource waste. Some even present it as a means to promote social democratization or protect individual rights. However, no matter how they frame it, their efforts ultimately converge toward profit. They are simply finding ways to satisfy consumer desires to serve their own profits.

Their use of new technologies to pursue profit is quintessentially capitalist behavior. The information revolution remains firmly within the bounds of capitalism. In fact, it might be more accurate to say that the information revolution is converging toward an idealized vision of capitalism. So, where does this information revolution, interpreted as a capitalist expansion meet insurance?

Ultimately, what firms do with the help of information

is to classify consumers and segment products and services accordingly. Whether it's called a niche market, a new market, efficiency improvement, or cost reduction, the essence is the same—they are creating classification systems. Whether by creating new categories that didn't exist before, further subdividing existing ones, or establishing new criteria, their primary task is the creation of these classification tables. For them, the information revolution is about creating classification tables. The reason they gather more information and process it faster is to create advantageous classifications before their competitors do.

Creating classification tables has been the very task of the episteme since the dawn of capitalism. For these firms, the information revolution is the resurgence of this old episteme, now in the name of artificial intelligence or big data. And here, their jealousy becomes apparent. They were jealous of the privileges that insurers enjoyed in the capitalist system. They envied the insurance market, which could freely discriminate against consumers and still claim to be fair. They also attempted to discriminate against consumers in the name of efficiency or consumer satisfaction, but the state sanctioned this discrimination as unfair. Thus, they have always envied the insurance market, coveting its privileges.

The information revolution has provided them with an opportunity. Under the banner of the information revolution, the lines between discrimination and innovation began to blur, and long-held frameworks of thought started to crumble. Firms have finally reached the brink of fully sharing the privileges once reserved for insurers. In this way, the information revolution has transformed all firms into insurers.

The information revolution is, therefore, an insurance revolution. It has allowed all firms to emulate the discriminatory and classificatory practices of insurers, enabling them to categorize and differentiate consumers at will. The long-standing aspiration of complete differentiation, which has been a desire since the dawn of capitalism, is now becoming a reality. As a result, the state and social solidarity, which were based on equity and identity, are gradually yielding to the capitalistic insurance ethos, which is grounded in discrimination and difference.

The embrace of discrimination and difference by all firms can be seen as "becoming insurers" of firms and also as the culmination of capitalistic ethos. In modern terms, this can be interpreted as the process of neoliberal ideology spreading even further. This trend raises critical questions about the future of social solidarity. Is social solidarity now succumbing to neoliberalism, or is it preparing for a new form of solidarity?

Information And Command

In the age of information, both money and language become information. Cryptocurrency, artificial intelligence, and big data are devices that interpret and convert money and language into information. In the age of information, let us think about information which is the common denominator of money and language.

Money serves as a means of exchanging goods, while language serves as a means of exchanging meaning. Both money and language thus become memory banks (Hart, 2000). Money remembers and preserves the value of goods, while language remembers and preserves the value of meanings. To remember and preserve these values, money and language must be recorded. It's no coincidence that the earliest human records on Mesopotamian clay tablets were of monetary value. In this way, money becomes language, and language becomes money. Money becomes the language that expresses the value of goods, and language becomes the money that gives value to meaning.

According to Ferdinand de Saussure (1959), language does not merely assign names to pre-existing objects; rather, objects come into existence through language. It is through being named by language that things are perceived and recognized. Saussure's concept of the linguistic sign is divided into the "signifier" (signifiant) and the "signified" (signifié). The signifier is the mark of a sign, and the signified refers to the meaning or concept of the sign. The differentiation of things doesn't inherently exist but is instead created through the differences between signifiers. The distinction between things, which doesn't inherently exist, comes to exist as a difference between the signifiers. As a result, things are created through language.

If money is akin to language, then money will also be like that. The value of goods that money signifies also does not inherently exist but is instead created and recognized through money. Just as language brings things into existence, the value of goods in the market exists as the value expressed by money and through differences in value. Two goods with the same price are perfectly interchangeable, making them indistinguishable from the perspective of money. For consumers, the value of goods is measured in terms of utility, which is an extension of money. It is no coincidence that in economics, two goods are said to be "indifferent" when they provide the same utilities.

However, speech act theory suggests that the purpose of language may not be merely the transmission of information, but rather action and command. Language is not just a simple means of communication for describing and conveying information; it must be understood within the context of its surrounding environment. In different contexts, the speaker commands or directs the listeners to perform different actions. This perspective in speech act theory may have already been implicit when Saussure argued that things are brought into existence through language. If the act of assigning a signifier had been initiated merely to describe the thing, it would have been beautiful but unproductive, and would have been possible only with rich literary sensibility.

However, human life was likely not so leisurely. The earliest records of humanity were not literary but highly calculative. When monetary values were inscribed on clay tablets, they were probably records of debts and essentially commands to repay the debts. The reason people crave more money than they need for consumption might be because money itself is a command. More money represents a stronger command with greater reach.

Money and language are not simply descriptions that label things, but involve actions and commands. Given that money and language are information, information must also be a command. This could explain why people and firms so desperately crave information. It is not because they view it as a mere tool for communication, but because the storage and accumulation of information, like the language in speech act theory or the money in capitalism, are meant to direct actions and give commands to others. In the age of information and capitalism, information is not leisurely exchanged for literary or artistic purposes. From the very beginning, information has been a language and money for command and profit. It is precisely this reason that money and language could both be absorbed under the name of information. Money and language become information, and information is no other than command and power.

Information Revolution And The Insurance Industry

If every firm becomes an insurer, what will the existing insurers become? Now, they must compete with countless new insurers. The insurance market no longer exists as a separate entity. Every market is now an insurance market and a competitive market. Automobile firms, IT firms, and pharmaceutical firms are now all insurance firms. The moment they discriminate and classify consumers, risk is produced. And as risk is produced, the role of the insurer begins.

If other firms become insurers due to the information revolution, insurers may have to either transform into other types of firms or connect with these new insurers. Alternatively, they will have to classify and manage risks in an even more segmented and multidimensional way. The role of an insurer is not exhausted merely by producing risk. Insurers must reduce as well as produce risks simultaneously. Therefore, when firms only produce risks, insurers must still address the remaining risks. The ultimate role of the insurer depends on whether it can possess the capacity to cover the risks. Although competition in the field of risk coverage may increase, the production of risk can also present new opportunities for true insurers. While the privileges of insurers are gradually diminishing, their role is not disappearing.

The information revolution is likely to increase uncertainty rather than reduce it, ultimately leading to a greater demand for insurance. However, the critical question is whether this demand can be met within the traditional insurance market. The risks introduced by the information revolution are uncalculable and interconnected risks and high-level uncertainties. Aren't these precisely the risks that insurers have historically claimed could not be turned into insurance products? Haven't insurers been saying that unquantifiable, unpredictable, and interconnected risks are traditionally considered uninsurable? Moreover, these risks are related to networks and relationships, which also encompass moral hazard—the very type of risk insurers have long sought to avoid. The new risks brought about by the information revolution are, in fact, the same kinds of risks that insurers have been trying to distance themselves from. With numerous competitors emerging to cover past risks and an apparent lack of preparedness to address new risks, where will the conventional insurers find their places in the future?

Information Revolution, Life And Personhood

Earlier, we decided to refer to the information age of the Fourth Industrial Revolution as an era of manipulation, going beyond mere discipline and control. The once indivisible individuals are now being fragmented into "dividuals", compelled to transform like chameleons, and forced to further divide and reduce themselves. In this era of manipulation, governments, corporations, and individuals surveil and control one another. Faced with heightened uncertainty, individuals, now interconnected within complex networks, also become agents who themselves generate uncertainty.

The more individuals break things down, look further ahead, and calculate more meticulously to reduce uncertainty, the more uncertainty is actually produced in society as a whole. As everyone meticulously calculates with the same determination to respond to uncertainty, the world only becomes more uncertain. This is because the calculation formula for one individual's objective function, on the interconnected network of diverse wefts and warps, plays as a constraint for others. And these constraints are so complex and diverse that properly considering and calculating them become impossible.

When all firms become insurers and implement micro-classification and discrimination, macro-level uncertainty increases. While insurance is genuinely needed to respond to this uncertainty, the irony is that as all firms aspire to become insurers, uncertainty is maximized. It is now time for individuals to shatter their illusions about insurance.

But what does it mean that an individual is a being that is no longer divisible? In the age of information, when individuals are sliced vertically, horizontally, or even diagonally as dividuals, can they still exist as such? Can the sum of these dividuals ever be restored to the original individual? The concept of dividuals originally emerged from the black islands of the Pacific, referring to the various social or cultural roles and meanings of an individual (Karl Smith, 2012). However, in the era of data, dividuals are coldly dissected, transforming individuals into something entirely different—mathematical or semiotic figures and symbols. However, in the era of data, dividuals are, quite literally, entities that coldly dissect individuals and transform them into mathematical or semiotic numbers and symbols.

The idea of the individual as indivisible likely pertains to life and personhood. This is because, in principle, life and personhood are intrinsic to the essential existence and meaning of the individual. The idea that an individual should be treated with dignity as a being with life and personhood, and the idea that one exercises rights and responsibilities as an individual, capture the essence of what it means to be an indivisible person, or individual.

On the other hand, it seems that personhood can be distributed among dividuals, leading to the concept of a digital persona. The insult directed at a dividual can thus be interpreted as an affront to the whole individual. Consequently, each dividual might sometimes represent not just a part but the entirety of an individual. It is at this point that the issues of personal data protection and digital privacy are connected. More precisely, the personhood is not merely divided and allocated among dividuals; rather, it is copied and revived within each dividual, like a form of duplication magic. However, this duplication does not occur with the same intensity in every dividual. The degree of personal data protection may vary depending on the context and the specific dividual in question. The copy of personhood into dividuals is not so precise, much like that from an old copy machine.

In any case, the personhood within dividuals is not the personhood itself but a copy of it. The significance of the copy lies in its ability to represent the original. The copy of the personhood within dividuals holds meaning only when it summons the original personhood. However, it is important to note that the original personhood exists outside the collection of dividuals, not within it.

On the other hand, life cannot be divided or distributed from the beginning. Therefore, the most precise meaning of an indivisible individual might be rooted in life itself. Ultimately, personhood will also be defined based on life. Life cannot be broken down into data or information, although it can be interpreted through them. Perhaps it is possible to plant an avatar of life within the network, but like personhood, an avatar is merely a replica of life, not life itself. The original life, alongside personhood, exists outside the collection of dividuals.

It is precisely at this point that life and personhood become the most important aspects in the information age. While life may have always been significant, in an era where everything is divided and processed as information, life and personhood—entities that remain indivisible—stand out as being of utmost importance. The more information and data proliferate, the greater the significance of life and personhood, which is not divisible.

Thus, the true value of information must be assessed from the perspective of life and personhood. While firms and individuals may invest in and seek profit from the dividuals, their frontal lobes should focus not on the set of dividuals, but on what lies beside them. That space beside is a pitch-black void, beneath which there is a steep cliff, and below that, the molten lava of life and personhood flows. If they become blind to information and data and stumbles, they will have to feel the intense heat of life and personhood. Unfortunately, the profit of a firm is also nothing more than a fictitious dividual, which will silently disintegrate and melt away in the lava.

Information Revolution And Metric Space

What, then, is the ultimate role of the information revolution? When the world clamors for digitalization and virtual spaces and tries to send data and artificial intelligence into dreams or into the clouds, what does information innovation fundamentally do?

Upon reflection, informatization is ultimately a matter of distance. The process of informatization begins by altering the positions of previously distant points, either connecting them or bringing them closer together. Friends and relatives who once lived far apart are now connected in the palm of your hand, and people who were complete strangers can become friends or even family. In virtual spaces, we experience a closeness with people who are distant in reality. Stores in virtual spaces are connected to more dots, making it possible to trade with consumers at a distance that was unimaginable in the past. Now, no matter where you are on the planet, consumers can position a vast array of online shops just a hand's breadth away.

However, it would be a mistake to think of informatization simply as a means of connecting existing distances more quickly or closely. The essence of informatization is not to make distances closer, but to redefine distances. In this sense, informatization is about distance, not speed. Of course, speed and accessibility can also be interpreted within the concept of distance, so distance will encompass speed. However, speed is merely about how quickly one can move across an already defined distance. The fundamental reason why informatization is not about speed is because informatization must redefine distance itself.

How important is distance? The events of the world are defined and distinguished by distance. The relationship between two people can, in fact, be expressed by the distance between them. Family ties, friendships, and collegial relationships—all these human connections are measured by the distance between individuals. This is why sociology, which is concerned with relationships between people, pays close attention to networks and distance.

Let's take an example of the firm. A department within a firm is essentially a set of a core task, a range of related tasks and people connected to them within a certain radius. Marketing, manufacturing, accounting, investment, and risk management departments are such examples. These various departments are each like a circle or sphere with a certain radius from a central point, consisting of a collection of points within that radius. This applies not only to the visible distinctions between departments but also to processes and functional classifications. Of course, a single task, process, or function is a point that may be included in multiple spheres. In the end, the act of differentiation or classification is reduced to a matter of distance.

The role of the information revolution is not merely to

reduce distances but to redefine them. After the information revolution, we don't just remain in the same space; we move into a newly defined metric space with newly defined distances. This redefinition of distance creates new spheres. It is why points that were once close may now be far apart, while points that were distant may become closer. Points embraced within a sphere in the new space do not necessarily have to be the same as those that were in the same sphere in the past. In the new distance space, the distance between two existing points may become closer or farther away.

When new spheres are created and classified within this new metric space, the boundaries of departments within a firm must be adjusted, and procedures and perspectives must also change. The information revolution is not just about connecting and integrating a firm's information or putting it into a virtual space; it demands a simultaneous shift in how that information is viewed and classified. Firms that ultimately succeed in informatization will not be those that simply take the fast route or boast the high speed, but those that understand the meaning of distance in the new space.

9. FIRM

A Solid Surrounded By Liquid And Directed Towards Gas

There is a solid object. This object is sometimes equated with a person, and at other times with a machine. Yet, it is also equated with money and is even considered invisible energy. Thus, this object can be a living object, a non-living object, a liquid, or even a gas. Still, people regard it as something solid, a solid entity. A firm is such a bundle of contradictions. This contradiction churns and boils internally, while externally, it emits intense heat and can even explode.

A firm is inherently solid. The Korean word for a firm, " (giup)", comes from the Chinese characters "企業". The first character (企) combines "person (人)" with "to stand still (止)", depicting a person standing firmly on the ground. Another Korean word for a firm, "회(hoesa)", corresponds to Chinese characters "會社", whose second character (社) combines "altar (示)" with "earth (土)", representing something grounded and immovable. Therefore, a firm becomes solid because it must be something stable, firmly rooted in the ground.

The English term "company" traces back to the Roman infantry unit, where infantrymen had to stand firmly on the ground. The term "stock" in stock company, both in Eastern and Western contexts, carries the meaning of the stump of a tree. Traditionally, a company was the ground and the feet or trees standing firmly on it. A company, therefore, had to be solid. Another English term for a company, "firm," itself declares this idea of solidity. "Firm" has the meaning of being strong and stable, thus implies trust or an act of giving trust (such as a signature). Therefore, above all else, a firm should be a solid entity with stability that can be trusted.

On the other hand, a firm takes on risks and embarks on ventures to seek profit. Inside the firm are people referred to as workers, entrepreneurs, executives, and employees, and capital is accumulated from both internal and external sources. This capital will eventually be converted into new machinery, desks, factories, offices, or wages. In its form, a firm is a collection of people and money. The term "company," both in Eastern and Western contexts, includes the meaning of gathering or being together.

Firms do not exist independently of other entities within the economy or, more broadly, within society. Firms constantly move toward the outside. This is because the purpose of establishing a firm is not to promote friendship among insiders. Rather, the firm must distribute goods or produce products to sell to external consumers. From the very beginning, the existence of a firm is based on the presence of an external environment, with which it interacts and to which it is oriented.

Risk is something unseen in the future, something that does not stay still but wavers. A company's profit can only be gained by passing through such risk. Profit only becomes profit when the its opportunity is seized from amidst the risk and drawn into the firm. Therefore, the opportunity for profit shares an essential characteristic with risk. Above all, both risk and the opportunity for profit are like ghosts. It is the human desire to turn these ghosts into something visible that created the insurance market, firms, and capitalism. Under capitalism, risk flows backward from the future into the present, shifting from an invisible realm to a visible one, and the wavering of uncertainty is transformed into money, the certainty of the present.

A ghost is a being that drifts in the invisible realm of the void. So, a ghost is like a gas. On the other hand, money is like water that must flow continuously to prove its existence and create value. Therefore, what the firm does is a magical act of transforming gas in the air into a fluid liquid and collecting it. Profit is the result of that liquefaction. Corporate profit refers to the result of the liquefaction process that creates liquid called money from the gas of risks and opportunities.

Nevertheless, the firm itself is a solid. Workers, entrepreneurs, and capitalists bind themselves within numerous contracts and promises. No one can escape the confines of these contracts, making the firm a solid. Thus, the firm becomes firm.

This is the essence of a firm: transforming a gas into a liquid while asserting itself as a solid. A gas seeks to rise endlessly, defying gravity, while a liquid flows continuously across or downward on the surface. A solid, however, desires to remain stable under the greater force of gravity. Yet, this does not mean that a solid has weaker mobility than a liquid. It just struggles and holds on to its own weight constantly toward the center of the Earth.

Workers within a firm form the very core of such a solid. They constantly bear their own weight, enduring the pull of gravity. They seek stability because they experience fatigue. Workers become the foundation of the firm's existence, holding the center of gravity. However, as is often the case, once they settle into their roles, they inevitably become the weaker party. In the ever-changing landscape of modern capitalism, the position of strength belongs to gases and liquids that can move and adapt quickly.

The upper layer of a firm does not tolerate the stabilization of the firm's solid core. This is because the upper layer must constantly move toward the outside of the atmosphere, as the ghosts of risk and opportunity are always somewhere in or beyond the atmosphere. The strings of contracts meant to bind the gas are easily rendered ineffective because, from the outset, such strings cannot truly restrain the gas. These bonds are always most strongly applied to the workers, who, heavily influenced by gravity, find it difficult to move. Consequently, these binding strings become the harshest constraints on the workers.

Water, holding onto its liquidity, flows gently, mediating the conflict between gas rising toward the atmosphere and the solid gravitating toward the Earth's core. Flowing water brings life because it carries vitality within it. While water flows downward, it is always seeking opportunities to evaporate and rise upward.

Through the monetary rewards in their hands, workers gradually forget their own confinement and come to believe that the essence of the firm is the liquefaction of gases that has nothing to do with the solid. Workers feel pleasure in capturing vaporized ghosts and accumulating them as money. Satisfied and comforted by the meager flow of liquid that brushes past them, they sometimes laugh and sometimes cry. A lucky few may find the opportunity to shed their heavy iron coats and move upwards with lighter bodies. Eventually, they might even rise into the air. This is the only way they can escape the oppressive weight of gravity.

Money and finance define and sustain firms as they move between solids and gases. Therefore, money is not just liquidity, but also the water of life. Without this water of life, a firm will not be able to withstand its thirst and will die.

However, liquid can change its shape freely and will flow wherever it can find a path. Thus, money, while being the water of life, can also take life away. If it finds a more favorable place, it will flow there without hesitation. Therefore, even though a firm claims to be a solid, it is ultimately subject to the dominance of liquid. In reality, a firm is like a ship floating on the sea. No matter how sturdy the ship claims to be, its fate is determined by the whims of the sea. In this sense, modern firms are not much different from the medieval Islamic merchant ships that navigated the vast and unpredictable oceans.

The essence of a firm lies in the interplay between gas and solid, with liquid flowing between them to create unity. Liquid can both pit gas against solid and reconcile them. And liquid possesses the most powerful force because liquidity can flow anywhere, enjoying the ultimate freedom, and all participants crave this freedom. A life free from constraints, a life where one can command others at will—this is the gift and power that the highest form of freedom offers. Moreover, liquid can transform at any time. It can become gas, solid, or another liquid and then revert back again. Still, everything has meaning only when it can be reduced to liquid. In this way, liquid becomes the most essential matter in capitalism.

Understanding a firm must begin with grasping the diverse material transformations it undergoes. To truly comprehend the essence of a firm, one must see it as an entity that, grounded in solid, pursues and captures gas, continuously reducing and transforming it into liquid. This dynamic process of conversion and change is key to understanding the true nature of a firm.

Modern Firms: Eros And Thanatos

The defining feature of modern capitalism is the hegemony of finance. Understanding the nature of finance as a liquid helps explain this phenomenon. Gas is elusive, rising into the sky, while solid merely stands firm, enduring gravity. Only liquid has the capacity to flow freely across the surface. Thus, liquid defies human-made borders, moving constantly toward places where it detects a fragrance. It lingers in these fragrant areas, indulging in the scent, and prepares to move again when the fragrance begins to fade. Liquid is light enough to flow freely but heavy enough to remain in place when needed.

Capitalism initially began by traversing the surface in search of empty opportunities for profit, daring to face ghostly risks. As it flowed sideways, the gaze of merchants and capitalists was fixed solely upward and toward the gas. They were so preoccupied with avoiding risk and seizing profit that they had no time to look around. Blinded by greed, they engaged in violence and exploitation. The gleaming stones they accumulated thus became the seed money of capitalism.

The early capitalist era, focused solely on the gas, was an age of gas, where slaves had no voice of their own. Though they were solid, they were treated as if they were invisible, transparent gas, ignored and dehumanized. The importance of the solid only emerged with the Industrial Revolution, which shifted the center of gravity toward solidity. Workers in factories, producing goods, bore the weight and became the cogs in the wheel. Liquid still found its meaning in existence only in parasitizing the solid, unable to be fully independent from it. The confrontation between the alchemists attempting to extract liquid from the solid and the solid resisting them constantly amplified the conflict and exploded into a revolution.

By the late 20th century, the struggle between solid and liquid was declared a victory for liquid. The era of liquid had finally arrived, and the solid could only flounder in desperation, trying to avoid drowning. Liquid became even freer, able to move across horizons and landscapes, whether over rugged terrain or smooth surfaces. The advancement of information technology further lightened the weight of liquid, enabling it to flow even more effortlessly. Sometimes, like a viscous liquid crystal, it adhered to solids, leading the process of liquefaction. When liquefaction became too difficult, it would lighten itself without hesitation and flow toward a new host. The now-familiar aspects of the financial market—such as mergers and acquisitions (M&A), corporate governance, and financial derivatives and innovations— are all manifestations of liquid asserting and reinforcing its dominance, serving as a declaration of its triumph.

Take a look at any business textbook. Mergers and acquisitions are advocated as a way to increase corporate efficiency and firm value. In these discussions, efficiency and value are always defined and measured from the perspective of liquid. The solid within a firm may be torn apart or pushed out, but this poses no issue. From the liquid's perspective, any solid that cannot be liquefied must be discarded. This is precisely where the conflict between solid and liquid intensifies in the context of mergers and acquisitions.

What about corporate governance? It also aims to enhance firm value, but the value measured here is purely liquid value; solids are not incorporated as part of this value. Instead, they are treated as costs that drain the value. At times, corporate governance may appear to uphold justice, but this is merely justice defined for liquid or simply a coincidence. The actions and strategies described as enhancing the firm value in mergers and acquisitions and corporate governance are ultimately just fueling the liquid. The liquid, enriched by fuel, prepares once again to move toward a new host.

Derivatives and financial innovation using them also facilitate the liquefaction of solids, making the liquid lighter and more mobile. These instruments show off the power of liquid by enticing speculation and attracting more liquid. As liquids attract each other, they swirl together, generating stronger currents that extract more liquid and churn through the solid structures with even greater destructive force. It may seem as though liquid, rather than merely parasitizing solids, is generating new liquid through its own momentum. However, liquid cannot produce more liquid on its own, nor can it become a perpetual source of energy. The self-generation of liquid only results in bubbles, and it is a law of nature that those bubbles must eventually burst.

A firm is born from the supply of the water of life, and when that supply is cut off, it withers and dries up. The problem is that the water of life doesn't need to remain loyal to a single host. Freud speaks of Eros and Thanatos (Sigmund Freud, 1961). Eros is the life drive that breathes life into inorganic matter and maintains that life. A firm gains its life as a legal entity thanks to Eros. However, when a firm goes bankrupt or is absorbed by another through mergers and acquisitions, it is the result of the death drive, or Thanatos, the god of death and destruction. Which force—Eros or Thanatos—will prevail is ultimately determined by the liquid. The stronger a firm's solid characteristics, the weaker the liquid's determining power becomes. However, as a firm becomes more exposed and vulnerable to the liquid, the liquid's dominance grows stronger. In the current era when finance has become the center of capitalism, the power of the liquid is becoming stronger.

Liquid can both bring life and end life. While the birth of life exists only as a distant memory, death always lingers nearby, approaching as an ever-present anxiety and pain. Thus, liquid is often imprinted as an incarnation of Thanatos rather than Eros. The era of finance seeks to liquefy firms and assets through securitization. Excessive liquefaction, which destabilizes the center of gravity, leads to the evaporation of the water of life, forcing firms to succumb to Thanatos. Thanatos manifests in the forms of corporate raiders, restructuring, downsizing, private equity funds, business closures, and bankruptcies. In fact, the life drive in a living being cannot be stronger than the death drive. A living being can only postpone the death drive, but in the end, it must inevitably succumb to it. In this era of financial capitalism, where liquidity is venerated, liquid transforms into Eros and Thanatos, constantly oscillating between life and death.

Therefore, firms today must always be prepared for liquefaction. To remain as a solid, a firm must either possess the abilities to attract liquid or to survive independently of liquid. Most firms, lacking such abilities, must soften their rigidity and be ready to mix with or accept liquid at any moment. This is the only means of survival. Firms must segment or soften themselves. Otherwise, they will face the inevitable fate of being dismantled by the merciless liquid. However, transforming into liquids means relinquishing their centers of gravity and giving up being solids, ultimately leading them to surrender their fate to Thanatos.

Genealogy Of The Firm

Let us briefly explore the genealogy of the firm, from ancient Roman enterprises to modern joint-stock companies. In ancient

Rome, people formed associations for common interests. These associations aimed to enter into contracts with the Roman government and undertake various government projects. They collected and farmed taxes, developed gold mines, and built roads on behalf of the government. These associations were known as "societas publicanorum", which would correspond to partnerships or cooperatives in modern terms. We might call this the prototype of the firm—or simply a firm in its own right.

These early firms were rigid and inflexible, much like the helmets or shields of the Roman infantry. They were bound by contracts with the government, and the parties to these contracts could not be easily changed. The contract had to be upheld. If a partner left the firm or passed away, the contract had to be rewritten and revalidated. This rigidity gradually led to a softening of the corporate structure. Rather than strictly adhering to legal texts, the focus shifted towards ensuring the practicality of contracts. We may guess that the Roman laws were not necessarily enforced as written. As a result, a representative of the partners was elected, and the authority and responsibility of the other partners were reduced. Operations became separated from financing. Shares were traded and speculated on and became a tool for cronyism and illicit accumulation of wealth. The speculation and greed we witness in modern financial markets are, therefore, not entirely new phenomena.

As the rational administration of society grew increasingly strained, Rome eventually fragmented, and by the end of the 5th century, the Western Roman Empire fell. Only the Eastern Roman Empire, armed with gold and fortresses, managed to survive for a thousand years, but historians had already diagnosed the end of the ancient Roman era. Societas, the Roman corporate organization, also shared the fate of Rome, fading away along with the empire.

With the fall of the Western Roman, Europe transitioned into the medieval period. Unlike the Eastern Roman region, where the Byzantine Empire continued, the rest of Europe became centered around agriculture and rural life rather than commerce and urban centers. This shift marked the beginning of the feudal era in Europe. Under feudalism, local lords pledged loyalty to the king and paid taxes in exchange for territorial control and governance rights. This economic system was known as the manorial system, where the economy was self-sufficient, revolving around the lord and the peasants subordinate to the territory.

With the decline of commerce and the rise of an agriculture-based, self-sufficient economy, Rome's societas failed to continue its legacy. While commercial activities waned in Europe, medieval Islamic merchants thrived in the Middle East and beyond. These merchants were highly active, engaging in trade not only within the Middle Eastern region but also extending their commercial reach to West Africa and even to Korea and Japan at the eastern end of Asia. They were indeed adventurous merchants, traversing the entirety of the Old World.

The driving force behind the global trade ventures of Islamic merchants was the "qirad" or "mudarabah". Qirad represents a partnership between investors who provide capital and an entrepreneur or merchant who manages the business operations. While qirad can be viewed as a form of corporate organization, it can also be considered a financial technique, depending on the context. This arrangement is similar to modern limited partnerships.

Merchants who received investment capital through qirad engaged in trade and then distributed the profits between the investors and themselves according to their agreed-upon share. The distribution of profits in the form of pro-rated shares rather than debt with fixed interest would have been a highly significant and meaningful system in Islamic regions, where interest is prohibited. By raising funds through shares, merchants could share the risks of the trade with the investors. This allowed the merchants to focus on their trade without excessive concern over the business outcomes. This may have been an institutional mechanism that supported the vigorous and enterprising trade activities of Islamic merchants.

Qirad functioned both as a financial mechanism for raising capital and as an insurance mechanism for risk-sharing. Through this commercial innovation, Islamic merchants were able to traverse the globe. It is not difficult to see the resemblance between the share investment in qirad and the today's stocks in a stock company. In this way, qirad can be seen as a precursor to the stock company, laying the groundwork for its eventual emergence.

The advanced commerce and finance of medieval Islamic merchants, much like their contributions to science, likely influenced Europe, particularly the Italian region. In coastal cities like Venice and Genoa in northern Italy, organizations similar to qirad emerged. These were known as "colleganza" or "commenda". Like qirad, they involved raising investment capital and conducting maritime trade, with profits being distributed according to the equity shares. The success of Venice, which enjoyed immense wealth and glory during the Middle Ages, was underpinned by colleganza. As the modern era approached, the decline of colleganza paralleled the decline of Venice itself.

Meanwhile, the inland city of Florence focused not on maritime trade but on land-based commerce and finance. This focus led to the rise of the Medici banking family, which played a central role in leading the Renaissance in 15th-century Europe. The business structure employed by Florence's financiers was known as "compagnia". The compagnia expanded capital through a combination of the entrepreneur's own funds and external loans, which were then used to conduct business. Profits from the business could be retained internally to further expand operations. Additionally, large banking families established branches or divisions across various regions of Europe. The financial statements issued by the Medici Bank, which utilized double-entry bookkeeping, clearly distinguished between capital and liabilities (additional capital, more precisely), much like a modern corporation. Furthermore, the results of various divisions' operations were consolidated into a unified financial statement, resembling modern consolidated financial statements.

Stock Company

A stock company is an organizational structure that raises capital by issuing shares called stocks. However, a modern stock company is not just about raising capital through stocks; it also possesses crucial features such as limited liability for shareholders and legal personality. Raising capital through shares is not inherently difficult to conceptualize. This is because when business partners pool funds together to start a business, capital is naturally raised through shares. However, the concepts of limited liability and legal personality are legal constructs and products of human imagination. Upon reflection, they are quite unnatural. Limited liability implies that one can borrow money and yet not be obligated to repay it fully. Granting legal personality to a firm is essentially declaring that the firm will be treated as if it were a person. These two concepts are by no means natural.

Anyway, the stock company took its current form through the interaction of two business organizations in northern Italy: compagnia and the colleganza. However, this combination did not happen in Italy but in the western part of Europe, specifically in the East India companies of England and the Netherlands. These companies, like the colleganza, were primarily focused on maritime trade and, like the compagnia, were capable of raising capital from a variety of sources. The reason why the modern stock company began with these East India companies is that they had to plan for long-term, risky trade ventures. As a result, they were recognized as independent legal persons that could continue their business operations over time, and they introduced the concept of limited liability to share the risks with creditors, not just with shareholders. Now, the risk of business ventures was shared not only between entrepreneurs and shareholders but also with creditors. The stock company is not merely a fusion of the compagnia and colleganza; it is the product of a deliberate effort to pursue long-term business goals and actively seek ways to share risk.

Long-term business ventures naturally entail a high degree of risk and uncertainty, and without proper risk distribution, it would be challenging to sustain the business. The stock company was likely an invention of entrepreneurs to cope with this uncertainty. Therefore, a stock company is not only a profit-seeking business organization but also an insurance mechanism for managing, transferring, and sharing the risks associated with long-term business operations.

The concepts of legal personality and limited liability are directly tied to the essential characteristics of a stock company. The idea of legal personality originated in ancient Rome as a practical solution for ensuring the continuity of business operations. Without the concept of a legal person, there was the inconvenience of contracts being terminated prematurely whenever a partner changed during the business period. Legal personality was thus necessary to maintain business continuity.

However, the legal personality granted to modern firms is not a direct legacy of ancient Rome. The concept of a "persona ficta"—a fictional person—was introduced to the world anew by Pope Innocent IV in the 13th century (1250). This fictional person was a religious entity, capable of eternal life, much like the divine. As the era of science and governance gradually replaced the age of religion in the modern era, this persona ficta—once endowed with eternal life by divine authority—was reimagined as a legal entity, now granted life by law. The fact that a stock firm can possess legal personality and the capacity of eternal life will only mean business continuity in the secular world. In contemporary language, stripped of its religious connotations, the modern stock company refers to this capacity for business continuity indirectly as a "going concern," instead directly as eternal life.

In the case of limited liability, it has been debated for a long time due to its unnaturalness and the moral problem of not paying off debts. But it was eventually accepted. Above all, this may be because the transfer and sharing of risks arising from long-term business were absolutely crucial for the survival of stock companies.

A stock company, on the surface, appears to be a business entity that raises capital through the issuance of stocks. However, the essence of a stock company lies not in its stocks but in its business continuity and the transfer and sharing of risk. The importance of stocks stems not just from their role as a means of raising capital through share investment but from their ability to represent this essence of a stock company. Stocks represent eternal life through infinite maturity and also represent limited liability by transferring risk to creditors through default and bankruptcy.

Stock companies began as a means of making money and taking risks for entrepreneurs and investors. However, their actions outside of Europe led to violence, war, and colonization. In this way, stock companies became the leading organizations driving European imperialist expansion. As imperialist ambitions intertwined with capitalist desires, capitalism spread across the globe—this was likely the violence of capitalism that Marx witnessed. If capitalism is violent, it is because stock companies are inherently violent. Perhaps this is why, even now, the harms and violence of capitalism are always inseparable from the problems of stock companies.

10. FIRM THEORY

Anti-Market Firm

Originally, the existence of firms was not of great interest in economics. This aligns with the ideal of perfect competition in economics. In a perfectly competitive market, firms can be easily replaced by others at any time. Therefore, under perfect competition, the specific nature of a firm doesn't seem important, as the firm only needs to barely survive as a producer.

However, reality is not perfect competition. Firms have become more diverse and larger, and their internal structures have grown increasingly complex. As a result, understanding firms has become important, and the management and administration of firms have gained significance. This led to the emergence of not only business studies as a field of study focusing on the management of firms, but also the theory of the firm within economics in the 20th century.

What is Coase's theory of the firm, which is regarded as the orthodox view in economics? Coase's theory seeks to find the significance of the firm's existence by comparing the transfer of goods through market transactions with the transfer or production of goods within the firm. If transferring goods through production within the firm incurs lower costs than through market transactions, then production is chosen over transactions, and this choice represents the firm. To compare these two methods of transfer, the concept of "transaction costs" is introduced. Transaction costs are the costs associated with market transactions. If the production costs of a good are lower than the transaction costs incurred from purchasing the good in the market, the firm will come into existence. Upon closer examination, it becomes clear that this is not a particularly novel story. In essence, if it is cheaper to produce something yourself rather than buying it from someone else, you will produce it yourself. Buying from someone else corresponds to market transactions, while producing it yourself corresponds to production within the firm. While the content itself may not be groundbreaking, later economists have focused on the concept and details of transaction costs, expanding Coase's theory of the firm to further understand firms.

Perhaps the lack of particularly novel content in Coase's theory provided later scholars with various possibilities for expansion. The truly important point of Coase's theory is that it highlights how firms, like any other product, can be subjected to cost analysis. Whether it's market transactions or running a firm, both incur costs, and these costs must be considered to choose the alternative that yields the greatest benefit. Wouldn't rational economic agents behave in such a way? This is precisely why Coase's approach, though seemingly distinct from neoclassical economics, ultimately became integrated into mainstream economics. Rational decision-making based on cost considerations is the cornerstone of modern economics. Consequently, modern theories of the firm, built upon Coase's foundation, offer a variety of meaningful analytical tools for understanding firms.

Coase's theory of the firm can be considered useful in the sense that it provided a starting point for analyzing firms. However, its utility has led to a rather lenient attitude towards the fundamental problems of the theory. Let us briefly examine some of these potential problems (see Seog, 2014, 2020c).

First, there is an issue of historical inconsistency. Coase's theory of the firm is reminiscent of a kind of origin myth for the birth of a firm, ending with "That's how the firm came to be." However, firms appear to have existed long before the point in history that Coase describes as their inception. In Coase's theory, the firm emerges primarily as a producer—an entity that opts to produce goods directly rather than purchase them in the market. Yet, historically, firms did not originate as producers; they began as contractors and merchants.

Scholars often trace the origins of the firm to the societas of ancient Rome. The societas emerged not as a producer but as a contractor with the government. In modern terms, it played a role similar to that of a party in government procurement contracts or public construction projects. This ancient form of business organization was created to fulfill tasks on behalf of the government, such as collecting taxes or developing gold mines. It did not come into existence as a result of weighing the decision to purchase goods from the market or produce them directly, unlike Coase suggests. Instead, it was formed to carry out work that was assigned through contracts.

Moreover, these tasks were not something an individual could accomplish physically alone; they required collective efforts, which necessitated the creation of an organization rather than relying on a single person. Beyond the physical aspects, there was also the challenge of bearing risk. Bearing the entirety of a business's risk alone was difficult, so firms were established to facilitate mutual aid through cooperation and risk-sharing. Coase would have imagined firms as producers operating in a (factor) market where numerous unspecified buyers and sellers existed. However, the earliest firms were cooperative organizations created to perform specific tasks demanded by specific consumers.

Are the firms of ancient Rome just stories of a bygone era? If so, what about the merchant guilds of the East Asia, the qirad in the Islamic regions, the compagnia or colleganza in Northern Italy, or the early modern joint-stock companies? It is true that these firms operated with the assumption of an unspecified large number of consumers. However, they did not emerge as producers. Rather, they were merchant organizations that sought to profit by moving goods from one place to another. These organizations were not born as a result of a Coasean deliberation on whether to purchase parts in the market or produce them directly. Instead, they were formed because trading required cooperation and it was not feasible to trade alone and also because the risks involved were too great for one individual to bear alone, necessitating risk sharing among people.

The essential foundations for both ancient and early modern firms were cooperation and risk-sharing. These aspects did not presuppose the firm as a producer, nor did they necessitate decisions about whether to buy or produce. It wasn't until after the Industrial Revolution that firms primarily as producers emerged. Coase's theory of the firm, with its focus on the producer, is, like most origin myths, intriguing and instructive but ultimately a fiction.

Second, another aspect of the historical inconsistency is the issue of the market's existence. Coase not only positions the firm within the production process but also presupposes the existence of the market within that process. However, markets are neither self-evident nor easily established. It was only after the rise of capitalism that markets began to expand significantly. The existence of firms does not necessarily require the existence of markets. History bears witness to how difficult it is to establish markets. According to anthropological evidence, market trades are neither universal nor natural; they are merely a mode of exchange that became widespread with the expansion of capitalism (David Graeber, 2011).

The reason Coase's narrative seems so natural is probably because, to us living in the modern era, the existence of markets appears entirely self-evident. This is either because we are so accustomed to the age of capitalism or because we have been captivated by the magic of economics.

Third, beyond the issue of historical discrepancies, Coase's theory also contains a potential contradiction that might be easily overlooked. As suggested by the title of Coase's paper, many interpret his theory as an explanation of the nature of the firm. In Coase's world, market transactions and firm production are set in opposition to each other. If an entrepreneur purchases a needed product from the market, he is utilizing the mechanisms of the market; if he produces it himself, he is utilizing the mechanisms of the firm. This is often referred to as the "make-or-buy" decision and is considered the core of the firm's origin story.

If we accept this narrative at face value, it's easy to interpret it as follows. If an entrepreneur producing directly signifies the birth of a firm, then their purchasing from the market implies the absence of a firm. However, this interpretation raises some questions. If this interpretation is correct, why is it that the other entrepreneur, who manufactured and sold the product the entrepreneur purchased, cannot be qualified as a firm? Buying a product from the market presupposes the existence of another entrepreneur who produced and sold that product. Within the make-or-buy framework, that entrepreneur should be also a firm. Therefore, understanding Coase's narrative of the firm's origin purely through the simple make-or-buy framework inherently leads to a contradiction.

In a world governed by the simple make-or-buy framework, firms must have already existed from the outset. Within this framework, Coase's narrative might be about whether there are one or two firms or about the size of the firm, but it doesn't reveal the secret of a firm's origin. The secret of a firm's birth is revealed not when it goes from one to two, but when it goes from zero to one. In the make-or-buy framework, firms already exist; they aren't newly created.

Therefore, the simple make-or-buy framework cannot adequately explain the birth or nature of the firm. Perhaps this is why Coase and subsequent economists had to focus on the boundaries and size of firms, as well as the contracts between employers and employees, or even among stakeholders. It might be easier for the myth of a firm's origin to survive within the make-or-buy framework, if we accept the following scenario: the market must be a place where individual entrepreneurs trade what they have each produced alone; and only when these multiple entrepreneurs decide to produce together instead of separately does a firm finally come into existence.

Transaction costs can explain the choice of production over purchasing, but they do not necessarily impl an increase in the number of people involved in the production process. If we genuinely wish to understand the firm as a relationship among multiple people, it must inevitably be linked to the perspective of viewing the firm as a mechanism of cooperation. However, the intriguing myth that a firm was born as an antithesis to the market must be abandoned. Instead, what remains in hand is only the dry birth certificate proving that the firm is merely a mechanism of cooperation.

Structuralist Firm

Coase's approach to comparing markets and firms appears to be unconsciously close to the dichotomous framework of structuralist methodologies, particularly those of linguist Ferdinand de Saussure and anthropologist Claude Lévi-Strauss. In structuralism, concepts are often understood through binary oppositions, where each term is defined in relation to its opposite. Just as "clean" is understood in contrast to "dirty," or "good" in contrast to "bad," Coase’s framework suggests that the understanding of firms and markets is mutually dependent. The firm is understood in relation to the market, and vice versa, similar to how structuralism posits that language and concepts are perceived and defined through these dualistic relationships.

Under Coase's project, the firm is defined in relation to the market and only through the market. This raises the question: how should the market itself be defined? The market's definition is also contingent upon the existence of firms because the market presupposes the presence of suppliers. In other words, the symbolic signs of market and firm are mutually referential, each relying on the other for its definition. This interdependence underscores the structuralist idea that concepts can only be fully understood through their relationships with opposing or complementary terms.

In Coase's world, however, the market is treated as if it inherently exists, serving as the foundational premise for his argument. The market is defined in and of itself, almost as if it possesses a divine or inherent quality—this could be seen as the fetishization of the market or perhaps its mathematical axiomatization. All entities of nature are creations of God, and all mathematical results are derived from axioms. Likewise, firms are merely outcomes of the divine or axiomatic market. Coase's theory suggests that firms are the rebellious offspring of this market deity, portraying them as heroic yet inevitable creations. This narrative, however, seems to echo a common theme in mythology, which is not particularly novel or exceptional.

Coase's theory, by deifying and axiomatizing the market, presents firms as emerging from the market while simultaneously positioning them in a binary opposition with the market. This raises a fundamental question: Is the firm merely an offspring of the market, or is it a conflicting competitor? On the one hand, Coase attempts to frame firms in a dichotomous opposition to the market, yet on the other hand, he places them within a linear genealogy extending from the market. The inherent contradiction in Coase's theory stems from this incomplete structuralist approach.

Just as the market precedes the firm, the firm also precedes the market. In the binary framework where the existence of the firm depends on the market, the existence of the market must equally depend on the firm. A market can only come into being when it becomes cheaper to buy something from others than to produce it oneself. Thus, from the firm, the market emerges. Before determining which came first—the firm or the market—all we can ascertain is the difference between them. And perhaps, the history of self-producing what is needed precedes the history of acquiring it through trades with others.

As long as we understand the firm as an abstract organization that produces something, then it is the firm, not the market, that should function as the axiom. Instead of pondering the origins of the firm, we should have been questioning the origins of the market. However, Coase's theory, by axiomatizing the market, imposes the assumption of its inherent existence. Because the existence of the market was not questioned, the firm could only be contrasted not with the market but with transactions. The act of trading was awkwardly compared to the institution of the firm. As a result, it has become difficult to properly recognize the contradictions within the incomplete structuralist perspective.

Insurer Firm

Frank Knight's exploration of risk and insurance provides a foundational perspective on the firm, especially in how they manage uncertainty, the high level of risk that cannot be easily quantified (Frank Knight, 2009). For Knight, the ability of a firm to handle uncertainty is what justifies its existence and enables it to generate profit. Additionally, he mentions the "unlimited" potential for capital raising and business scope in stock companies due to their advantages in managing risk.

However, when Knight mentioned the unlimited nature of stock companies, it was a rhetoric. This should be understood to mean that stock companies can take on costly ventures because they can easily secure external capital. It was never meant to imply that they could grow infinitely in a literal sense.

Knight was also the economist who most seriously considered moral hazard as a key factor limiting the infinite expansion of firms due to internal inefficiencies. He pointed out, before Coase, that a firm's size is constrained by these internal inefficiencies.

Knight's theory of the firm, despite being criticized and overshadowed by Coase's more popular approach, delves into critical aspects that Coase's framework tends to overlook. Above all, Knight linked the nature of corporate activities with uncertainty and the firm's capacity to manage it, including insurance. A firm's profits can only be created if it has superior capabilities in responding to and handling uncertainty. A successful entrepreneur or manager should possess such superior ability and judgment. This perspective was pioneering at a time when the importance of risk in business was not fully appreciated in mainstream economics.

Knight extends the principles of insurance to the firm, using them to explain corporate profit. The insurance principle involves managing risk through integration and diversification. Knight expands this concept to address the incentive problems associated with insurance and the highly uncertain risks that cannot be commodified as insurance products, as well as the abilities of the entrepreneur. By pooling risks according to the law of large numbers and concentrating them with experts, firms can achieve greater efficiency in risk management. Additionally, shareholders in stock companies can manage risk through diversified investments. These various mechanisms of risk management and sharing enhance the firm's efficiency. Beyond conventional insurance and risk management, it is the management of uncertainty and decision-making that generates profit for the firm. According to Knight, the firm can be understood as a mechanism for risk management and insurance.

Entrepreneurs are required to perform functions of managerial decision-making and control. As the problems of information and uncertainty are inseparable from management, the entrepreneur's abilities cannot be directly contracted. In other words, the entrepreneur cannot sell their abilities in the market (Nicolai Foss, 1993). From a Coasean perspective, this could be interpreted as a consequence of transaction costs, which prevent such abilities from being traded. Therefore, the entrepreneur must plan production themselves and collaborate with workers to realize these plans. This is how the firm comes into existence.

Unlike Coase, Knight conceived of the firm not as a substitute for market transactions but as a result of uncertainty in the market. The criterion of efficiency that determines the existence of a firm is not transaction costs but the ability to respond to uncertainty. In this context, the market refers to the consumer market where products are traded, not the market within the production process as Coase envisioned. Uncertainty is not limited to the production process but also includes uncertainty in the consumer market. Therefore, in Knight's view, the firm does not necessarily have to be a producer, unlike in Coase's case.

It may be said that Knight focused on the operation of the firm or the distribution of risk and control within the firm rather than why a firm exists. In other words, with the existence of the firm admitted, he seemed to be interested in the function of a firm and the source of its profits. It is true that his approach has indirect implications as to why firms exist. But Knight did not explicitly define the firm's existence, which is why Coase is often seen as the foundational thinker in firm theory.

Knight not only explained a firm's profits through the principles of risk and insurance but also compared and explained different firm organizations such as sole proprietorships, partnerships, and corporations. He discussed the importance of moral hazard and incentive systems, which foreshadowed what later became known as agency theory and corporate governance. However, by sidelining Knight's insights, subsequent scholars recognized moral hazard as a persistent problem in firms but failed to grasp that the risk, which gives rise to moral hazard, fundamentally constitutes the essence of the firm.

The connection between risk and profit is a crucial mechanism through which a firm transforms future ghosts into present liquidity. At the very least, Knight was imagining a connection between gas and liquid in the firm. Compared to Coase's epistemologically contradictory view of the firm, Knight's perspective might be seen as a theory that more closely approaches the nature of the firm.

Of course, even if Knight sensed the nature of gases and liquids through the connection between risk and profit, he did not have a sufficient understanding of the nature of firms. Profit is merely a monetary representation of value attributed to shareholders, and risk extends beyond mere uncertainty to encompass various dimensions. Knight's focus on only uncertainty and profit as the core concepts of the firm reveals a partial grasp of its essence. Furthermore, he showed no interests in the firm's solid aspects. As a result, although Knight acknowledged the significance of moral hazard and discussed corporate governance, his analysis remained confined to the issues between shareholders (capitalists) and managers (entrepreneurs) without advancing further.

We need to distinguish between different concepts of the firm. The firm as a group that produces something is an abstract concept, which indeed precedes the market. Coase's concept of the firm is closer to this abstract idea. On the other hand, Knight's interest is in the concrete firm, i.e., the kind of firm we commonly refer to. It's true that scholars after Coase have expanded on his theory to deepen our understanding of firms. Only when Coase's theory is expanded in this way will Coase's firm finally become closer to Knight's firm.

As previously mentioned, in fact, Coase's theory does not address the nature of the firm. This is because Coase's theory conflicts with historical context and lacks epistemological rigor. Nonetheless, Coase's theory is often considered fundamental in economics because economics is also built upon the common axiom that market trades naturally exist. Another important reason for its prominence may be that the expanded view of the firm in Coase's theory proves quite useful under the axiom.

A Community Of Risk And Cooperation

Coase's view of the firm as a substitute for market transactions and Knight's view of the firm through the lens of insurance principles are either insufficient or prone to misunderstanding. Was it because defining the firm as a mechanism for cooperation to pursue common interests seemed too ordinary and uninspiring? However, this cooperation encompasses not only the practical, operational cooperation necessary for conducting business but also the capital cooperation achieved by sourcing capital from multiple investors, and finally, the cooperation in risk-sharing in various forms.

Operational cooperation within a firm typically takes the form of decision-making and the allocation of responsibilities and authority within the framework of partnerships or bureaucracies. Bureaucracy, in turn, is combined with a hierarchy of command. Superiors issue authoritative commands to subordinates and sometimes delegate authority, while subordinates follow these orders and exercise the delegated authority.

Cooperation does not only mean collaboration. Cooperation often takes the form of the division of labor, where tasks are distributed, leading to increased efficiency. When Adam Smith mentioned the importance of the division of labor, it was neither surprising nor new. Humanity had known about it for a long time.

Operational cooperation is applied within a firm through the division of decision-making and tasks. Meanwhile, capital cooperation is achieved when external investors provide the funds necessary for business activities. This represents a division of labor between external investors and internal managers and workers. The cooperation between external and internal parties is imperfectly achieved through the pursuit of profit and mutual monitoring or checks, rather than a sense of community. From the moment cooperation is promised, the two sides begin to distrust each other.

In contrast, cooperation in risk-sharing is more subtle. This is because risk is like a gas or a ghost—it is not confined to a single place but is dispersed everywhere. Risk permeates both operational and capital cooperation. Even when it is not explicitly named as such, risk is inherently present within these processes. The division of labor and the division of decision-making between managers and workers inherently involve the sharing of risk.

In capital cooperation, risk is a primary consideration. Shareholders provide capital to the firm, but in doing so, they set up various barriers to protect themselves from risk. Limited liability, shareholder rights, class actions, voting rights, and bankruptcy are all mechanisms designed to protect shareholders' rights and minimize potential losses. The same applies to creditors. Workers, who provide human capital instead of financial capital, also protect themselves from risk through labor laws, commercial laws, civil laws, and social insurance. While each party takes steps to defend themselves against risk, they ultimately share and bear the risks associated with the firm together.

In this sense, they form a risk community. Thus, a firm exists as a community of risk and cooperation. From this perspective, a firm does not necessarily originate from the production process or need to be a producer. It is sufficient simply to be an entity that facilitates the movement of goods. Moreover, the sharing of risk is not limited to managers or shareholders alone. A company is a community of various stakeholders and cannot be the exclusive property of any single group of stakeholders.

From the perspective of a firm as a community that shares risk, there is a similarity to Knight's view of the firm as an insurance mechanism. Both perspectives focus on the role of the firm in managing risk, not merely to reduce it but as a means to generate profit. However, the point that diverges from or extends Knight's concept is that a firm does not just respond to risk efficiently to make an immediate profit; rather, this risk response becomes a tool for pursuing further risks. Risk response serves as a means for the continuous pursuit of new risks. A firm is thus a community aimed at profit, with profit opportunities arising from the relentless pursuit of risk.

Risk-sharing mechanisms and insurance ultimately exist as tools for pursuing risk. In this sense, it might be more accurate to describe a firm not as an insurance machine that reduces risk, but as a gambling machine that actively seeks out risk. While insurance may seem to reduce risk when viewed in isolation, the true reason a firm requires insurance is to capture even more risk. Insurance and gambling are essentially indistinguishable twins from the outset.

Paranoid Firm

Describing a firm as a community of cooperation might lead to an overly relaxed view of the firm, evoking images of people helping each other out of affection and camaraderie. However, a firm is not a community based on such bonds but on a hierarchical order grounded in commands and directives. While the term "cooperation" can still be applied, it does not reflect a harmonious community. Instead, the stock company, the crown jewel of capitalism, is a battleground where relentless competition, checks, and struggles are constantly repeated both internally and externally.

Economists' focus on the processes of command, control, and authority in corporate decision-making is both significant and accurate. Corporate decision-making is distinctly different from decision-making in the market. But why must decisions within a firm be based on a hierarchy of commands and authority? This necessity is often justified from the perspectives of efficiency and rationality, as is commonly accepted.

However, efficiency and rationality do not have a single direction. We often witness cases where reality is justified solely by a narrow view of efficiency and rationality. It will be insufficient and overly simplistic to use financial performance and visible outcomes as a paramount measure of efficiency or rationality. This approach is likely related to capitalism's overconfidence on monetary measurement.

Firms may seem to have escaped market transactions, but they could not escape money, the market's foundation. Even when corporate decisions are justified in the name of efficiency and rationality, they are still evaluated and measured in monetary terms. Firms might appear distinct from markets. From the perspective of money, however, firms and markets are similar, becoming indistinguishable in a slightly dark place.

Why, then, must modern firms be organizations that pursue

narrow efficiency and rationality? That may, perhaps, be related to the genealogy of power shifts. Before capitalism, absolute power was held by monarchs. As capitalism emerged, these monarchs had to cede their power to capitalists. Whether through bourgeois revolutions, civil revolutions, or democratization processes, the transition marked a shift where the absolute rights of monarchs were distributed to capitalists and citizens.

However, absolute power was a sweet temptation for everyone. The distribution of the power does not simply lead to fragmentation into small pieces. The nostalgia for the absolute power that was disappearing might have driven a desire for a new kingdom where such power could be reestablished. Perhaps the reason why absolute monarchy gradually faded is not because it collapsed, but rather because it sought new territories and moved across the surface. The new territory it found was the stock company. Under capitalism, while absolute power was fragmented in political domains, it grew even more pronounced in the kingdom of stock company.

When the Dutch and English East India Companies established colonies and exercised imperial rule, those stock companies reigned as the absolute monarchs of the new kingdoms. The stock company became the new kingdom of the capitalist era, succeeding the political kingdom that once dominated physical territories. This new kingdom rules over a liquid territory rather than a solid territory, a new and peculiar form of kingdom that appears for the first time in history.

According to Gilles Deleuze and Félix Guattari, the despotic state exhibits symptoms of paranoia (Deleuze and Guattari, 2014). All desires are directed solely towards the despot. A despot is wary of the dispersion or spread of desires, and constantly suspects and monitors his surroundings. The despot occupies the apex of the pyramid of desire.

Firms that admire despotic monarchies are also unable to escape this paranoia. Inside a firm, the CEO occupies the position of despot. All desires must be directed towards the CEO, who holds ultimate authority and issues commands to subordinates. The CEO's commands then cascade down the pyramid of the corporate hierarchy.

Desire converges and ascends toward the pinnacle of the pyramid, while commands descend and spread broadly below. This reciprocal motion of ascending desire and descending commands, brushing past each other, is what defines the hierarchical order. To facilitate the smooth transmission and execution of commands and directives, authority is delegated, and discipline is enforced within the organization. This structure is called bureaucracy.

Bureaucracy is generally regarded as a product of rationality. On the other hand, however, it also serves as a mechanism to maximize the desires captured by the despot and to alleviate the fatigue of the despot. This is precisely why bureaucracy was implemented in Asian despotism before the advent of capitalism.

In a bureaucracy, the delegation of authority is accompanied by the delegation of responsibility. When roles and responsibilities are properly allocated according to authority, it is considered a rational distribution of decision-making. However, this represents at best a partial rationality. The authority and responsibility allocated to them are merely distributions within the chain of command. No matter how rationally authority is distributed within the chain of command, desires are never distributed sufficiently among them. Desires continuously converge toward the despot and must not leak out along the way. As long as desires are not distributed, the delegation of authority and responsibility within the chain of command remains asymmetrical and, therefore, irrational.

To justify the convergence of desire, the firm should constantly reaffirm the despot's power. The closer one is to the despot's position, the greater the chance to capture a portion of this desire. Thus, the despot moves loyal subordinates to positions close to him. Because the number of close positions is inevitably limited, subordinates compete in loyalty to gain the opportunity to move closer. This is why the hierarchical order takes the shape of a triangular pyramid—because it functions as a mechanism to foster competition in loyalty. Additionally, to instill fear of constant surveillance, the despot measures and pressures subordinates on their loyalty and performance. In this way, the firm becomes a panopticon.

All measurements are gauged solely by the magnitude of desire contributed to the despot. The basic yardstick for all measurements taught in the business school is precisely this size of desire converging toward the despot. This is why the magnitude of this desire is always quantified in monetary value. Monetary value can be calculated in numbers, and numbers can be arranged in a single line. Only after they are lined up can they be compared to each other, and only then can an order table of efficiency and rationality be attached to see who is ahead of others. In the end, the ranking of efficiency and rationality is another name for the order determined by the measure of this desire.

On the other hand, this observation might apply only when looking exclusively inside the firm. However, a firm is not a closed organization that exists solely within itself. While the CEO may hold the position of a despotic monarch, desire does not stop there. Doesn't the power of a despot is derived from ruling over a territory with the blessing or in place of a deity? Likewise, in a firm, there exists a deity that reigns above the despot. In this position of deity stands the shareholders, with the majority shareholders being the most supreme. The desire that converges toward the despot is not ultimately owned by the despot but is instead offered as a ritual tribute to the deity. Of course, in this ritual process, the despot receives a significant share of desire, likely leaving them with little reason to complain.

To produce the desire that will be offered as tribute to the deity, firms continually compete with one another, distributing commands and responsibilities. The reason desire is measured solely in monetary terms is not because the despot directly demands it, but because it is ultimately the shareholders—the deity—who crave this measure of desire. The insatiable thirst for desire and the anxiety to fulfill it, shared by both the deity and the despot, drive the firm to exhibit paranoid pathological behaviors. Modern firms become paranoid machines, spurring on self-destructive competition, mutual surveillance, and internal conflicts. From the perspective of desire, bureaucracy and hierarchy rush towards the entrenchment of paranoia. So-called rationality and efficiency may serve to mask the paranoia, but in fact, they only exacerbate it. In addition, the obsession with rationality and efficiency also attaches itself to the paranoia.

Linear Firm

The linear firm follows in the footsteps of the paranoid firm. The paranoid firm mirrors the triangular pyramid of a despotic monarchy. At the apex sits the despot, with the structure broadening downward to include nobles, vassals, commoners, and slaves. Thus, the paranoid firm takes the shape of a triangle. The despot, by drawing a vertical line upward, connects with the deity. As long as the deity permits, the despot can claim to be almost divine.

The reason why the linear firm originates from the paranoid firm is because the direction of movement on the triangle of the paranoid firm is always a straight line. The concentration of desire toward the despot signifies that the movement of desire must proceed in a straight line, not sideways, but toward the apex of the triangle. On the other hand, command and authority are transmitted downward in a straight line through the bureaucratic hierarchy. Desire moves upward toward the apex, while commands move downward toward the broad base, both moving in straight lines. Because desire and command must move in straight lines on the geometric shape of the triangle, the paranoid firm becomes a linear firm.

The efficiency, profit, or stock prices measured in monetary terms always move with a linear perspective in mind. This is because these are devices for lining up the object of measurement in a straight line. It is no coincidence that the Chinese character for "straight" (直) also means measured "value". In addition, the Chinese character for "value" (値) also contains "straight". This is because the measurement of money is a linear movement.

Economics also knows the beauty of these straight lines. Therefore, complex reality is transformed into a straight line by using monetary value. The reason why economics equates risk with actuarial probability is not because risk can only be expressed mathematically. Rather, only actuarial probability can line up highly complex and multidimensional risks on a closed straight line. The reason why economics advocates profit maximization and utility maximization is not because firms or consumers behave that way in reality. Rather, it is because a curve can be converted into a straight line only by solving the maximization problem. This is why modern economics admires mathematicians' differential calculus and differential equations, which are far from the real economy. If you look at a curve infinitely close with the eye of differentiation, the curve, at some point, becomes a straight line.

Another reason why a paranoid firm is linear lies in the inheritance of bloodlines. When a despot passes the throne to direct lineal descendants, it is an act of practicing linearity. Similarly, a corporate executive's desperate efforts to pass on the reins of the firm to their lineal successors reflect the linear nature of the firm. The same goes for major shareholders who, under the illusion that they own the firm, attempt to pass it down to their direct lineal descendants. A paranoid machine always moves in a straight line.

The direct lineage succession is not limited to people. Capital forms an even more relentless bloodline, and moves in a straight line. Money and capital give birth to "beneficial offspring" called interest, preparing for direct lineage succession. Capital does not grow simply because the return on investment is high. The growth of capital is a process in which money continually forms direct lineage. As interest begets more interest and capital begets more capital, capital is passed down and the lineage of capital expands ever more.

This is precisely why capitalism needed the revival of interest. In capitalism, capital admires a living organism that practice the preservation and prosperity of the species. Therefore, capital, like a living organism, longed for the proliferation of its lineage, and for that, capital also had to be able to reproduce and extend its lineage. In this way, "bloodline capital" became the basic unit of building the capitalist era.

Therefore, when capital increases with compound interest, this is direct lineage, and therefore linear motion. Investment textbooks might say that compound interest is not a straight line. Interest that increases with compound interest grows exponentially or geometrically, and this is depicted by a curve that becomes increasingly steep.

However, the exponential form is the outward appearance revealed by linear motion. While compound growth may not seem linear, in fact, this perception is merely a matter of what is placed on the horizontal axis. If the capital amount is aligned on the horizontal axis, compound growth is simply moving in a straight line according to the capital amount. The only difference is that as the amount increases, it accelerates and therefore travels farther. Although it races away at a fast pace, it is still moving along a straight line. The reason compound growth appears to us as exponential rather than linear is because time is placed on the horizontal axis. Because they run away faster and faster as each day passes, when lined up in sequence, they only appear to take on an exponential form.

Likewise, consider the reproductive model of biological lineage. If one parent continues to have two children, it results in a linear motion, yet the number of direct descendants increases exponentially. Exponential growth exists not by denying linear motion but rather as its creation.

The succession of direct lineage in positions of power and the compound succession of bloodline capital both represent the linear motion. This linear motion was practiced in despotic monarchies and is being replicated by paranoid communities that admire them. Therefore, the modern firm becomes a paranoid community engaging in linear motion.

Violent Firm

For Max Weber, the state is a community that successfully claims the monopoly on the legitimate use of physical force within a given territory (Max Weber, 2019). The law of the state inherently demands coercion, and thus, it becomes a signifier of this monopolized physical force, that is, violence.

If a firm is born out of admiration for the state, then it must also resemble the characteristics of the state. Thus, the firm should become a community that exercises legitimate violence within its own territory. While this legitimate violence cannot extend to the physical violence monopolized by the state, it can manifest as economic violence. Economic violence can be as powerful, if not more so, than physical violence at times. A firm can now be defined as a community that legitimately exercises economic violence. This is, of course, an homage to Weber.

In a despotic state, the legitimacy of violence originates from the despot's command. Analogously, in a firm, the CEO takes on the role of the despot. Under the constraints of the state's monopoly on violence, the firm compromises and sometimes colludes with the state to justify its own use of violence. "Contracts" were born as a result of that compromise. Contracts may appear to establish relationships among the firm's stakeholders, and they indeed do so. However, before that, they serve as a link between the state and the firm.

In economics, firms are often understood as a nexus of contracts (e.g., Jensen and Meckling, 1976). A firm is a community where stakeholders are intertwined in various explicit or implicit contractual relationships. The term "contract" implies a binding connection between the parties involved. The Chinese character for "contract" (契約) reflects this concept: "契" (promise) suggests something carved in stone, irreversible and inescapable, while "約" (agreement) signifies being bound by a thread. Similarly, the English word "contract" shares this essence, derived from the Latin "contractus," meaning to draw together or to bring separate entities into one place. Thus, the word "contract" not only signifies an agreement but also implies a contraction or tightening. After pulling entities together, they must be bound tightly to prevent escape, ensuring that a proper contract is always binding.

A contract binds the parties involved, implying that one can enforce the agreement through coercion, which is, in essence, a form of physical violence. Although a contract may appear to be an agreement between two stakeholders, the power to bind them does not rest with the parties themselves but with the state. The act of affixing a seal or signing a contract serves to assert one's innocence in front of the state, which wields the power of violence. Thus, a contract is not merely an agreement between two parties. All contracts become contracts between individuals and the state. Without the backing of state-enforced violence, a contract is not truly a contract.

A firm can exercise its power within the limits permitted by the state, wielding economic violence in ways such as raising or lowering wages, promoting or dismissing employees. In modern times, where it is nearly impossible to live without being connected to the market or firms, economic violence can often inflict more severe suffering than physical violence. Examples of people enduring physical violence to avoid economic violence are commonplace. A manager serving jail time on behalf of a major shareholder, a worker silently enduring mistreatment, or an employee smiling through a customer's insults—all these instances likely stem from the recognition that the pain of economic violence can surpass even that of physical violence.

When economics describes a firm as a collection of contracts, it conjures an image of a beautiful promise made by autonomous will. However, contracts function more on the basis of violence than on the elegance of promises. If a promise were truly beautiful, it wouldn't require paperwork and signatures; a simple exchange of words and a shared glance would suffice.

The violence that makes contracts possible is the economic violence exercised by firms, and is fundamentally rooted in the physical violence of the state, called law. The reason contracts in economics appear as beautiful promises is not because they are upheld out of goodwill in the absence of law. Rather, it is because the legal enforcement is so powerful that no one dares to break the law, ensuring that contracts are always honored. Accordingly, contracts may appear as if they would be fulfilled even without the law—but this is true only within economics, not in reality.

11. FIRM VALUE

The Value Of The Firm

The value of the firm, as the term suggests, refers to the worth of the firm. It is likely the most important concept in business studies. While the concept itself is straightforward, actually measuring the value of something is not an easy task. Economics, in the end, can be seen as the study of the value of goods or commodities. Classical economics distinguished between exchange value and use value, and it held that the value of goods should be measured and interpreted based on the labor value embedded within them. In contrast, modern economics seeks to fix value to market price. Although the distinction between value and price can be important, we will set aside that issue for now, as the aim here is not to delve into the conceptual differences.

Our interest begins with the methods of calculating firm value in business studies and economics. Conceptually speaking, firm value is determined by discounting the future revenues generated by the firm to their present value. Simply put, it refers to the value that the firm would contribute to my wealth if I were to own the entire firm.

Business management traditionally aims to enhance firm value. However, firm value is often equated with shareholder value or stock value (stock price). More frequently, the increase in firm value is regarded as identical to the increase in shareholder value. This is peculiar because a firm and its stock are not the same concept, so equating firm value with stock price requires explanation. Despite this, it's challenging to find textbooks that adequately explains this. Even among the few that do, the logical rigor is not satisfactory. (Much of the following content is referenced from Seog, 2018a.)

First of all, in textbooks, firm value is often equated with the sum of shareholder value and creditor value (Park, Jeong-Sik et al., 2015; Brealey and Myers, 2003). The balance sheet, also known as the statement of financial position, suggests that the firm value is equal to the sum of the value attributed to shareholders and creditors. In a balance sheet, the firm's assets are listed on the left side, while liabilities and equity are listed on the right side. The total on the left must equal the total on the right. If the left side is called the firm value, then the right side represents the creditor value (liabilities) and shareholder value (equity).

So, a question arises: If the firm value is the sum of the value of its debt and equity, how can the firm's value and shareholder value be considered the same? Where does that leave the creditors? Are they such insignificant beings that they can be ignored? Both debt and equity are liquids, so why should debt be considered inferior to equity? Some may argue that firm value is equated with equity only for convenience, although it technically includes both. Or they may point out that in cases where there is no debt, there's no issue. This reasoning might be acceptable among those who are familiar with such conventions. However, for those unaware, this could lead to misunderstandings. The confusion around these terms may not be entirely accidental; there could be a degree of intentionality or at least willful negligence. We will revisit this potential confusion around terminology below.

What is most intriguing is the perspective on firm value itself. What is a firm? Isn't a firm a combination of labor and capital, essentially a combination of a solid and a liquid? Capital stays and flows within the firm, and the management and workers collaborate to pursue profit. If that is the case, shouldn't firm value represent the value of both the solid and the liquid? So why is it argued that firm value only refers to the value of the liquid?

Where is the solid?

If a firm is called a "firm" as in the English expression, it implies a solid rather than a liquid. Yet, firm value measures only the weight of the liquid, excluding the solid. There are no textbooks that address this apparent contradiction.

Viewing a firm solely as a liquid is, in fact, outdated. This perspective might apply to family-run businesses or small shops where the entrepreneur operates with their own capital and labor, meaning the liquid and the solid are not separated. In such cases, the entrepreneur is both the solid and the liquid. However, in modern corporations, the liquid and the solid are separated. The separation of liquid and solid is a defining feature of modern businesses. Modern corporations are designed to pursue larger and long-term ventures through this separation. The significance of stock companies in modern capitalism lies in their ability to best realize the separation of liquid and solid.

As a result, for modern corporations, the legal entity (legal person) is of paramount importance. Although the solid and the liquid have been separated, it is necessary to bind them under a firm, thus requiring one name and one bundle. Therefore, a separate name and legal personality were assigned to the corporation. A legal entity is a fictitious personality recognized by law.

It is not always possible for two inherently different entities to be in harmony. In a firm where the solid and the liquid are separated yet bound together, they begin to struggle for dominance. Marx was the one who most sharply criticized this issue. He denounced the exploitation of the solid by the liquid. Squeezing a solid to extract a new liquid is precisely the exploitation he referred to.

Despite its logical inconsistencies, the view of a firm solely as a liquid seems to stem from the hegemony of the liquid. Or maybe it simply reflects an outdated perception that remains at the level of a small corner shop. Therefore, when it is said that the goal of a firm is to maximize firm value, this value should be understood not as the inherent value of the firm itself, but rather as the value of liquid only, from the perspective of the liquid. At this point, firm value intersects with linguistics.

When discussing firm value, the liquid must be the subject and the speaker, and it should be considered the core reason for the existence of the firm. Since only the liquid can be placed entirely in the subject position, the solid, as another potential subject, is relegated to the position of an object. This object, distanced from the subject and excluded, no longer exists as an active being but rather becomes a replaceable component. This is the power enjoyed by the subject. Those who can successfully impose their language as a common language and encode their perspective into a code can gain power (Pierre Bourdieu, 2020). Through the structuring devices (modus operandi) of myth and ritual, the liquid has produced the structured outcomes (opus operatum) of liquid language and perspective, ultimately acquiring symbolic dominance. When the language of the liquid becomes the common language and the grammar of the liquid is codified, the liquid can seize symbolic power and achieve hegemony.

The Goal Of The Firm

In business studies and economics, maximizing firm value is often cited as the primary goal of management. If they assert maximizing firm value based on the false assumption of equating firm value with shareholder value, then the assertion is simply flawed in itself. This is because a firm is an organization with legally independent personality. Yet, there is a subtle twist here. For example, they may still argue that even if firm value and shareholder value are different, maximizing shareholder value can still "lead to" the maximization of firm value. How could this happen?

The argument is as follows: Even if a firm is composed of a solid and a liquid, let's assume that the solid can secure its share first and foremost. Then, the liquid takes what's left. Among the liquid, creditors take their share first, and only what remains is left for shareholders. Under these assumptions, maximizing the shareholders' value would be equivalent to maximizing the total value. This is because shareholders take what is left after everyone else, so maximizing the remaining amount is the same as maximizing the total amount. In this scenario, even if the firm and its shareholders are not identical, maximizing firm value and maximizing shareholder value would lead to the same outcome.

This beautiful happy-ending fairy tale is the main content featured in textbooks. The title of this tale is the "residual claimant theory." The idea is that since shareholders claim the residual value—what's left after others have taken their portions—maximizing that residual also maximizes the total. At first glance, this theory does not seem problematic. Moreover, for those familiar with accounting practices, this logic is easy to accept. The income statement, after all, clearly shows that after deducting production costs from revenue and then subtracting interest expenses and taxes, the remainder—net income—is allocated to the shareholders. Doesn't the income statement clearly demonstrate that the remainder belongs to the shareholders?

If shareholders were truly forced to take only what others left behind, then the logic above might be roughly valid. That is, the logic may be valid if shareholders were powerless and ranked at the very bottom. But are shareholders really such weak and insignificant being? On the contrary, aren't shareholders the most powerful being? How could those who wield enough hegemony to equate themselves with the firm be considered the weakest rank? Who has the power to replace a CEO who wields absolute authority within a firm? If the CEO is a despot, then aren't shareholders gods?

If the one who takes the leftovers actually holds a power, he can increase his share by reducing what others receive. What becomes important here is not simply who takes the remainder, but who holds the power. One cannot view a powerful being that squeezes the solid to collect the spilled liquid in a jar, as the same residual claimant as the weak being who can only take what is left over. Focusing solely on the order of claims without considering the magnitude and position of power will only obscure understanding of the essence.

In response to this, there is a counterargument that even if shareholders are not weak, it doesn't matter. The reasoning is that other stakeholders ultimately enter into contracts with shareholders, and they can protect themselves by anticipating shareholders' behavior in advance when signing these contracts. Given that participation in contracts is voluntary, rational stakeholders can reflect their interests and concerns in the contracts.

Well, this counterargument is not entirely wrong on its own. However, a fundamental issue arises when we ask the following question: If each stakeholder is capable of protecting their own interests, why should we uniformly focus on maximizing shareholder value? Even if we were to maximize the value of any other stakeholder, couldn't the others still protect their own interests? Isn't this precisely the kind of outcome that Coase's theorem reveals about contracts? When a worker contracts with a shareholder, the shareholder also contracts with the worker. Therefore, maximizing worker value should be possible for the goal of the firm, just as maximizing shareholder value is.

In fact, a more accurate point is that stakeholders enter into contracts through the entity called a firm. The critical flaw in the concept of maximizing shareholder value lies in the fact that it overlooks the role of the firm. It deliberately ignores the personification of the firm, which is undeniably a cornerstone of modern capitalism.

Residual Claimant

The reason the most powerful shareholders cosplay as the weak lowest-ranked is rooted in their desire to maintain the efficacy of the magical spell of equating the firm with themselves. Those enchanted by this spell continue to chant the mantra that the firm is synonymous with its shareholders, and that firm value is equivalent to shareholder value. The world in which this magical realm is confused with reality is no other than financial capitalism.

The position of the residual claimant is by no means for the weak. Just look at those who historically occupied the so-called the lowest position of the residual claimant. Following the story of Jacob Hollander (1903), in the late 18th century during the era of "The Wealth of Nations" and Physiocracy, it was the landlords who claimed this position. In the 19th century, during the Industrial Revolution, it was the capitalists who took this role. By the late 19th century, in the context of the socialist movement, Francis Walker placed the worker in this position, and at the dawn of the modern American corporation, John Clark positioned the entrepreneur as the residual claimant.

Were the landlords of the Physiocratic era weak figures? Wasn't the ultimate goal of the free trade, as advocated by the Physiocrats, aligned with the interests of the landlords? During the Physiocratic era, the hegemony belonged to none other than the landlords. As the Industrial Revolution marked a new leap for capitalism, capitalists gained new dominance in Britain. At that time, capitalists were also often the entrepreneurs. David Ricardo interpreted the profits received by the capitalist-entrepreneur as interest that included compensation for risk. Traditionally, capitalists implied creditors, like bankers who lent money. As capitalists ascended to hegemony, the lowest position of the residual claimant also belonged to them. This interpretation is related to the popular theories of the time, such as the wage fund theory and the wage subsistence theory. These theories implied that the total wages received by workers at any given time were fixed. After paying the predetermined rent and wages from the revenue generated by the firm, the remaining profit belonged to the capitalist.

Walker advocates for the worker's position as a residual claimant through his residual theory of wage. In his argument,

Walker conceptually distinguishes between the capitalist and the entrepreneur. When an entrepreneur invests his own capital, he can be seen as fulfilling a dual role: both as a capitalist and as the entrepreneur responsible for managing the business. In this framework, the income generated by the firm is allocated by first paying rent to the landlord, interest to the capitalist, and the entrepreneur's share to the entrepreneur. The entrepreneur's share is determined similarly to rent or interest, based on what another entrepreneur with the same amount of capital and labor could earn in the market. After these allocations, the remaining residual income is ultimately designated as the worker's wage.

Around the same time, Clark assigned the position of residual claimant to the entrepreneur. After paying rent to the landlord, wages to the workers, and interest to the capitalists, the remaining profit was attributed to the entrepreneur. Clark further subdivided the entrepreneur's role. The entrepreneur was not only a capitalist who provided capital but also a worker engaged in management, and a merchant who owned and sold the products. As a capitalist, he received interest, and as a worker, he earned wages. However, the merchant’s profit was not predetermined; it was ultimately determined by external factors. Thus, the residual income of the business should be allocated to the entrepreneur in their role as a merchant. The approaches of Walker and Clark likely represented different responses to the increasing need to distinguish between the various functions of capitalists and entrepreneurs in the late 19th century, a period when firms required more substantial capital.

Finally, in the early 20th century, when the separation of management and capital became more visible, Frank Knight declared that it was not the entrepreneur, but the shareholder, who held the position of residual claimant. Knight argued that a firm's profits arise from managing uncertainty and making decisions. In other words, profits are captured by the managerial ability to navigate uncertainty. He referred to this process as "cephalization," a term borrowed from evolutionary biology, describing the concentration of nerve tissues in the head leading to the development of the brain and intelligence. If an entrepreneur were to combine both capital and management roles, the core of this "cephalization" would reside in that entrepreneur. In such a scenario, the firm's profits should belong to the entrepreneur.

But if capital and management are separated, who should own the profits? Knight offers this perspective: while the success or failure of a firm depends on the abilities of its managers, what is even more critical is the shareholders' judgment in selecting competent managers. The "judgment of judgment"—the shareholders' ability to discern the managerial abilities of executives—is of utmost importance. Shareholders must bear the high risks associated with this judgment, particularly the uncertainty that cannot be measured. Because shareholders ultimately bear this immeasurable uncertainty, they should be the residual claimants. This idea forms the basis of what we learn today in modern business studies and economics.

In the past, those positioned at the bottom, or the so-called residual claimants, were not the weak, but those who held hegemonic power in each respective era. During the era of Physiocracy, it was the landowners; as industrial capitalism developed, it was the creditors, workers, and entrepreneurs; and in the era of clear separation between capital and management, it was the shareholders who held the hegemony. The ones who wielded hegemony occupied the lowest position. They did not simply take what others left behind; they secured their share through their own power and claimed it. The position at the bottom, the last in the chain, was not for the weak but for the strongest. When the strongest claims the remainder, it is only natural that they would attempt to reduce the share of the weaker ones to increase their own portion. This is precisely where the true firm value and the shareholder value diverge.

Legal Entity

However, those who seek to occupy the lowest position in the rank often forget an important fact: the firm is a legal entity. Being a legal entity means that the firm is an independent living entity, and therefore, the lowest position does not belong to any single stakeholder. This means that what remains after distributing each stakeholder's share belongs to the firm itself, not to anyone else. This is precisely why modern firms are defined as legal entities.

The firm was officially born as a demigod, a being between gods and humans. Although it may not be a god, it was created as a being that could enjoy eternal life, much like angels. The firm was a distinctly Christian creation declared by the Pope. Perhaps from the beginning, firms were considered superior to humans. However, in the era when the death of God was proclaimed, the firm received a new form of life within the legal framework of the human world. The firm transitioned from a religious construct to a legal entity, changing its protective mantle from religion to law.

Modern firms, especially stock companies, are organizations endowed with legal personality. Like natural persons, firms can be the subjects of rights and obligations in contracts and litigation (Jang, Deok-jo, 2017). A key principle here is the concept of "separate patrimony," which means that the rights to a firm's assets belong to the firm itself, not to its shareholders (Kim, Geon-sik et al., 2018). Important concepts in understanding separate patrimony include: "entity shielding," meaning that creditors of individual shareholders cannot enforce claims against the firm's assets; "priority rule," meaning that creditors of the firm have priority over the firm's assets compared to shareholders; and "liquidation protection," meaning that shareholders cannot arbitrarily dispose of the firm's assets that correspond to their shareholding. In summary, these institutional mechanisms assert that shareholders cannot exercise ownership rights over the firm's assets, which belong to the firm itself. Firms, like natural persons, hold rights and obligations regarding their own assets.

In that sense, the residual claimant is not any individual but the firm itself. The rights to the remaining assets that are not distributed externally belong to the firm. Of course, ultimately, this internally reserved portion is destined to be distributed to stakeholders. What is important is that this reserved share never belongs to any one stakeholder, including shareholders.

The residual assets reserved within a firm are ultimately distributed to all stakeholders in various forms. When a firm retains more of its assets, consumers benefit from a more stable supply of products and potentially more reliable repair services. Suppliers can enjoy stable business relationships and opportunities for revenues. Creditors benefit from lower bankruptcy risks, and the government can collect taxes more reliably. The situation is even more desperate for workers. For workers, reduced bankruptcy or closure risks mean greater job security and potential increases in employment and wages. Shareholders, too, may receive higher dividends and enjoy lower risks.

In the end, all stakeholders ultimately have claims to the residual assets of the firm. Therefore, saying that a firm has a residual claim is essentially the same as saying that all stakeholders are residual claimants. At this point, we encounter theories like the "enterprise theory" in accounting or the "stakeholder theory" developed by Edward Freeman (1984). According to the stakeholder theory, a firm serves not only its shareholders but also a variety of stakeholders. Following this theory, the goal of a firm should be to maximize the value for all stakeholders, not just shareholder value. Of course, more practical discussion will be needed about which and what to extent stakeholders should be included in this maximization. It is common to contrast the stakeholder value maximization as a European model with the shareholder value maximization as an American model and discuss the differences between the two.

In any case, if many stakeholders share the position of claimants to residual assets, then acting as if shareholders are the only ones to claim residual assets can only be said to be the result of ignorance about the legal personality of modern firms. Perhaps this mindset might stem from outdated thinking, viewing modern firms as if they were still mom-and-pop shop or family-run enterprises.

On the other hand, due to the granting of legal personality, shareholders cannot easily access the firm's assets, but in return, they are granted the privilege of limited liability. This means that while creditors have priority over the firm's assets, they cannot exercise their claims against individual shareholders. If the firm's assets are insufficient to cover debts, creditors cannot pursue claims against individual shareholders. Shareholders' liability is limited to the extent of their investment in the company. Limited liability is the most brilliant—and consequently critical—features of modern firms. Without limited liability, such a vast amount of capital could not be invested in stock companies. If shareholders were liable for the company's management results without limit, who would be willing to easily buy and sell stocks?

Residual Risk: Workers

The logic behind shareholders' residual claim is often justified as a consequence of their residual risk-bearing. According to this argument, shareholders bear the residual risk of the firm and therefore have a right to the residual assets. However, this argument is flawed in that it overlooks the fact that other stakeholders also share the risk. Most importantly, it ignores the concept of limited liability for shareholders. Shareholders do not bear all residual risk; limited liability implies that they are not fully responsible for the residual risk. Residual risk-bearing would be truly meaningful only under unlimited liability. The argument for shareholders' residual claim thus finds itself caught in a contradiction—praising limited liability on the one hand, while emphasizing unlimited liability through residual risk-bearing on the other.

All stakeholders share residual risk collectively. And those who bear residual risk more critically than shareholders are the workers. Can the impact of dividend cuts and stock price declines be considered a greater threat than worker layoffs? Moreover, can shareholders not mitigate their risk through diversification?

If a single claimant had to be chosen based on the burden of residual risk, that position should go to the workers rather than the shareholders. Remember, workers are solids. Solids must hold their ground, absorbing and enduring the full weight of risk. As a result, they must bear the greatest pain and suffering. In contrast, liquids can simply flow and move away when pressed by a heavy object, though they may have to endure some contamination in the process.

Shareholders, the strongest predators, always possess the ability to shift more of the burden onto the weaker stakeholders. Yet, they often feel the need to portray themselves as the vulnerable ones, likely as a strategy to maximize their own power. After all, shouldn't society offer support and encouragement to those who ultimately bear the burden of risk? This is why wage cuts or layoffs are often framed as protective measures for the firm. Furthermore, such measures are often framed as being for the interest of workers themselves. After all, isn't it essential for the firm to survive in order to employ more workers in the future? It is a fascinating irony to lay off workers while claiming it is for their benefit.

There is a similar irony revolving around labor. Workers, in order to resist the power of shareholders and managers, may choose to strike, also gain the justification of protecting workers by ceasing to be workers themselves. This is because capitalism forces paranoid purity on workers, so that they can claim their rights only through self-destructive means. For capitalists, the pursuit of profit serves as the standard of morality, but for workers, it is purity that becomes the standard. When workers involuntarily stop their labor, it is for the sake of future workers, and when they stop voluntarily, it is for the sake of present workers. In this way, workers become the protagonist of modern capitalism as paradoxical and self-destructive beings, where their gestures become for workers only when they deny being workers.

Workers, as a solid, form the essence of the firm yet remain alienated beings, excluded from the calculation of the firm value. While workers are the key to creating value through labor, they are forced to be pure so that they can claim their rights only when labor is denied. This is the unfortunate reality of the position workers occupy in modern capitalism.

Speaker And Scapegoat

Why is shareholder value often packaged as firm value? It's not surprising that shareholders, having gained hegemony, would argue that for increasing their own value. However, muddling the distinct concepts of firm value and shareholder value is both uncomfortable and inappropriate.

This muddling is a deliberate attempt to hide shareholder value within the more socially accepted concept of firm value. Such confusion of terms can be linked to Francis Bacon's "idols of the marketplace," which refer to logical fallacies arising from the use of imprecise or misleading language. Firm value, in this context, represents a harmful idol of the marketplace, intentionally designed to mislead. It is akin to unscrupulous merchants in a marketplace using confusing terms and skewed scales to deceive their customers or counterparts.

In modern capitalism, where all economic activity is conducted through the market, the market essentially becomes synonymous with the economy itself. The idols of the marketplace do not merely create confusion within the market; they lead to a broader confusion in the economy and society. As a result, government officials, the media, judges, and prosecutors, under the guise of enhancing firm value, end up serving the interests of shareholders. The greatest culpability, however, may lie with academia and education, which, instead of correcting this confusion, often perpetuate it. The worship of these idols in the marketplace fosters unfairness and inequity in the economy and society, but due to the confusion of terms, people may not even realize the fallacies in their thinking.

Seeing the firm as belonging to the shareholders means viewing the firm through the eyes of the shareholders. In this perspective, the shareholder is the speaker and the subject. Subjectifying the shareholder, in turn, objectifies other stakeholders. The shareholder, as the subject, claims ownership of the firm and genuinely believes in this ownership. Stakeholders who challenge this ownership are becoming outsiders or "others" who must be subdued.

Just as to René Girard, the "other" is another name for the scapegoat (René Girard, 2007). The scapegoat must be sacrificed to complete the ritual. The violence inflicted on the scapegoat is justified in the name of the ritual, leaving no sense of guilt. Contaminants are merely objects that must be disinfected and purified (Douglas, 2001).

The means used in this purification ritual range from codified measurements, regulations, and laws to decodified, direct violence. Anyone whose actions harm firm value is subject to various legal or violent sanctions, such as discipline, pay cuts, dismissal, lawsuits, or public condemnation. The methods of measurement cleverly exploit mechanisms of objectification. According to accounting practices and regulations, the share of the "others"—those who are not shareholders—is treated and recognized as an expense that diminishes firm value. Only the portion allocated to shareholders is recorded as increasing firm value. For example, the share of workers is measured and recorded as something that damages firm value.

This purification ritual is represented in the form of a typical tale in which the subject is good and the other is evil. In this tale, or within the purification ritual that represents the tale, the other becomes evil and the target of punishment. As a result, there is no room for guilt associated with this punishment. Thus, the other becomes the scapegoat, but both those who participate in the ritual and those who observe it from outside may not recognize this fact or experience any sense of guilt. That is because when the blade of the sacrificial ritual flashes, it is carried out in the name of justice, efficiency, enhancement of firm value, or economic growth.

The ultimate scapegoat in the purification ritual is always the solid, burdened by the weight of gravity, unable to leave its place. They are like the lamb already bound to the altar. Liquids, on the other hand, can simply flow away to find other prey if necessary. Solids, which provide the most crucial capital to the firm, are recorded only as costs in the form of labor expenses and wages, not as capital themselves. Despite being fundamentally capital, they become prisoners of the firm because they cannot move and must withstand gravity. Capital, therefore, is not a name given to those who maintain their place while creating profitability. Instead, it is a privileged name reserved for liquids that have the ability to flow and move across the surface of the earth.

Polarization

Capitalism has indeed brought material abundance, but it has not resolved the deepening divide between the rich and the poor, nor the growing polarization between oppressors and the oppressed. This trend has only intensified since the late 20th century. The corporate ecosystem, often seen as the pinnacle of capitalism, might naturally lead to this polarization. In this system, the gas is liquefied and returned to the capitalist, but for workers who are bound by gravity and cannot move, the liquid merely passes by, wetting their collars. The liquid that belongs to capitalists only flows to other places in pursuit of profit. Capitalism is such a dynamic era that it is harsh on those with heavy bodies.

News about fortunate a few solids that have finally increased their liquidity and transformed into liquids rarely makes headlines, and even when it does, it holds little significance. Such news would be meaningful only if it became so commonplace that it ceased to be newsworthy. While many express concerns over growing polarization, they, too, tend to view and speak of it from the perspective of the liquid. Everyone agrees on the principle of reducing polarization, but when it comes to actual implementation, hesitation often arises. The primary reasons for this reluctance are concerns over a potential decline in the competitiveness, value, or efficiency of the firm.

However, they fail to realize that these thoughts, which seem to prioritize the nation and the economy, are actually captured by linguistic manipulation. When they discuss the value and competitiveness of the firm, it's hard to recognize that they are, in fact, talking about shareholder interests. When speaking about the firm, they do not understand the importance of changing the speaker or the subject of the sentence. Thus, ultimately, they end up back where they started.

If people's thinking is limited, and they aren't even aware of it, then this is also a problem of education. Economics and business studies often depict firms from the perspective of the liquid, equating firm value with that of the liquid. However, we must not forget that the true center of gravity in a firm comes from the solid. The fact that firm value is expressed in liquid terms does not mean that a firm is made entirely of the liquid.

12. CORPORATE GOVERNANCE AND SOCIAL RESPONSIBILITY

Corporate Governance

The discussion on so-called corporate governance is an important economic topic. It has already been mentioned that the concept of firm value and the maximization of shareholder value, which are taken as prerequisites in corporate governance discussions, contain serious epistemological and linguistic errors. Discussions on corporate governance built on this faulty foundation cannot avoid fundamental errors and limitations. Since much of this has already been investigated earlier, it seems unnecessary to repeat it here. Instead, let us discuss additionally about other aspects of consideration.

The topic of corporate governance refers to discussions on how to resolve or mitigate conflicts among a firm's stakeholders in order to enhance the firm value. These conflicts often arise because information is asymmetrically distributed among the stakeholders. Therefore, discussions on corporate governance in economics or business studies often reduce to the issue of information asymmetry.

In principle, discussions on corporate governance can address all conflicts among diverse stakeholders, but the main focus in economics tends to revolve around two major types of problems. The first concerns the relationship between shareholders and management, while the second deals with the relationship between large and minority shareholders. The first category discusses how to ensure that management makes investments and operates the firm for the benefit of the shareholders rather than misappropriating the funds provided by them. The second category addresses how to prevent the decrease in firm value caused by the abuses of large shareholders and how to protect minority shareholders from such actions.

By now, it should be clear that the core of corporate governance issues is always centered around liquids. The components of a firm—gas, liquid, and solid—are in constant conflict with one another. The liquid commands the worker, who strives to return to the planet's core, to defy gravity in order to capture the opportunities and profits that evaporate into the atmosphere.

Not all solid components, the workers, are the same. Some of them succumb to the influence of the liquid and seek to dissolve, inevitably coming into conflict with other solid components. These individuals receive liquid fuel, overcome the risks in the atmosphere, and pursue profit, viewing it as their given mission. Perhaps they started as solid, but now they might appear as liquid crystals, half solid and half liquid. They strive to break free from their solid state, measuring their success by their affinity with the liquid. Sometimes, they urge other solid components that are struggling under the weight of gravity, wielding a whip sometimes harsher than the liquid itself does.

However, if they fail to reach the stars in the sky, they will no longer be able to remain in the organization of the firm and will either voluntarily or involuntarily experience a free fall. Those who once seemed light enough to keep rising will only then feel the full weight of gravity on their entire being. But because of this, the firm, which has become somewhat lighter as a result, will be able to recruit new solids and move towards a brighter future.

This is the problem of corporate governance between managers and workers, which forms another axis of the governance problem. It is the problem between a liquid crystal, which is a solid that has approached the state of a liquid, and a solid that still firmly remains on the ground, resisting liquefaction. A manager who, despite being a solid, considers himself as a liquid and assigns the meaning of existence to liquefaction cannot resolve this contradiction. As a result, he is continuously caught in conflict between the liquid and the solid.

This contradiction and conflict, from another perspective, produce distrust between managers and shareholders. Liquid crystal might think of itself as similar to a liquid, but from the perspective of the liquid that has always been swirling around the outside of the firm, it still cannot be trusted. Because of its origin as a solid, the liquid cannot fully trust it. As a result, the liquid is always anxious and nervous, and when it worsens, it may experience panic disorder.

To treat this, sometimes more liquid fuel is injected into the liquid crystal as a conciliatory measure to further assimilate it into a liquid, and in other times, the reins of surveillance are tightened. Look at the measures implemented under the pretext of benefiting the firm in corporate governance discussions. External audits, disclosures, incentives, and stock options are the lists of treatments or vaccines developed to alleviate the chronic condition of panic disorder that plagues the liquids.

If they ultimately become disappointed with the liquid crystal, the true liquids may stop supplying fuel and dispose of it. Once discarded, the liquid crystal, unable to combine with other solid components, will likely choose to jump off on its own. Knowing the consequences of such disposal, the molecules in the position of the liquid crystal have no time to look back. It must simply think and feel like a liquid, pretending to be more melted, as if it were liquid itself. The problem of corporate governance between managers and shareholders begins here. It is a problem between an unstable liquid crystal that has not fully become liquid and the liquid that is anxious and on the verge of panic disorder.

Not all liquids that flow around a firm are the same. Some liquids are so thin that they almost lose their viscosity, becoming lighter and lighter, while in other places where many liquids gather, they consistently flow cold and majestically. Low-viscosity liquids can give up their liquidity and disappear at any time. Liquids that are about to disappear are essentially like gases and are therefore naturally excluded from decision-making as liquids. In the world of water, it is only natural that the deep blue sea is the master. Weak, low-viscosity liquid molecules cannot, by their own strength, overcome the force of the crashing waves and tsunamis. The society that permits the existence of firms declares that all liquids are the same, regardless of viscosity. However, since in reality, not all liquids are the same, conflicts arise. Then, to what extent should we protect low-viscosity liquids? This is precisely the problem of governance between large and minority shareholders. Ultimately, this problem is about the viscosity differences among the liquids.

Among liquids, liquids that are closer to solids have power. Now, what is emphasized among the liquids is their affinity with solids. Those who once opposed solids now reject liquids with weaker viscosity than their own, claiming that their viscosity is closer to that of solids. Liquids now compete to prove who is closer to the solid. The so-called large shareholders find themselves in this paradoxical position. They demand the dissolution and liquefaction of solids, while simultaneously criticizing the liquids for lacking viscosity. They compel solids to become liquid and liquids to become solid. This is the fundamental contradiction of large shareholders. However, it's not that large shareholders impose this contradiction because they truly want it. They are simply leveraging their power to increase the amount of liquid that belongs to them.

Is the essence of corporate governance really about increasing a firm's value? Sometimes, it may be. However, the reality of corporate governance is an ongoing conflict and struggle between solids and solids, liquids and solids, and liquids and liquids. They compete and criticize each other over their viscosity. Once the value of the firm is equated with the value of its shareholders, the liquid has already seized hegemony in this battle. Therefore, the solid must dissolve itself and flow toward the liquid. This becomes the survival strategy for the solid.

The maximization of shareholder value might just be a slogan for appearances. If shareholder value were truly pursued, it should be for the minority shareholders, as they are the ones who most embody the characteristics of a liquid. However, the competition among liquids now flows in the opposite direction. Instead of striving to embody the essence of liquidity, they compete over who has viscosity closer to that of a solid. Few recognize this irony.

Just as with the determination of the position of the residual claimants of a firm, corporate governance also serves the interests of those who hold hegemony. In the corporate world, hegemony lies with the liquid. However, not all liquids can possess this hegemony—only those with viscosity and the ability to manipulate it at will can truly enjoy it. Therefore, despite the loud slogans, corporate governance truly for minority shareholders inevitably struggles. After all, isn't it the solid that truly generates the firm value? It is this very point that gives power to those liquids that have an affinity with solids, leading them to hold power among liquids.

The irony of corporate governance lies at the intersection of hegemony and firm value. And it is a double intersection space where shareholders and the legal entity also cross each other at the same time. In this intersecting space, they clash and generate contradictions, but it is difficult to accurately recognize these contradictions.

Social Responsibility

One might question whether a corporation should fulfill social responsibilities and, if so, what those responsibilities should be. Milton Friedman would argue that a corporation's only social responsibility is to maximize its profits. On the other hand, Edward Freeman would advocate for a broader approach, demanding that corporations consider the interests of various stakeholders. With such diverse perspectives, a wide range of answers is possible.

Corporate Social Responsibility (CSR) appears to be a concept that emerged as a reflection on the pursuit of corporate profits. Howard Bowen (1953) is said to have marked the formal starting point of serious consideration regarding the social responsibilities of businesses (Archie Carroll, 2016).

Indeed, the concept of social responsibility is not clearly defined, leading to the emergence of various interpretations. For instance, Alexander Dahlsrud (2006) identified 37 different definitions of social responsibility. Archie Carroll (1979) conceptualized social responsibility as encompassing economic, legal, ethical, and philanthropic responsibilities. This broad view highlights the multifaceted nature of what it means for a corporation to be socially responsible.

Generally, the concept of social responsibility can be understood as encompassing more than just the basic duties of a corporation as an economic entity. The basic duties aligned with a firm's objectives can include economic and legal responsibilities, based on Carroll's classification. The "something more" beyond these can be seen as encompassing ethical and philanthropic responsibilities. In a broad sense, social responsibility includes the firm's inherent pursuit of profits. But the essence of the social responsibility discourse is with discussing whether firms should go beyond profit-making, rather than with denying the pursuit of profits. Let us discuss social responsibility with this broader understanding in mind.

Milton Friedman (1970, 2007) and Theodore Levitt (1958) understand the social responsibility of a firm as being focused on maximizing profits. Friedman, in particular, stands at one extreme of the social responsibility debate by arguing that the discussion itself is unnecessary. His argument is not difficult to understand: if the market functions well, everyone will take care of his own interests, leading to the best possible outcome. Therefore, firms only need to focus on their original purpose of generating profit. For Friedman, the market either works well or should be made to do so. Thus, it is undesirable to demand anything from firms beyond generating profit.

If the assumptions underlying Friedman's argument held true in reality, the world would not be complicated. It would be a world without hegemony struggles, conflicts, or contradictions. If reality were such a beautiful world, as Friedman suggests, everyone would simply do his own job, and excessive demands beyond that would indeed be undesirable. If that were the case, however, no one would have argued for social responsibility in the first place, which obviously contradicts reality.

Friedman's perspective aligns closely with modern mainstream economics and neoliberal thinking, making it very familiar to economics students. It is based on the ideas that the market is beautiful, that firms should serve the interests of their shareholders, and that other stakeholders will take care of their own interests. This belief, according to Friedman, should also be realized in practice.

However, the truly bizarre claim is that firms should fulfill social responsibility because it helps their profits. The discussion on social responsibility in business studies often revolves around whether it contributes to the profit or value of the firm. It seeks to understand the meaning of social responsibility from the perspective of profit. The logic that social responsibility should be carried out in a way that benefits the firm raises the question: what kind of epistemological framework makes this logic possible?

When we act responsibly, is it because the outcome benefits us? The answer is no. Responsible behavior is simply about doing what must be done, even if not to the strict extent of Kant's categorical imperative. Responsible behavior is simply about doing what is right, even if it doesn't fully align with strict Kantian categorical imperative. Of course, such an action may ultimately bring benefits. But regardless of whether it is profitable or not, the action must still be carried out. The moment profit is calculated, the action ceases to be a responsible one. It becomes merely an action driven by calculated self-interest.

The same applies to corporate social responsibility. If a firm calculates gains and losses when fulfilling its social responsibilities, it is no longer truly carrying out its social responsibilities. All corporate actions preached in business studies are ultimately directed toward shareholder value. Shareholder value is the objective function of management. The only actions a manager should take are those that increase shareholder value and profits. Within this framework, a firm can never truly engage in socially responsible behavior.

Therefore, even when a firm engages in socially beneficial actions, it is not acting out of responsibility. It is merely the "invisible hand" of Adam Smith guiding the firm's self-interest to align with societal benefit. In other words, the firm is simply doing what it has always done. If social responsibility is sought solely within the framework of shareholder value, it is an extension of Friedman's plan. When social responsibility is pursued only when it benefits shareholders, it becomes merely a reiteration of shareholder value maximization, unrelated to social responsibility. In that case, it would be cleaner, like Friedman suggests, to say that firms need not concern themselves with social responsibility at all.

If social responsibility truly increases corporate profits (or even if it does the opposite), should social responsibility be interpreted as meaningful or as meaningless? Taking responsibility is not about doing something because it brings benefits to oneself, but about doing it to help or benefit others. Responsibility always presupposes the existence of an "other." It is judged from the perspective of the other, not based on whether it benefits the one taking responsibility. In the context of social responsibility, the "other" is society. Firms are responsible to society. They must act to avoid causing harm to society and, furthermore, to contribute positively to society. Therefore, social responsibility holds true meaning only when it is carried out despite potential losses, rather than being carried out after calculating the firm's profits.

And often, when firms say they are carrying out social

responsibilities, it is workers who bear the weight. This is because social responsibility is pursued only when it contributes to liquid representations of profit and stock prices. Some of the increased profits will likely be distributed to workers. However, the distribution does not increase proportionally compared to the worker's effort. If profits decrease or losses occur due to the performance of social responsibilities, the share of damages to workers will be increased. It would be sad if profits belong to shareholders and responsibility to workers.

Of course, this doesn't mean that firms should not engage in actions that benefit society nor pursue profit. Rather, the point is that there's no need to interpret profit-maximizing actions as social responsibility. It would be pitiful if profit maximization is disguised or believed as social responsibility.

In such a situation, Friedman's argument might have to be described as naïve. When firms fulfill social responsibility, it is precisely to increase profits, just as Friedman intended. In other words, firms can gain more by appearing socially responsible rather than openly declaring they won't engage in such activities, which would draw public disfavor. Thus, firms should not agree to Friedman's argument that the only social responsibility is to generate profit. Instead, they must be prepared to demonstrate a willingness to engage in any form of social responsibility. The only thing that matters is keeping hands and eyes focused solely on profit. In this way, firms practice Friedman by denying Friedman.

When people fail to understand the inherent nature of firms, the belief that firms truly fulfill their social responsibility can deceive others and even themselves. Perhaps it's better for firms to remain as beings that simply pursue profit. Instead of holding onto the illusion that they fulfill social responsibilities, it might be more natural to continue viewing them with suspicion. The theme of social responsibility could be seen as a new kind of enchantment in the 21st century—one that confuses the eyes and minds of those who watch over these firms.

Thus, it is a pity to strive to find evidence that a firm's stock price or profits increase because of its social responsibility. It is also unfortunate to argue for or against the importance of social responsibility based on such findings. This is because the issue of social responsibility lies in its moral obligation, not in its connection to the firm's profit.

In a world where all measurements and judgments are made from the perspective of liquid, the concept of social responsibility is increasingly being surrounded and absorbed by liquid, diverging from its original intent. The lesson we can draw from discussions on social responsibility is that firms are progressively infiltrating more domains of moral judgment, extracting profit and liquidity from them.

Perhaps the concept of social responsibility might function as a simulacrum—a distorted copy of the essence. By presenting an illusion, the simulacrum obscures our understanding of the essence. When social responsibility operates as a simulacrum that obscures the firm's profits, the firm may be willing to take on social responsibility. This phenomenon is not necessarily a bad thing. If this is harnessed positively, society may be able to push firms in a good direction.

Probably, the simulacrum is an inherent aspect of capitalism. The changes in capitalism may not be driven by an emphasis on morality or responsibility, but rather through the provision of simulacrum disguised as morality. The reason why social responsibility emerges as a key issue is not because it is truly an expression of morality or responsibility, but probably because it operates as a simulacrum of profit.

The Moral Deconstruction Of Shareholder Ownership

It was previously observed that contracts bind the parties involved, and that a firm can be considered a community where stakeholders are intertwined through various contractual relationships. The discussion of corporate governance also reflects the view that firms are built upon diverse contractual relationships among stakeholders. However, it seems that only solids are inevitably bound tightly by the strings of contracts. Can gases or liquids truly be bound by the strings of contracts? The framework of contracts is, by its very nature, disadvantageous to solids.

The work of the firm which is a solid that transforms gas into liquid, gives birth to the fundamental contradiction of the firm. This is because the very act of turning a gas into a liquid and the idea that such a transformation could be bound by the strings of a contract are inherently contradictory. How could things that cannot be grasped by hand and that slip through the fingers possibly be tied down with just a few strands of string?

To contain liquid, one needs a jar, not a string. A jar is a tool for holding that which falls. Perhaps that is why liquid seeks to call itself the residual claimant. The jar that claims all that falls as its own, the jar that claims the firm as its property. But not everything that falls is liquid. Among the falling objects, there are solid fragments and remnants of ash. One must be cautious, for solid fragments can pierce holes in that jar.

Discussions on corporate governance are based on an outdated view of the corporation as owned by shareholders, along with a misunderstanding regarding residual claimants. As a result, corporate governance is designed through the lens of liquid. However, we already know that a corporation, as a legal entity, does not belong to its shareholders but to itself. The fact that a corporation is its own entity means that the interests of various stakeholders are embedded within it. Yet, corporate governance discussions, dominated by this outdated perspective, seek to maximize shareholder value under the guise of firm value maximization.

The protection of shareholder wealth from other stakeholders, who have been relegated to the status of "the other," is judged as both virtuous and moral. Consequently, the portion allocated to these others is labeled as costs and inefficiencies, while only the portion that benefits shareholders is deemed valuable and efficient. In this way, people become personally assimilated to shareholders, perceiving what is good for the shareholders as inherently good.

What the corporate governance debate overlooks is the fact that viewing the corporation as the exclusive property of shareholders is not only outdated but also immoral. How can it be considered ethical if one insists that a common property is solely one's? And can it truly be called evil if others assert their rightful claim to this property that has been selfishly declared as one's own?

Therefore, the discussion of corporate governance must be reconsidered from its very starting point. Instead of viewing the corporation as the property of shareholders, the debate should begin with the corporation as an entity permitted by society, whose existence is justified only by its contribution to societal value. The value of a firm should be centered on its worth as a legal entity, and corporate governance should be discussed with a focus on the firm as an independent legal entity.

Viewing a corporation as the property of shareholders ignores the fundamental principles of legal personality and limited liability that form the basis of the modern capitalist view of corporations. This outdated perspective is akin to viewing a large corporation through the lens of running a small corner shop, and is also immoral as it involves claiming something that belongs to others as one's own. However, it is difficult to clearly recognize this, perhaps due to moral insensitivity. This perspective must be dismantled. This is why we need moral deconstruction.

13. MONEY AND FINANCE

Financial Market

Money, after securing its status as liquid, leaps to the next stage. Liquid attracts other liquid, becoming an even larger liquid. A single drop of water may be insignificant, but a flowing river or the vast ocean is incomparably powerful. The ocean differs from a single drop not only in quantity but also in quality. It possesses an aura that a single droplet could never mimic. A droplet on a table is merely a contaminant or doomed to disappear, but in the ocean, water becomes the protagonist, expanding itself and commanding all around it.

Water meets other water, mixing and expanding, but at the same time, it contracts through mutual affinity, forming surface tension and cohesion. In this way, it creates a protective barrier to separate itself from the outside. However, when it encounters a hydrophilic object, it bonds and cooperates. Liquid thus gradually expands its influence, advancing steadily.

The same is true for money which is a liquid. Money relentlessly seeks to merge with other money. Once merged, it is integrated into the power of a single, larger money. This explains the saying, "It takes money to make money," as seen in the nature of liquid. It also sheds light on why Marx and Weber were so focused on the formation of initial capital. Money continuously consolidates, growing its power, and eventually establishes its own world. This world is operating in a semi-transparent state, semi-isolated from the outside world. The world is called the financial market or the capital market.

The financial market is closely connected to the real world, but this interaction occurs only through the process of osmosis. The financial market, separated by a semipermeable membrane from the real world, forms its own unique ecosystem. The financial market is an independent ecosystem, within which matter and energy circulate through creation, growth, decline, and extinction.

The boundary between a liquid and its external environment is formed by a weak membrane, determined by the balance between external pressure and surface tension. While this membrane separates the inside from the outside, it is a fragile surface, always ready to collapse. Similarly, financial markets and the outside world are separated by a fragile boundary that is always on the verge of collapsing.

The financial market is a market where money is traded. In the real market, money had to be content with playing the role of a medium of exchange, intervening in the transaction of goods. However, in the financial market, money itself becomes the main actor of the transaction, going beyond being a mere medium of exchange and transforming itself into a good to be exchanged. Money is traded with money. Here, a serious question arises about the nature of money: what does it mean to use money as a medium of exchange while trading money as a good? Giving and receiving the same thing has no meaning as an exchange.

So, what becomes important in the financial market is time. For the exchange of money for money to have meaning, there must be a time difference in the exchange. Thus, the financial market becomes a space where not only money is traded, but also time. Since prices are originally expressed in money, the price of money is simply its own quantity. The price of 1 won is 1 won, and the price of 1000 won is 1000 won. Therefore, the focus of interest in the financial market is not the price of money itself. What truly matters now is the so-called price of time. People call it interest.

It is precisely from this point of understanding that the prohibition of interest in medieval Europe and the Islamic world originates. If what is being traded in the financial market is not money but time, and thus if a price is placed on time, it goes against divine providence. Time is a sacred gift from God. Thus, pricing and trading time with money, a human invention, was a blasphemy against the sacred.

In any case, the financial market, while ostensibly trading money, have become spaces where time is truly traded. Therefore, the financial market is essentially a debt market. Whether we are making deposits, taking out loans, trading bonds, or even trading stocks, all of these are different names for debt contracts that trade time. Moreover, time inherently forces us to think about the future, and the future contains uncertainty. To determine an accurate price, we must consider not only the passage of time but also uncertainty. What modern finance does is precisely to assign prices to time and uncertainty.

What finance does within the boundaries of liquid is, first, to maintain liquidity, and second, to continuously expand the scope of the liquid. It must not remain as a small droplet; it must flow powerfully and gather to become rough waves, and ultimately the ocean. The nature of liquid is different from that of solid. A solid stays in place, content with itself. However, liquid displays and expands its power by constantly flowing and seeking, and sometimes by gathering in one place. This is the principle by which all water circulates, assimilates, and eventually converges into one ocean. A small amount of water in a bottle may seem separate from other water for a moment, but ultimately all water is one. What the financial market dreams of is precisely this—a world of liquid that, like a vast, unified ocean, gathers together as one.

Contradictions In Finance

Money is a liquid that proves its existence by flowing. It produces value when it flows between real goods. Sometimes, money flows between money. That flow of money is what we call finance. The space where money flows between money and becomes an object of exchange, is called the financial market. When money flows only between money, it cannot directly produce value. To generate value and wealth, one end of the flow must inevitably touch the real goods. When money swirls only between money, bubbles form and amplify.

Originally, money was either a scale to measure value or a jar to contain value. This granted money the privilege of flowing between real goods. Thus, when money began to flow only between money rather than real goods, it was an unexpected occurrence. It was as if the scale tried to weigh itself or the jar tried to contain itself.

However, this strange phenomenon may have been inevitable, as long as money is liquid. Nothing is more natural than water combining with water to form a larger body of water. Money, which originally began with the function of measuring and storing values, gradually became a liquid as it perceived flowing as the essence of its role. As soon as money became a liquid, it naturally attracted other money, which led inevitably to the birth of finance.

Thus, the financial market is fundamentally a market of contradictions. Money is merely a signifier, a numerical indicator for measuring value. Pointing to this signifier with the same signifier is meaningless. What sense does it make to trade 1,000 won for 1,000 won? Value is produced, and utility is created only when what is exchanged is different. Trading the same thing back and forth is both meaningless and inefficient.

The idea that the same thing must be exchanged but must also be different—this contradiction is the first principle of the financial market. The concept that emerged to fulfill this role is time. It is time that makes the same thing different. We all consider ourselves to be the same person, yet the "me" of today and the "me" of tomorrow are different by the amount of time that separates them. Likewise, today's money and tomorrow's money are the same, yet not the same. Time has the power to make anything different. Ultimately, the financial market discovered a clever solution to trade the same thing. Time is the ingenious scheme that can resolve the inherent contradiction of finance.

Thus, finance finds its raison d'être only on the foundation of time. While the trade of debt may appear as a transaction of borrowing and lending money, its essence lies in the exchange between money and the exchange of time difference. This time difference demands additional money in the form of interest. Debt transactions are mediated by IOUs, which serves as the link between present and future money. Similarly, when investing in bonds like corporate bonds, one may feel like paying money for an asset. But the bond is merely a sign, a promise to pay money in the future. A sign is needed to bridge the gap between present and future money. Like the IOU, a bond is not an asset like a real good, but simply exists as a link between present and future money.

Stock trading may appear as exchanging money for the sign called a stock, but this, too, is an exchange of time difference, as a stock ultimately represents a promise of future money. In this case, the additional money demanded by the time difference is called a dividend rather than interest. In places where stock trading is active, one can also gain profit through selling the stock, known as capital gains, instead of receiving dividends. As long as capital gains replace dividends, there is no need to insist on dividends. Now, interest is divided into dividends and capital gains.

Forward or futures trading starkly reveals the inherent contradiction of money exchange. In futures trading, if values are exchanged at a current price, there is no need for actual money to be exchanged. The money itself is not exchanged, yet the transaction is still valid. Futures trading involves nothing but the flow of future money and the conditions attached to it. What is being traded are essentially different bets on the future. This futures trading could be interpreted as a mutual debt contract in which the interest cancels each other out. In any case, it is an exchange without exchange and a trade without trade. While futures trading clearly exposes the contradiction of finance, every financial trading is contradictory in itself. Only time can resolve this contradiction.

Meanwhile, time never arrives alone. It always comes accompanied by risk or uncertainty. The future is not just a time of waiting; it is also a time of risk. Interest, then, is both the price of time and the price of risk. A serious contemplation of interest is inseparable from considerations of time and risk. Time and risk are fundamental problems that humanity has always faced, closely tied to humanity's most essential questions. Thus, discussions about interest extend beyond the realm of economics and enter the domain of philosophy.

Financial Innovation And Financial Engineering

Just as a water droplet merges with another droplet to form a larger one, finance grows larger as it blends with other forms of finance. What so-called financial innovation or financial engineering does is precisely to create this larger droplet. When new financial products are created by synthesizing futures or options, it is akin to combining small droplets to form a larger one. The way futures and options combine is like a chemical formula for the combination of two substances. Just as different chemical combinations create different compounds, the combination of futures and options in new ways gives birth to new financial products. In this sense, financial engineering is chemistry rather than engineering.

A powerful way for water to expand its power is to extract moisture out of other objects. Much of the moisture within living organisms evaporates and recirculates when the organism dies, eventually returning to the ocean. Likewise, finance seeks to grow by extracting the liquid within organisms that have lost vitality. It should identify assets that have been losing vitality, and extract their liquidity. This process is called "securitization". Securitization involves drawing liquidity from assets. A prime example is the Mortgage-backed Security (MBS), where banks issue securities based on loans secured by housing mortgages. Investors who purchase these securities gain rights to the mortgage payments that the banks' borrowers make. In exchange for transferring these rights, the banks receive a lump sum of money from the sales of the securities.

For banks, the mortgage loan was originally an asset that would slowly trickle in as cash over the course of 20 to 30 years. While it was a source of income, it lacked vitality. Through securitization, banks could transform this slow trickle of small payments into a torrent of capital, injecting new energy into its financial system. Of course, not only mortgage-backed securities but also any form of loan or asset can be securitized, leading to what is known as Asset-backed Securities (ABS).

Securitization, contrary to popular belief, does not infuse assets with liquidity. It doesn't breathe new life into assets by making them liquid; instead, it extracts the water of life from them, effectively declaring them dead. The asset itself does not become liquid. The debtor's obligation cannot flow and remains in the same place. Securitization is merely a mechanism that draws the water of life from an asset and merges it into the sea of speculation. In this process, the asset itself loses vitality and withers.

Originally, a debt contract was a matter between the debtor and the creditor. With securitization, however, the debtor now faces numerous anonymous creditors. These distant, hidden creditors remain indifferent to both the debtor and the asset. Abandoned in indifference, the asset slowly withers. What gains vitality through securitization is not the asset itself, but the liquid parasitic on the asset. In the financial market, heavy objects are cumbersome, and only the liquid is needed.

Herein lies the risk of securitization, and by extension, financial engineering. In their eyes, assets or real goods are invisible; all they see is the liquid residing within. Even if extracting that liquid causes the asset itself to wither and die, they either turn a blind eye or remain completely unaware of this fact. From the start, they had no interest in the asset itself.

The 2008 global financial crisis vividly illustrated how

financial innovations, such as securitization and financial engineering, led to the withering of real assets, through excessive extraction of the water of life from those real assets. As many commentators say, it may be more convenient to explain the crisis as a result of the speculative nature of the financial market. However, speculation only addresses the behavior of market participants, not the nature of the objects being speculated on. The object of their speculation was not the liquid representing the assets, but the liquid separated from the assets. As more liquid flowed away from the assets and became the object of speculation, the assets themselves inevitably withered away.

Speculation is represented by bubbles. A turbulent river or sea creates bubbles. When the liquid separated from assets swirls as the object of speculation, bubbles are formed. Bubbles generate larger bubbles and may cluster together or merge. It is natural to call speculative markets bubbles because the object of speculation is liquid.

In responding to the 2008 financial crisis, focusing only on the issues of speculation and analyzing the problem solely as a matter of bubbles led to a neglect of the withering assets. Excessive bubbles were mistaken for the waves themselves. Bubbles are merely small droplets clinging to the edge of the wave. In efforts to save the speculators trapped in the bubbles, there was indifference to the assets that were drying up from thirst. Fearing the collapse of bubbles, continuous supplies of liquid were provided. But where did this newly supplied liquid come from? Ultimately, it had to be extracted once again from real assets. Taxes, too, must be supported by someone's real assets. As a result, the assets continued to wither from increased thirst, while more liquid was injected into the speculators riding the bubbles under the guise of soft landings or financial stability.

The true solution should have been to refill dying assets with life-giving water. On the contrary, however, more water of life was extracted from these assets and poured into the bubbles.

They didn't seem to realize that the problem with the bubbles was caused by too much liquid being separated out. Rather, they focused on making the size of the bubbles appear smaller by pouring more liquid onto them.

However, the increased accumulation of liquid inevitably harbors the potential for even larger bubbles in the future. In the post-financial crisis world, genuine real assets continued to wither, while the liquid separated from assets only accumulated further. This widened the gap of polarization. Many people are groaning in pain beneath the dry, twisted and collapsing assets. However, for those who are busy savoring the seaside scenery, the moaning sound cannot be heard because it is obscured by the sound of the waves. Many assets that had been robbed of their water of life were tottering to the point where they would crumble if touched. Eventually, the COVID-19 virus of 2020 struck and passed through this weakened link.

14. INTEREST: TIME AND RISK

Interest And Time

For those familiar with modern finance, interest is calculated as follows: it is the sum of the interest portion under the assumption of no risk and the interest portion added due to risk. The interest in the absence of risk is often called the risk-free interest. This risk-free interest is considered the price of time. Additionally, a consideration for risk is inserted. Thus, the interest is increased by the amount corresponding to the risk. This portion is often called the risk premium. In the case of ordinary loans, the risk premium increases if the borrower's creditworthiness is low. For stocks, it increases if there is a high level of uncertainty about the performance of the firm issuing the stock. In this way, interest is described as the arithmetic sum of the risk-free interest and the risk premium.

It is not a bad thing that both time and risk factors are included in the calculation of modern interest. On the other hand, the fact that the two are arithmetically added together shows a simplistic view of time and risk. This also confirms that the essence of so-called capitalist calculation is closer to naivete than to rationality. In reality, the future cannot exist without risk, and risk always approaches from the future. Therefore, time and risk are not the kinds of things that can be separated in an additive formula.

In any case, the idea that time and risk are embedded in interest is an old one. But which is more important, time or risk? It is at this point that Islam and Christianity diverge. Islam placed emphasis on both risk and time, while medieval

Christianity seemed to place its emphasis mostly on time.

Medieval Christianity focused on time, and it was in this context that the aversion to interest was practiced within Christian regions. Time was considered something granted by God to humans, and thus human time was not really humanity's but God's. Yet, isn't interest the price of money trade with time difference? Interest is, in essence, a price attached to time. It is at this very point that interest was interpreted as blasphemy (Geisst, 2013).

What could be more insulting to God than placing a human-made price tag on time, which belongs to Him, and trading it? With this line of thinking, it became a natural step for the all-powerful medieval Church to prohibit interest. Moreover, trades were seen as the domain of greedy merchants, and thus, sacred time could not be made into the object of greedy dealings. The pathological prohibition of interest in medieval Christianity was justified through the abhorrence of merchants and the sanctification of time.

However, this view of interest in Christianity was destined to collapse with the arrival of the capitalist era. In capitalism, merchants were no longer objects of disdain, and interest was to be regarded as the legitimate profit of merchants or entrepreneurs. In other words, interest became a rightful byproduct of commercial or investment activities. Since capitalism viewed the efforts of merchants and entrepreneurs positively, interest, like profit, was set to be interpreted as a legitimate reward.

Or, the order might be reversed. The capitalist perspective on interest may not have been formed after capitalism emerged, but rather, capitalism may have been created only after such a perspective already existed. At least Max Weber had something similar in mind. According to Weber, a shift in religious perception preceded the rise of capitalism. The phenomenon of changing religious perception in early modern Europe is what we call the Reformation. The Reformation arrived in Europe before capitalism did.

The shift in the perception of interest also began with the Reformation. Reformers like Luther and Calvin opposed usury but did not reject interest itself. Interest was no longer seen as blasphemy but as a legitimate compensation. How did interest gain its legitimacy? It was likely justified by the benefit it provided to borrowers facing financial difficulty. After all, there would be no financier willing to lend money without receiving interest. If interest were prohibited, it would put potential borrowers in need of funds in a dire situation. Allowing interest, then, would be seen as helping the borrower. With this shift in perspective—seeing interest as a means of aiding rather than burdening borrowers—the sharp accusation of blasphemy must have begun to dull.

And interest began to be justified from the merchant's perspective. Just as a merchant earns profit through effort, interest is seen as the result of the financier's efforts. Just as a merchant's efforts are rewarded with profit, so too should the financier's efforts be compensated. Merchants carefully choose where to invest and earn profits as a result. To select investments with higher returns, merchants must forgo other alternatives with lower returns. Merchants compare investment opportunities and calculate the costs.

The same applies to financiers. Interest is the profit determined by comparing investment opportunities. In this way, interest became opportunity cost. The interest charged must be compared to the profit the financiers could have earned had they invested elsewhere instead of lending the money. Thus, the equation that interest is compensation for the profit forgone due to lending began to be established.

It is difficult to determine whether the shift in the perception of interest justified commerce, or, conversely, whether a more favorable view of commerce altered the perception of interest. Likely, the two influenced each other, creating a kind of positive feedback loop or virtuous cycle. In any case, the interest's "becoming" an opportunity cost was an event that occurred as capitalism gradually permeated Europe.

Interest: From Life To Matter

The medieval Christian critique that interest was a greedy price tag on sacred time gradually collapsed with the advent of the Reformation and capitalism. While time remained within God's domain, interest was no longer interpreted as a blasphemous challenge to that domain. Instead, it came to be seen as a means of helping borrowers or as a legitimate reward for a merchant's investment opportunities.

Of course, the idea of interest as a means of helping the borrower did not always carry a purely positive image. Interest was not seen as something inherently good, but rather as a necessary "lesser evil" that one had to endure for the sake of something better. In interest as opportunity cost, time was no longer the central focus. While time was always involved in the concept of opportunity cost, the primary concern was no longer about time itself, but about comparing different investment opportunities. The moment attention shifted slightly away from religious and philosophical questions about time toward practical considerations, the notion of blasphemy began to fade into obscurity.

Interest was no longer interpreted within the framework of blasphemy but began to be understood as the result of mutual cooperation between individuals or the outcome of diligent investment. Although the shadow of usury and its negative consequences may have lingered nearby, the capitalist era embraced the revival of interest with a more positive outlook. In hindsight, didn't interest effectively exist in the Middle Ages through various methods of circumventing the interest ban? The only change in the capitalist era was that people became more honest and revealed their desires, rather than that entirely new interest was created.

Let us pay a little more attention to the shift in perspectives on interest. When Aristotle famously stated the so-called "sterility theory of money" that money cannot beget money, he was expressing disdain for interest. Modern individuals see interest as a byproduct of debt contracts, but they don't attach life force to it. However, Aristotle viewed interest as the offspring of money, a perspective shared by many ancient cultures across both East and West. The Greek word for interest, "tokos", and the even older Mesopotamian term "mas" were both synonymous with the word for the offspring of livestock. Similarly, the Chinese character for interest (利子) also carries the meaning of "offspring." In the past, people believed that money could reproduce like a living being, whereas in the modern capitalist system, interest is seen as a byproduct of investment activity. Interest, a by-product of debt, is now understood not as offspring linked by blood, but rather as a material surplus.

Aristotle rejected the idea of interest by expressing contempt for the unnaturalness of viewing money as a living being. When he condemned interest, he did not explicitly consider factors like time or risk. Instead, he emphasized its inconsistency with the natural order. In nature, living beings go through cycles of birth, growth, and death, while money, as an artificial creation of humans, lacks life. How could anything be more unnatural than the idea of lifeless money becoming pregnant and giving birth? Aristotle's disdain for interest points to its unnaturalness.

In medieval Christianity, time was considered to belong to God and thus sacred. Additionally, in medieval Scholastic philosophy, which inherited Aristotle's tradition, the idea of lifeless money giving birth was seen as unnatural and abhorrent. Thus, interest was blasphemous, unnatural and disgusting.

However, with new perspectives, money and interest began to be viewed not as living beings but as material substances. Interest was seen as either an auxiliary material that satisfies the needs of those in need of funds or as a byproduct of investment activities and opportunities. This shift in perception transformed interest from a blasphemy against God or against living beings created by God, as in the medieval view, into something simply interpreted as a necessary matter for human life. While we often criticize capitalism as an era obsessed with materialism, the process of materializing life had already begun with money and interest before capitalism emerged.

The materialization of objects might also be related to the so-called Scientific Revolution that swept through Europe in the 16th and 17th centuries. When Descartes proclaimed that the fundamental attribute of the mind is thought and the fundamental attribute of matter is extension, Aristotle's view of nature collapsed. Nature is extension, and extension is space. Nature is merely space with length, width, and depth. In Descartes' universal mathematics (Mathesis universalis) approach to nature, the Aristotelian life that possessed its own purpose (telos) did not exist. Nature was merely matter and mathematics.

Through the Scientific Revolution, the life force of nature disappeared, and nature had already become matter. Therefore, there was no longer any reason to consider money and interest unnatural simply because they lacked life force. Freed from the shackles of Aristotle and Christianity, interest was able to be reborn, not as the offspring of life, but as a material byproduct of opportunity. Interest now became part of Descartes' extension and thus something natural. As the Scientific Revolution began to view nature through the lens of mathematics, interest, too, was poised to be expressed mathematically. Finally, interest was to be represented through compound interest calculations. Compound interest is a tool that embodies exponential growth, and this is the financial representation of Cartesian geometry.

If we go back further, perhaps the materialization of time had already begun long before the Scientific Revolution. In the Middle Ages, Leonardo Fibonacci introduced the mathematics of Islamic merchants to Europe in his "Liber Abaci" (Book of Calculation, 1202). This book explained compound interest and present value calculations, and at that time, the concept of time had already intersected with the concept of space. The idea of interest earned after one year was not much different from the idea of profits earned by traveling from one city to the next.

Compound interest earned after two years was akin to making profits after traveling to yet another city. Medieval merchants realized that interest over time and profits from spatial movement were essentially the same. Although Christianity and Islam strictly prohibited interest at the time, merchants may have already erased the word "blasphemy" from their minds by understanding interest in terms of spatial profit. The last thing they needed was the scientific justification that time, too, is a form of space and that interest is just another matter. The Scientific Revolution of the 17th century finally provided this justification, completing the task.

Interest And Risk

The perspective on interest in medieval Christianity did pay attention to the meaning of time, but it was ignorant of another important factor, risk. Interest highlights not only the theme of time but also that of risk, because time always comes with uncertainty. Did they think there was no uncertainty because it was predetermined by God? There may be no uncertainty for God, but for humans, the future is always uncertain.

Medieval Islam likely scoffed at the narrow-minded views of their Christian neighbors. The task of serious consideration of both interest and risk was imposed upon Islam. While medieval Christianity overlooked the gravity of risk intertwined with time, Muslims were much more attuned to the weight of risk. Certainly, they were familiar with Aristotle's view of nature and the sanctity of time. However, unlike Christians, Muslims could not ignore the additional dimension of risk.

In Islam, the issue of risk seems to extend across various dimensions. First, there is a problem of risk as uncertainty regarding the future. Modern economics reduces this to a problem of probability calculation, solving it by adding a risk premium to the risk-free interest rate. However, Islam does not view it so simplistically. Instead of focusing on how to calculate the uncertain future, it reflects on how to distribute it.

Risk inevitably leads to inequality in outcomes. Some may suffer accidents, becoming injured or even losing their lives. Others may fall ill due to disease, potentially facing long-term disability or death. A fortunate merchant might strike it rich, while another could lose everything and see their family enslaved. Even though people face the same risk beforehand, the realization of risk can result in dramatically different outcomes afterward. The central issue becomes how to mitigate the inequality resulting from these divergent outcomes of risk.

Now, interest emerges from the axis of time and takes its place in the grand discourse of risk. Interest is typically expressed as a fixed amount to be repaid at a predetermined future time. As a result of the debt contract, the debtor is obligated to pay the creditor this fixed amount, regardless of the debtor's business outcomes or harvest yields. If the debtor earns low income or experiences a loss, the payment of interest amplifies the loss for the debtor. However, if the debtor achieves high earnings, he can retain all profits beyond the interest payment, leading to potentially high gains. Modern economics refers to this as the "leverage effect" of debt. Just as a lever moves up and down around its fulcrum, debt amplifies the debtor's gains and losses. The leverage effect magnifies the profits and losses that the debtor experiences, resulting in a higher level of risk for the debtor due to the debt contract.

In modern economics, the leverage effect is depicted as a strategy where entrepreneurs or investors borrow others' funds to increase their capital and thereby amplify their profits. When risk is considered in relation to interest, it is framed as part of an investment strategy, where the investor calculates how to reflect risk in the interest they charge. However, for most of human history, borrowers did not take loans to exploit the leverage effect and increase profits but simply to survive. In some ways, the leverage effect may have been a life-threatening gamble. The precarious position of borrowers under the leverage effect may have provided a fundamental reason for the prohibition of interest, not only in Islam but also in medieval Christianity.

In any case, Islam's approach to interest, placing it within the realm of risk, diverged from that of medieval Christianity. The prohibition of interest in Islam was rooted not only in the sanctity of time but also in the justification in fairness. Risk inevitably leads to unequal outcomes, and interest, through the leverage effect, disproportionately burdens the borrower with that risk. This excessive inequality is unjust. To ensure the fair distribution of risk, interest must be prohibited.

The principle that the distribution of risk must be fair would not be limited only to monetary debt. After all, didn't medieval Islam already recognize that money is merely a social contract? If so, anything could serve as money, not just gold or silver. Therefore, in any transaction where the same goods are exchanged but with unequal amounts or values, the difference would all be considered interest. The Islamic concept of interest, "riba", applies to both money and general goods alike. Thus, the prohibition of riba is not restricted to money. It applies to any unequal exchanges, whether in gold-for-gold, silver-for-silver, or even dates-for-dates. In trading general goods, any unjust profit also becomes riba.

That is not all. Since debt is merely one type of contract between two parties, the understanding of risk distribution can be extended beyond debt contracts to more general agreements. In situations where two merchants enter into a contract, if the terms of the contract or its fulfillment involve excessive ambiguity or uncertainty ("gharar"), or if the nature of the business itself carries a gambling-like character ("maisir"), such contracts are prohibited. The reason for the prohibition is clear. Uncertainty in contract terms unfairly allocates risk to the weaker party, and the gambling nature of a business produces and distributes excessive risk without value creation.

Interest, on the one hand, passes through the realm of the divine as it moves along the axis of time, and on the other hand, passes through the realm of humanity as it moves along the axis of risk. As it traverses the axis of risk, interest intersects with contractual uncertainty and gambling. In the space of risk, interest confronts the complex issue of justice in risk distribution.

Furthermore, since interest is inseparable from time, time and risk could not be thought of independently either. This inseparability of time and risk is precisely what distinguishes the Islamic understanding of interest from that of medieval Christianity. Paradoxically, this difference in perception becomes a crucial factor for the birth of capitalism in Europe, a region of relatively naïve views, rather than in the Islamic world where commerce was flourishing. We will examine this further later on.

Islam And Risk

Islam may have been fixated on the fair distribution of risk, but this should not be interpreted as a rejection or fear of risk. As the phrase "Islamic merchant" suggests, Muslims were not afraid to pursue risk for commercial gain. The commerce practiced by medieval Islamic merchants included not only local trade but also long-distance trade, stretching from Africa to the end of East Asia, including Korea and Japan. In the medieval period, Islamic merchants were the ones who understood risk the best and were the most enterprising in the world. It was not because they were afraid of risk, but because they understood it so well that they were able to place interest in the space of risk.

Muslims seemed to encourage the pursuit of legitimate and enterprising risks, but such risks should not be shifted onto one party alone. Doing so would violate the principle of brotherhood, which was highly valued in Islam. True brotherhood means sharing not only profits but also losses. The method of risk distribution that they advocated was risk sharing. While they prohibited debt arrangements that transferred excessive risk to one side, they permitted the mechanism in which risks were mutually shared.

Merchants raised the capital needed for their businesses through "qirad" or "mudarabah". In modern terms, qirad can be viewed as a form of equity sharing, similar to stocks. In equity-based contracts, profits are distributed according to the agreed-upon share ratio. If the borrower's profit is high, both parties share in those large profits, and if the profit is low, they share in the smaller profits or even losses. This equity sharing method ensures that risks are not transferred to one party but are shared by both. Qirad resembles the structure of a debt-free stock company and, in fact, served as the foundation for the development of stock companies. The stock company, often seen as the pinnacle of modern capitalism, has its roots in the organizations of medieval Islamic merchants.

Interest And Opportunity Cost

In medieval Christianity, interest was positioned solely within the dimension of time. This sacred time, however, was gradually replaced by matter and mathematics as the modern era unfolded. The prohibition of interest eventually gave way, and its acceptance became a natural development.

On the other hand, in Islam, interest was placed not only in the space of time but also in the space of risk. Thus, the replacement of life with matter and mathematics as the essence of nature could not serve as a justification for permitting interest. The future remained uncertain, and with that uncertainty, it was always possible that the vulnerable had to bear excessive risks. In some sense, the more capitalism has developed, the greater the uncertainty and risk have increased. The issue of interest, situated in the space of risk, increasingly revealed the harshness and problematic nature of interest itself. While modern Christianity has proudly liberated interest and taken it for granted, abandoning biblical teachings, modern Islam still has no choice but to grapple with interest as it remains in the space of risk.

For those familiar with economics, interest is an opportunity cost. Opportunity cost refers to the profit that must be forfeited due to the lost (investment) opportunity. As an opportunity cost, interest represents the return a lender could have earned by investing the loaned amount elsewhere. This seems reasonable when you think about it. Isn't it rational for the lender to be compensated with interest that reflects the profit they could have gained by investing the money elsewhere? A rational lender would naturally compare the relative returns between two possible uses of their money.

Thus, we tend to view the prohibition of interest in medieval Christianity and Islam as a result of ignorance or irrationality. Did they not understand the concept of opportunity cost? Or were they simply incapable of making such calculations? In any case, we assume they were irrational. We never doubt that, while they were ignorant, we are now enlightened and rational economic actors. This perspective produces the misconception that they lacked the concept of opportunity cost.

However, opportunity cost is not a special or complex concept. It is the kind of basic concepts that humans likely had even when drawing in caves. Flowing time and the limited resources have always compelled us to make decisions based on opportunity costs. Did they not realize, while spending time and effort drawing in caves, that they could not simultaneously be out hunting? Believing that only we understand such a simple concept is nothing more than an irrational inference. Then, do we correctly understand opportunity cost? Is it not possible that, on the contrary, we are misunderstanding about opportunity cost?

The profit that could have been earned from a forgone investment constitutes the opportunity cost. Thus, to justify the interest as opportunity cost, there must be an alternative investment opportunity that could yield profit. But how is this profit calculated? Economics tells us that this, too, is an opportunity cost. It is a substitute for the interest that could be earned by lending that amount instead of investing it there.

Then, opportunity cost is not an independent concept. Every opportunity cost always presupposes the existence of another opportunity cost, that is, the existence of something else. Thus, isn't opportunity cost something that can only exist by referring to each other? Interest refers to profit, and profit, in turn, refers to interest for its existence to be revealed. Opportunity cost 1 must refer to opportunity cost 2, and opportunity cost 2 must refer back to opportunity cost 1. It is a system of infinitely repeating cycles. Opportunity costs form a small celestial system, orbiting each other while illuminating each other.

The system of opportunity costs, which exists only by referring to one another, is ultimately related to the fact that opportunity cost is essentially a form of promise. This parallels the idea that a price represents only the exchange ratio between two goods, rather than indicating the inherent value of the goods themselves. Opportunity cost is a promise and merely a relative ratio between opportunities. After establishing a reference point, opportunity costs can be calculated as relative ratios between different opportunities.

Therefore, there is no definitive answer to what the reference point should be. Opportunity cost does not concern itself with the reference point itself. What matters to opportunity cost is merely the difference in distance or the ratio of distances from the given reference point. It resembles the way various planets orbit around a central star. Opportunity costs are simply the ratios of distances between the star and the various planets.

The reference point for opportunity cost is, in other words, the zero point, or, origin and it is quite natural to position this origin as zero. In medieval Christianity and Islam, the zero point was placed at zero. The prohibition of interest was simply a promise to place zero as the reference point and as the central star around which the planets revolve. The perception that it was irrational then and it is rational now stems from a misunderstanding of the essence of opportunity cost. Such a perception is a manifestation of irrational prejudice. It might have been irrational then, but even now, it can also be irrational in a different sense.

While people think that the zero interest rates of the Middle Ages and Islam were irrational, they do not think the zero or negative interest rates that keep emerging in the 21st century, following the global financial crisis and the COVID-19 crisis, are irrational. They find it fascinating and surprising as a new experience, but they do not feel it's irrational. They view it as a nation's effort to respond to crises and sometimes even demand a more drastic drop in interest rates. Although interest rates are zero both now and then, it is thought to be rational now, but irrational then. Wrong then, but right now? You are wrong, but I am right?

The fact that opportunity cost is not absolute but relative is familiar even in modern capitalist economies. Opportunity cost is the relative distance from a reference point. The base interest rate is the most important reference point for interest, which is determined by each country's central bank. When a central bank positions the base interest rate, there is no room to justify it with the conventional concept of opportunity cost. The central bank's base interest rate can come up to us only when it parts ways with opportunity cost.

The central bank sets the reference point based on the state of the economy, economic views, and economic philosophy, while also considering the direction in which the economy should move. Economic views and philosophy include moral and ethical considerations. What is socially and morally unacceptable is defined as illegal, and if discovered, it is confiscated. When setting the reference point, the central bank does not take illegal and immoral trades into account. Since illegal trades should not exist, they cannot be considered. As it determines how much to receive in the future, opportunity cost is a future tense and also an expression of oughtness. Oughtness cannot part ways with morality.

Thus, the fact that medieval Christianity and Islam prohibited interest is not so different from today's monetary policies. This may be as natural as setting the zero point at zero. In light of their moral and economic views, it may be only natural. Just as illegal trades are not subject to consideration, immoral trades should not be considered either. Their zero point was pointing exactly at zero.

Was the zero point back then wrong? If we do not want to declare that today's zero point is wrong, we should not say so. They just viewed the world through different standards and set their zero point within that world. They wanted a moral world, and their standards were rational. This principle applies equally today. Can we really say that the zero interest of the past was less rational than today's zero interest?

Moreover, the opportunity cost we consider today is almost always based on market trades. If we do not lend money here, we could lend it there, or invest or deposit it elsewhere to gain profit. Investment opportunities are never exhausted. However, in a time when the market was not routine and financial trades were not commonplace, interest would not have escaped far from zero even if it had become an opportunity cost in the modern sense. If there are no other investment opportunities, it would not be unusual for the opportunity cost to be zero.

The problem that medieval Christianity and Islam could not directly resolve, and which was a source of concern, was the practical aspect that no one was willing to lend money at zero interest. In other words, their contradiction arose not from a failure to understand opportunity cost, but from the gap between theoretical outcomes and practical realities. Unlike their theoretical calculations, in reality, interest can arise due to the burdens or costs associated with managing a loan after it is issued. This could also be called opportunity cost in some sense (well, every cost can be interpreted as opportunity cost in economics), but it is not the concept of opportunity cost related to the loss of investment opportunities that modern economics takes for granted.

One important reason why interest was declared as zero in the Middle Ages was likely to reduce the harmful effects arising from the differences in status and power between lenders and borrowers. However, it remained relatively silent on the management costs of lending that are inevitably incurred. Modern Christianity could undermine the prohibition of interest by addressing such issues. In contrast, in Islam, the prohibition of interest remained in place because it had in mind another moral axis of risk sharing. The difference in attitudes toward interest between modern Christianity and Islam diverges precisely at this point.

15. CAPITALISM: INTEREST AND INSURANCE

The Beginning Of Capitalism: Prohibition Of Interest

Europe, which was relatively underdeveloped before the modern era, gradually began to gain economic and social superiority over the Islamic and Asian regions. And the economic system known as capitalism began to emerge, centered around the Netherlands and England.

Adam Smith saw the origin of capitalism in the division of labor, Marx in violence and exploitation, and Weber in Calvinist Protestantism and rationality. But did capitalism have to begin only by breaking away from earlier times or other regions? Division of labor, violence, and exploitation existed long before capitalism, and rationality is not exclusive to Europe. A slight difference and a small shift, when met with chance, can cause the collapse of an old system and the birth of a new one. Looking back after time has passed, it may seem as though the change had its own rationale or purpose, but the people of the time may not have been aware of or intended these shifts. Every moment flows, as it always has, simply passing by.

Perhaps the groundwork for the creation of capitalism, though it may have been coincidental, began in the Middle Ages. When medieval Christianity prohibited interest, no one could have noticed, but the roots of capitalism were already being planted. Capitalism likely cannot exist without interest.

However, capitalism may have possibly begun only when interest was revived, not simply when interest existed. (We will explore this in more detail later.) If so, the groundwork for capitalism may have begun with the prohibition of interest.

Like most major religions, Christianity was hostile to interest. The Old Testament is full of provisions prohibiting interest. In the New Testament, Jesus' anger and resentment towards moneylenders also appear. This is likely a reflection of the abuses of lending and finance that prevailed in the ancient Roman Empire. At the Council of Nicaea in 325, the lending of money at interest by clergy was prohibited, and at the Third Lateran Council in 1179, moneylenders were excommunicated (Choi, Wonoh, 2019; Ferguson, 2008). In 1234, Catholic Pope Gregory IX issued a papal decree prohibiting usury. This was the era when Alighieri Dante cast usurers into a desert hell with flames flying, as described in his works.

The Fifth Lateran Council, held between 1512 and 1517, defined usury as 'gain or profit drawn from the use of things that are sterile in nature, profit obtained without any effort, cost, or risk' (Seog, 2014; Steinmetz, 2015). In this definition, we can simultaneously read the two opposing perspectives on interest.

According to Aristotle's theory of the sterility of money, money cannot reproduce, so in the first half of the definition of usury, interest becomes usury and therefore provides grounds for prohibition. This may have been the stance of medieval Christianity on the prohibition of interest. Along with this, the sanctity of time was a logical basis for medieval Christianity to maintain the prohibition on interest.

On the other hand, looking at the second half of the definition of usury, it states that if interest is tied to effort, cost, and risk, it may no longer be considered usury. In Europe, during a period when commerce and finance were beginning to awaken, interest was preparing to free itself from the constraints of usury. After all, isn't commerce an enterprise that involves effort, cost, and risk? The definition of usury in the early 16th century may have simultaneously contained the medieval prohibition of interest and the modern allowance of it. The difference between the two may have been where the emphasis was placed in the definition of usury—whether at the first half or the second half.

As Europe entered the modern era, the emphasis on usury shifted from the first half to the second half, and accordingly, the Christian perspective on the prohibition of interest began to collapse. Capitalism gradually emerged to take its place as the dominant force.

The Key To Capitalism: Separation Of Time And Risk

From the Middle Ages to the modern era, the concept of interest in Europe was detached from the notion of risk. Interest was seen as something that went against divine providence related to time and pregnancy. Only God governs time, and only life, as permitted by God, could conceive and give birth. Interest was considered blasphemous because it assigned a price to time and was an offspring of money—a non-living being. The medieval prohibition of interest was strictly enforced under the hegemony of Christianity.

During the period when capitalistic thinking was spreading, in a region where the hegemony of merchants was growing, the suffering of bankers who lent money and the compensation for that suffering came into view. Although interest was originally seen as blasphemous, if it was compensation for the effort, cost, and risk that bankers had to bear, it could be forgiven. The justification of interest as compensation for the banker's suffering inevitably converged with the concept of opportunity cost.

Above all, thinking of interest as separate from risk forms a key point of divergence from Islam. Can interest truly be separated from risk? One might initially think of it this way: if a borrower comes to a banker to borrow money and has no choice but to repay the money, then there is no risk. In ancient or medieval times, when tenant farmers borrowed money from landowners, they could not arbitrarily choose not to repay the debt. Defaulting meant falling into slavery. In that case, isn't interest, in effect, separated from risk?

The view of interest in modern economics also begins with interest that is separated from risk. Interest that exists solely over time, independent of risk, is referred to as the risk-free interest in modern economics. Risk is then added to the risk-free interest in the form of arithmetic addition. Thus, on the surface, it appears that modern interest is no longer considered separately from risk.

However, it has not strayed far from the medieval interest in that interest is possible even without risk. In fact, interest continually moves in the direction of eliminating risk. Securing collateral or assigning credit ratings are laborious efforts to offset risk within the debt system. Even in modern capitalism, risk is not seen as the essence of interest but rather as something to be eliminated.

The modern view on interest may seem vastly different from the medieval Christian perspective that prohibited it. However, while the permissibility of interest may differ, in attempting to strip away the risk and confine interest solely to the dimension of time, the modern view on interest is not so different from that of the Middle Ages. In fact, far from being distinct, modern interest views the Middle Ages as a utopia. Modern interest, which strives tirelessly to cast off the burden of risk, is a pitiful being longing to converge with the medieval interest.

The Emergence Of Capitalism: De-Interest And Insurance

If interest were completely prohibited today, modern capitalism could no longer be sustained. Therefore, one could argue that capitalism began with the permission of interest as a prerequisite. This perspective seems to explain why capitalism did not emerge in medieval Europe or Islamic regions where interest was forbidden. However, capitalism also did not emerge in the East, where the prohibition of interest was not enforced and commerce was flourishing.

Arguably, capitalism may not have been able to start without the prohibition of usury. With the ban on interest and a bit of coincidence, risk was unshackled, leading to the creation of another pillar of capitalism. When interest was finally revived, capitalism could have taken off. Capitalism required two wings: risk and debt. Since the place where these two elements were simultaneously present was modern Europe, capitalism could only have started there.

When usury was prohibited by canon law in 1234, "bottomry" was also banned. Bottomry was a method of finance used since ancient times, in which a banker would lend money to a merchant embarking on a voyage. Thus, bottomry was essentially a debt contract. However, unlike general debt, it came with a condition. The condition was that if the ship sank due to a storm or enemy attack, the interest and the principal would be waived. From the debtor's perspective, the debt would be forgiven on the condition of the ship's sinking, and in this aspect, bottomry was also an insurance contract.

In modern financial terms, bottomry could be called a structured bond or a contingent bond. Bottomry is structured in such a way that, in addition to the general debt contract, a kind of put option is granted to the debtor. This put option can be exercised if the event of the ship sinking occurs. Of course, if the merchant’s ship returns safely, the principal must be repaid along with the agreed-upon interest. Since the banker bears the risk of not receiving the principal, a relatively higher interest rate would be charged.

Thus, bottomry is a contract that simultaneously realizes both debt and insurance. As a debt contract that involves the payment of interest, bottomry became subject to prohibition when usury was banned. But what about the insurance function embedded in bottomry? Should insurance also be subject to prohibition? Nowhere in the Bible is there a prohibition against the function of insurance, is there? Insurance compensates those who suffer losses and damage, which, unlike interest, is desirable, isn't it? Shouldn't bottomry be prohibited as debt but encouraged as insurance? In that case, wouldn't it be acceptable if the debt portion were removed from bottomry and it functioned solely as insurance?

As later formalized by the papacy, if risk is involved, it is not usury. If the interest portion is not explicitly visible and risk is being traded, then no significant problem arises. From then on, in Europe, debt sought rationalization by somehow embracing risk. Two major directions can be considered for this rationalization. One is debt with emphasis on the presence of risk, and the other is trading solely risk without debt being involved. In either case, it was not debt and interest but risk and insurance that took center stage.

In emphasizing risk in debt, there were two important methods. One was the "bill of exchange". A bill of exchange is fundamentally something like an IOU, serving as a document for a debt contract. In addition, the holder of a bill of exchange gains the position of a creditor. In medieval northern Italy, when a bill of exchange was paid in a different currency, it became exposed to exchange rate risk. Therefore, a debt contract through a bill of exchange carried exchange rate risk, and the interest could no longer be viewed as usury, but rather as compensation for bearing exchange rate risk. Although it was essentially a debt contract, it was ostensibly able to shed the stigma of usury because it involved bearing risk.

Another method was the use of annuities. It was primarily utilized in government debt contracts. Royal families or states would borrow money from merchants to finance wars or pay reparations. The involvement of risk occurred not at the time of borrowing but at the time of repayment. Instead of repaying fixed interests regularly and principal at maturity, the borrower would make regular payments until the creditor's death—essentially repaying the loan in the form of an annuity. Since the risk of death was involved, this method could avoid the criticisms associated with usury.

The prohibition of interest placed interest within the framework of time while simultaneously positioning risk at the heart of finance. The moment interest was separated from risk, it reemerged wearing the mask of risk. Although interest became invisible on the axis of time, it did not vanish; it merely shifted its direction toward the axis of risk.

Bills of exchange and annuities are financial mechanisms closely tied to capitalism. The bill of exchange ultimately leads to modern paper money. It doesn't take much thought to realize that paper money is, in essence, a type of bill of exchange. When bills of exchange change owners by being used in trades and are no longer redeemed, we call them paper money or banknotes. Annuities involve the calculation of the present value of future cash flows, which inevitably leads to the calculation of risk. Calculating present value and risk is essentially the core of what modern financial markets do. In this sense, bills of exchange and annuities are directly connected to the basic framework of capitalism, modern money and finance.

And finally, risk itself was explored. This became the second method to dealing with the prohibition of interest. If interest was problematic, could one not simply trade risk itself without involving interest? In fact, the trading of risk had already existed since ancient times. Theft insurance, maritime insurance, and life insurance were traded even in ancient Rome, so the concept of trading risk was nothing new. Risk was explored in two ways: from a commercial perspective and from a mathematical perspective.

At this point, the insurance market began to take shape in earnest. The combination of debt and insurance, known as bottomry, was gradually replaced by marine insurance. Lloyd's of London thus became the birthplace of modern insurance. Additionally, frequent fire incidents in Europe, including the Great Fire of London in 1666, signaled the emergence of fire insurance. Thus, modern property insurance began with marine and fire insurance. On the other hand, while life insurance and annuities had already been established under the leadership of the state during the medieval period, private organizations gradually took over these roles.

Insurance trade, however, is not complete even with the formation of a commercial market. The reason is that while a market can exist through trades, insurance premiums and payouts cannot be accurately calculated without the ability to recognize and quantify risk. This is what distinguishes insurance from the general goods market. In a typical goods market, a business first produces or purchases goods, and then revenue is realized through sales. The cost of production is determined first, and the price is set to cover that cost. In contrast, for insurance products, the insurer first receives revenue in the form of insurance premiums, and only later, when an event occurs, does the insurer incur costs by paying out claims. From the consumer's perspective, they pay the premium (the price) upfront and can only expect to receive a benefit in the future. Furthermore, it is difficult to predict in advance whether, or when, a claim will be made. Accurately reflecting the cost of future events in the premium calculation is challenging. If trades occur based on inaccurately calculated premiums, it turns into speculation, not much different from gambling. Although insurance has been traded for centuries, the inability to calculate precise premiums blurred the line between insurance and gambling. In fact, the two have always been intertwined.

However, calculating risk was not something merchants could do. This was because risk, an invisible and elusive gas, could barely enter the realm of calculation only if it was represented in numbers. This task fell to mathematicians. While attempts may have been made as early as the 16th century, it wasn't until the mid-17th century that mathematicians began systematically calculating risk. Although they did not focus specifically on insurance, they became interested in the distribution of winnings in gambling which is the identical twin of insurance. In doing so, they opened the door to the mathematics of risk, that is, probability theory.

Since insurance was not fundamentally different from gambling, probability theory naturally became the foundation for actuarial science. Though it took more time for actuarial science to be applied in the insurance market, the development of commerce and markets and the development of actuarial science advanced hand in hand, mutually influencing each other. Only when these elements were combined could true capitalism finally emerge.

The Inseparability Of Interest And Risk

In medieval Christianity, interest was positioned solely in relation to time, and the prohibition of interest applied only along the axis of time. As a result, once risk was separated from interest, the trade of risk began to be thoroughly explored. This separation of time and risk remains valid in modern economics. In economics, risk is equated with the variability of states and is independent of time. Of course, even within economics, the distant future is marked by greater risk, but this is not because risk inherently contains time, but because time is added to risk. The effort to separate risk from time is likely due to mathematical convenience or old conventions. Are they unaware that risk exists only in relation to time? Since risk always pertains to future events, it cannot be separated from the axis of time (Seog, 2018b).

However, there was another misunderstanding they had. Even when interest exists solely along the axis of time, as they thought, the interest produces another risk. It is at this point that Islam's sharp observation begins. The idea that interest is separated from risk can be true only from the creditor's perspective. If the debtor always repays the debt, from the creditor's viewpoint, the debt and its interest are risk-free. However, from the debtor's perspective, debt and interest always generate risk. That the creditor receives risk-free debt repayment is equivalent to that the debtor must bear all the risk.

A capital contract, including a debt contract, always

transforms into an issue of distributing future returns between the two parties—the creditor and the debtor. Since the future is uncertain, risk always exists there. The absence of risk for the creditor means that the debtor must bear all the risk. The smaller the risk for the creditor, the greater the risk imposed on the debtor. From the perspective of the opposite side of the creditor, it becomes clear that debt separated from risk does not exist in the first place.

Christianity viewed debt from the perspective of the banker, the creditor, and thought that interest could be separated from risk and positioned solely along the axis of time. However, Islam had long viewed debt from the other side of the contract and thus saw through the fact that interest always produces risk. Islam recognized that the closer interest approaches risk-free interest, the more risk it inevitably produces. This recognition likely came from deep contemplation, or perhaps from viewing debt from the perspective of the Muslim merchant as the debtor. In any case, due to this difference in perspective, Islam's view of interest, while seemingly similar to that of Christianity, was fundamentally destined to follow a different path.

Now, attention shifts from the creditor's interest to the debtor's interest. Thus, the risk produced by interest and the debtor who must bear that risk take center stage in the discussion. Interest now sits within the framework of "risk transfer". Within this framework, interest cannot be separated from risk. It is merely a matter of who the risk is transferred to; there can be no interest that is independent of risk. The so-called risk-free interest is only risk-free in the sense that there is no risk for the creditor, but it does not mean that the risk disappears. Instead, all the risk is transferred to the debtor. Risk-free interest, as commonly understood, is not interest without risk, but interest in which the debtor bears all the risk.

Thus, Islamic law, Shariah, goes beyond prohibiting interest (riba) to also banning gambling contracts (maisir) and uncertain contracts (gharar) that could excessively transfer risk to one party. Furthermore, the prohibition of interest applies not only to monetary interest but also to exchanges of the same goods in unequal quantities. These various regulations exist as means to enforce the principle of prohibiting excessive risk transfer. The prohibition of interest is only one of these means. Accordingly, it was bound to be located, along with gambling and contracts, on the line segment of risk.

Interest cannot be separated from risk, and time and risk inevitably share the same line. However, if the insurance market, as a space where risk is traded, could only emerge once risk was separated from interest, then an insurance market could not have appeared in Islamic regions where risk and interest were never separated. The insurance market was, in the end, destined to emerge in Europe.

Insurance And Capitalism

Weber asked why capitalism began in Europe and found the answer in Calvinist Protestantism. According to Weber, the calling to labor and the ascetic lifestyle in Calvinism drove the initial accumulation of capital. He made great efforts to link Calvinism with rational calculation. Modern times are probably more rational and calculative than the past. However, it would have been premature to conclude that Europe at that time was more rational than other regions. This is because rational calculation was neither exclusive to Calvinism nor more developed in Europe.

It is undeniable that capitalism was triggered by the complex interplay of various factors. However, the ethical and epistemological foundation that propelled capitalism might have been more appropriately found in the trade of risk rather than in religion. The full-fledged risk trade, namely the insurance market, began in Europe. This was possible because Europe separated risk from interest and time. Moreover, the reason this separation began in Europe may not have been because Europe was more rational, but rather because it did not sufficiently reflect on risk. Whatever the reason was, once risk was separated from interest and began to be traded in the insurance market, it unintentionally influenced the mindset of the era.

This was precisely the insight Michel Foucault discovered regarding the episteme of the Classical Age. In the Classical Age, things were viewed primarily through the lens of identity and difference. The insurance market constantly categorizes risks, classifying things and people into those that are identical and those that are not. Insurance creates risk categories through tables and draws boundaries between identity and difference.

Insurance not only draws boundaries between identity and difference but also actively produces identity and difference itself. People who appear identical can be classified into different risks, while those who seem different can be grouped under the same risk. As a result, identity and difference are no longer fixed or certain; they continuously move and intersect.

Through the classification of risk, the insurance market not only manifests identity and difference but also opens up a new kind of market that had not existed before. The commodity traded in this market is risk, an elusive, invisible ghost-like gas. If one can trade ghosts, is there anything that cannot be traded? In a capitalism where ghosts and gases are commodified, there is no longer anything that cannot be captured by the market. Now everything is destined to be packaged and traded as a commodity.

The insurance market is not merely a market where insurance products are traded, but also a market where the spirit and perspective of capitalism are fully embedded. The insurance market is one that calculates and captures the gas called risk and pursues profit through it, and is the place in which capitalist perception is most purely represented. That is how the era of capitalism arrived.

Calvinism And Simulacrum

If capitalism began with the separation of risk and the

discovery of insurance, what, then, was the role of Calvinism? Where did the "elective affinity" between Calvinism and capitalism originate? As Weber observed, was it the calling to labor, ascetic behavior, and rational calculation in Calvinism that created this affinity? Why did early capitalists need Calvinism? Did they yearn for labor and asceticism, and need a sign of salvation in the form of capital accumulation in return? Is that how Calvinism unintentionally became linked to capital accumulation and the rise of capitalism? Here, let us imagine a different perspective on why early capitalists may have needed Calvinism.

Labor, diligence, and rationality are not exclusive to Calvinists. These traits can easily be found in other religions and ideologies as well. Weren't diligence and rationality also key values in Buddhism and Confucianism? In fact, isn't belief in an unproven monotheistic god a result of irrational thinking? Moreover, what about Islam, which shares the same roots as Christianity? Weren't the Muslim merchants of that time the most rational calculators of profit? Furthermore, they rejoiced in the acquisition of profit and capital as gifts from Allah, and considered helping the poor a duty. If the affinity with capitalism lies in labor, rationality, and profit, then capitalism should have had a closer affinity with Islamic regions or East Asia long before Calvinism.

Perhaps, in essence, capitalism could be said to have originated in the Islamic region rather than Europe. Capitalism did not begin abruptly, severed from the past; rather, it has developed through interconnected influences from various regions. Nevertheless, the desire to view capitalism as a product of Europe rather than the Islamic region might stem from a latent sense of European inferiority.

Anyway, let us just assume that capitalism began not in the Islamic region but in the Calvinist region. Given that, what were the distinguishing features of Calvinism that made it possible, compared to Islam or other religions and ideologies? As observed earlier, those differences do not lie in labor, asceticism, or rationality. Perhaps the most important distinction may be related to the moral justification of selfishness.

According to the doctrine of predestination of salvation, an important teaching of Calvinism, who will be saved has already been determined by God, and humans cannot change that. That is, those who will be saved have already been decided, whether they live miserably or happily in this world, or whether they are deeply religious or not.

Just because an individual's life is miserable does not mean they are to be pitied; it is merely the destiny that God has imposed upon him. From a worldly perspective, sharing my gains with him might seem like a good deed, but not only does it change nothing, it might even interfere with God's providence. If God has predestined that person to experience worldly misery and be saved in the afterlife, then helping him would be meaningless. Rather, I might be the one who should receive help from him. God has already predestined the salvation of each individual.

So, there is nothing I can do for someone living a miserable life. I work hard, earn money, and accumulate it, but there is no reason to spend it to help others. Capital keeps accumulating, because I, who live an ascetic life, do not spend it. In this way, I become a capitalist.

Of course, the teachings that Calvinism gives to its followers also include labor, diligence, and frugality. However, these are not unique to Calvinism. Unlike other religions or ideologies, the unique connection of Calvinism with capitalism is the perception that there is no secular obligation to be concerned for others. Humans cannot intervene in what God has predestined. Moreover, trying to intervene is itself impure.

The life of obedience to God is now indistinguishable from a self-interested life. Only Calvinism religiously justifies self-interest. This does not mean that Calvinists are particularly more self-interested people. Rather, self-interest itself is merely a worldly measure, and therefore ultimately meaningless. Armed with the doctrine of predestination, Calvinists do not perceive self-interested behavior as sinful; instead, they understand it as part of God's providence. Self-interest may be simply an act of conforming to divine will.

What Weber observed—that Calvinists regarded accumulated capital and profit as signs of salvation—is an expression of irrationality or a weak human mind, rather than something connected to rationality. Capitalism is distinct from pre-capitalism not because it is more rational, but because it justifies self-interest in a different way. Calvinism liberated self-interest by giving a religious indulgence to self-interest, which had been at least superficially condemned as sinful in the past and in other places. Although Calvinists may have sincerely believed their actions to be religious practices, their religious aspirations were destined to transform into self-interested desires, with just one step to the side at any time.

The elective affinity between Calvinism and capitalism is indeed linked, as often stated, to the doctrine of predestination. Although salvation is already determined, Calvinists face extreme uncertainty about their salvation, as they have no way of knowing whether they are saved or not. Individuals must feel powerlessness and experience intense inner loneliness. As a result, Calvinism is linked to a pessimistically tinted individualism (Max Weber, 1930).

The connection between predestination and capitalism may lie more in the self-interest liberated by individualism, rather than in the aspects of labor or asceticism. Individualism gives moral legitimacy to self-interest, and then aligns with capitalism through the affinity of desire. This affinity of desire was already predicted to pass through thinkers like Bernard Mandeville and Adam Smith. With the expansion of capitalism, the affinity of desire has also taken the same journey with the interpretation of individual self-interest as social virtue.

As a result, the affinity of desire extends in a straight line to the modern economics, where the axiom of the self-interested individual is accepted without question, along with the deification of the market where self-interest clashes with one another. If there is a change in this flow, it is that the realm where divine providence operates—originally in the predestination of salvation—has now transformed into self-interest and the market. When Adam Smith spoke of the "invisible hand," the object of salvation was no longer the individual but the market itself. This shift may not be a monumental change in which pure religious morality becomes imprisoned in the iron cage of material desire as Weber criticized. It may be just a small change such that self-interest changes its outerwear.

The interpretation of the affinity between Calvinism and capitalism might be a matter of directionality. Weber might have imagined the religious zeal of Calvinism transforming into the material desires of capitalism, but in fact, the direction may have flowed the other way. Material desires have always existed and are nothing special, but what the capitalist needed was a solid, steel-hard shell (stahlhartes Gehäuse) to morally cover those desires. Therefore, it was not that material desires intensified and transformed into a solid shell through the development of capitalism, but rather that the solid shell, which concealed material desires, was already put in place by Calvinism. Initially, this solid shell was God's providence, but as economics met the age of science, God's providence was replaced by the providence of the market, which was eventually supplanted by the providence of society.

Now, individual self-interest is no longer protected because of God's salvation, nor is it confined to the narrow realm of the market; it must be protected for the welfare of society and the public good. Material desires and self-interest have changed from being encased in the shell of religious zeal to the shell of social virtue. And the more people became included within that shell, the stronger it became. If that shell wasn't hard enough in Calvinism, it was simply because the number of people captured by it was small. And for capitalists who did not regard self-interest as a sin, accumulating capital among those who condemned self-interest would have been an easy task. That is how the early accumulation of capital might have begun.

In the end, what was necessary for the start of capitalism was a simulacrum, an illusion or a distorted copy, that could conceal self-interest. During Europe's modernization, Calvinism provided it. For Bernard Mandeville, it was the bees that played that role, and in modern economics, Adam Smith organized it. This is why Adam Smith became the founding father of modern economics.

As capitalism gradually advanced, its focus moved beyond the market to precise measurement and finance. This is because measurement and finance are the domains governed by simulacra. Measurement in terms of monetary value acquires the aura of mathematics and rationality, and regardless of its actual content, it is packaged as objective and scientific. Since finance is an extension of monetary value measurement, it also guarantees objectivity and scientific validity. Although the label 'scientific' is attached to GDP, corporate value, stocks, bonds, and various derivatives, in reality, they are merely simulacra —illusions trembling under the internal contradictions that collide within them.

The Factor Market And Insurance

Markets are not just places where goods are exchanged in the form of trades. Some markets also exist to reduce or transfer risks. When thinking of a market related to risk, one would most likely think of the insurance market. Of course, the insurance market is a representative market where risk is traded, and the significance of the insurance market under capitalism has been discussed above. Here, let us talk about the market for factors of production.

Land, labor, and capital are the three fundamental factors of production in a capitalist economy and are traded in factor markets. These can be said to be the basic elements necessary for a firm's production activities. Although some of these factors may become less or more important due to the development of information technology and the information revolution, it is not difficult to understand that proper production activities cannot take place without them.

However, Karl Polanyi observed that these markets were highly unnatural (Polanyi, 2001). This is because land which is a gift of nature, labor which cannot be separated from one's personality, and money which has no inherent value as it merely facilitates transactions and prices, are not things that are supposed to be objects of market trades. While there is no particular problem with markets where cultivated rice or manufactured goods are traded, the trades of land, labor, and money are inherently unnatural. Nevertheless, capitalism, especially after the Industrial Revolution, is a system built upon the trade of these three factors. Why have these unnatural markets become essential?

These markets, says Polanyi, are de facto insurance markets for producers' risks. Capitalist producers are not those who produce the goods they need and sell the remainder to others. From the beginning, they produce and manufacture with the purpose of selling. In doing so, they face long-term and extreme risks. They first encounter uncertainties related to consumption and competition. Additionally, they must bear the uncertainties that arise in the production process. Rent from the use of land, wages from the use of labor, and interest from the use of investment capital are all elements of uncertainty within the production process.

The factor markets serve as a means to minimize uncertainties in the production process. To fulfill their role as a form of insurance, factor markets must have an abundant supply of factors, and suppliers must compete with one another. This ensures that producers can access the necessary factors at low prices whenever needed for production. The markets that are enforced as mechanisms for risk management, are precisely what the factor markets are. Despite their unnaturalness, these markets have become essential for producers. In this way, the factor markets become insurance markets, and they deserve to be called the insurance markets for capitalism itself.

16. FINANCIAL THEORY AND RITUAL

Efficient Markets: Eikon And Idéa

For a long time and still now, economics has said that financial markets are efficient. The word "efficient" is a very convenient term. While "efficient" carries various meanings, it is a cure-all within the economic world. Efficiency can refer to an engineering perspective of the ratio between input and output, or it can refer to the economic perspective of profit or return relative to investment cost.

However, when an economist says that financial markets are efficient, he is probably talking about the prices of financial products and implying that these prices are appropriate. Here, "appropriate" means that the market correctly represents the so-called inherent value or intrinsic value of the financial product.

Many financial scholars believe in this notion of efficient markets, but they are often hesitant to confidently express it to others. Therefore, scholars tend to speak boldly about it only in gatherings of peers who share the same belief, while humbly referring to it as a hypothesis in public discourse. In any case, according to the efficient market hypothesis, the prices of financial products—particularly stock prices—are correct. Stock prices reflect the intrinsic value of the stock. So, one must trust in stock prices.

When they say that financial markets are efficient, they mean that prices are "eikon" (εἰκών). So they become Platonists. The essence of things is "idéa" (ἰδέα), and the intrinsic value of a stock is the idéa they have long dreamed of. Eikon refers to something that faithfully represents their idéa. Therefore, for financial markets to be efficient, stock prices must become the eikon that represents the idéa.

But how can we know the intrinsic value of a stock? Or does it even exist in the first place? The visible reality is not the essence itself, yet neither can the essence be fully known. Nevertheless, like Plato's yearning for the idéa (Plato, 2013), they believe that the idéa can be known. In the world of economics, the market must be rational and efficient, and therefore, stock prices must represent the intrinsic value of the stock. In this way, stock prices must be the eikon that represents the idéa.

The intrinsic value of a stock is uncertain, and even if it exists, it resides in the world of idéa beyond our reach. The idéa cannot be seen through the imperfect lens of this world. Thus, the proposition of an efficient market can never be conclusively proven. This is because even when counterexamples are observed, they will be overshadowed by examples in favor of the hypothesis. What to assume about the unseen and unprovable idéa is a matter of individual freedom and imagination. While Plato's philosopher might be able to perceive the idéa, the investor in financial markets seems to lack the time for such deep contemplation necessary to become such a philosopher.

The reason they cling to the idéa is because they seek to find the legitimacy of the capital market from it. They hoped that the capitalist economy and its markets would become the means and system to realize the idéa of humanity's economy. Thus, they aimed to give meaning to financial markets as the eikon that represents the idéa. At first, they might have struggled with the unproven nature of the idéa. But eventually, they came to a realization: just as it cannot be proven, it also cannot be disproven. Gödel's Incompleteness Theorem applies to the efficient market as well. If it can neither be proven nor disproven, then one can simply choose to believe in it.

Now, financial theory crosses over from science to religious ritual. Within the ritual, every action has meaning and reason, and causal relationships are established. However, from outside the ritual, these causal relationships are neither inevitable nor the only possibilities; they may even appear absurd at times.

Simulacrum

However, there is something they are misunderstanding. The existence of the stock market is originally unrelated to Plato's idéa. The fact that stock prices differ from the intrinsic value of stocks does not negate the existence of the stock market. The stock market can exist regardless of intrinsic value. Stock prices are not intended to replicate the idéa, but simply express themselves. Even if intrinsic value exists, stock prices are not an eikon that accurately replicates it, but rather a distorted representation, a simulacrum. The stock price would be a simulacrum which is a false image. Stocks do exist and are traded not as eikons, but rather as simulacra.

Think about it. Would any investor stop trading stocks simply because the stock price differs from intrinsic value? Stock trading occurs when a buyer and a seller intersect; people buy because they believe the price will rise, and sell because they believe it will fall. Intrinsic value is merely a reference point; it is not the main actor. It does not matter whether the stock price is the same as or different from the intrinsic value. What is important is whether there is another investor who will buy my stock at a higher price.

Then, we take it a step further. Is intrinsic value even a valid reference point? How can it be a reference if we do not know what intrinsic value actually is? At best, what can be referenced is the direction of a vector or the volatility of a pendulum's oscillation. What might matter is whether the arrow of the vector points upward or downward. In the market, the significance of intrinsic value is limited to that extent. Intrinsic value functions not as a value itself, but merely as a directional indicator.

Oh, no. That's not right. Don't philosophers like Foucault,

Deleuze, and Baudrillard (2012) say that simulacra do not mimic the original? A simulacrum is not a failed copy, but something that has meaning in and of itself. The original essence to be copied no longer exists, and even if it existed, it would be unknowable. Simulacra are no longer compared to the essence. Instead, they are compared and contrasted with other simulacra. What becomes important is not resemblance to the essence, but the similarity and difference between simulacra.

Look at stock prices. Stock prices are simulacra that are not evaluated based on their resemblance to intrinsic value. In stock prices, investors compare their own simulacrum with others' simulacra, but they are not interested in the resemblance to the idéa. The resemblance to the idéa is meaningful only to the extent that it is reflected in the simulacra, not as resemblance itself.

What matters in financial products, including stocks, is not the distance from each respective idéa, but the distance between simulacra. Look at derivatives based on underlying assets like stocks and bonds. If the underlying assets are already simulacra, these derivatives are layering other simulacra upon simulacra. They are another copy of a misaligned copy. The prices of these derivatives depend solely on the distance between simulacra. Or consider arbitrage, which claims to ensure efficiency. Arbitrage is not about intrinsic value, but about how much the distance between simulacra can be narrowed.

The value of options, a representative example of derivatives, is expressed through the Black-Scholes Model after passing through the heat equation of arbitrage, as if measuring the heat of speculation. Thus, the Black-Scholes Model is not about finding the true value of a simulacrum, but simply a formula for finding the fastest shortcut between simulacra. Just as heat is not energy but rather the movement of energy, the heat equation becomes a geometric formula for finding the fastest route in the metric space.

Amidst the heat of derivatives and financial innovation, the essence of finance is no longer important. Simulacra produce more simulacra and refer to each other, while the distance from or resemblance to the idéa is no longer of interest. Investors no longer visit or call the firms they are investing in. Many investors make their decisions solely by watching the movement of charts and arrows.

The financial market is a space of simulacra, where distance and difference are more important than essence. Furthermore, the distance between distances and the difference between differences are equally important. Distance produces new distances, and difference produces new differences. The financial market is not only a space of simulacra but also a space of différance.

With the development of information technology bringing faster and more abundant information, people expected to be able to know intrinsic value more accurately. However, what investors need is not information about the essence. For investors, only the similarities and differences between simulacra and the distance between them matter. The development of information technology has not provided more accurate information but has merely allowed faster movement between simulacra. As a result, they only look at the direction of charts and arrows and do not feel the need to know the essence of the firm. The more information there is, the faster or longer the charts can be drawn, but it does not lead to knowing more about the firm.

This phenomenon is not limited to the financial market. The development of information technology also creates the viral spread of fake news and rumors. The flood of information increases the number of cases for finding shortcuts, producing waves of multiple arrow vectors rather than simple straight lines.

Money Acts: Money Act Theory

Postmodernism may have discovered and admired the mysterious abilities of simulacra. It is clear that financial simulacra also possess remarkable abilities. This ability, which originally began with money itself, seems to have reached its peak in modern finance. However, merely being in awe of it overlooks the hidden sharpness of the blade, which causes countless people to be cut and suffer from the pain they must endure.

Humans are beings who exchange. Thoughts are exchanged through language, and goods are exchanged through money. Thus, as linguist Saussure pointed out, language is the money of thought, and money becomes the language of goods (Ferdinand de Saussure, 1959). The commonality between language and money is, above all, that they are both signs. As mentioned earlier, the sign in language is divided into the signifier (signifiant) and the signified (signifié). The signifier is the word spoken or written itself, and the signified refers to the meaning or image that the word represents. For example, if we see a tree and say 'tree,' the word 'tree' is the signifier, while the actual tree the word points to is the signified. Money, in the same way, is also a system of signs. Now, the signifier is the mark of economic value, while the signified is the amount of goods that can be purchased with that amount of money.

Another commonality is that both are arbitrary. The sound 'tree' has no inherent connection to an actual tree; it is merely an agreement. So, if people decide at some point to call a tree a 'dog,' then from that moment on, a tree will be called a dog. Money, too, is just a promise to measure or store the value of goods. Therefore, when people get tired of the existing currency and long for a new one, they adapt to new promises when they are made. This is why Korean 'won' could become 'hwan' and then return to 'won' again.

If there is a difference between money and language, it might be that language gains meaning through difference, whereas money gains meaning through identity. Language impresses different images and perceptions through distinct articulations and spellings. Thus, articulation becomes the segmentation that separates things. In contrast, money impresses its existence by placing different goods on a common measure, breaking down the boundaries between goods. The common measure becomes a common divisor (commensurability).

However, language does not exist simply to express the object of a signifier. As noted by John Austin (1962) and John Searle (1965, 1969) in their speech act theory, language induces action. A person's utterance is not merely something that conveys meaning. Depending on the environment or context, it may contain various illocutionary acts that reflect the speaker's intention, such as questions, promises, commands, or warnings. Furthermore, depending on the content of the utterance, it may actually provoke certain actions or emotions in the listener, which are known as perlocutionary acts.

Just like the speech act theory in language, the "money act theory" can be applied to money as well. Money does not merely remain a tool for measuring the value of goods. When money is handed over in a debt transaction, it could be a gesture of goodwill to provide help, or it could be a sharp leash tightening around one's neck. Additionally, it is both a promise and a command to repay with interest in the future, and also a warning that severe penalties will be imposed if repayment fails. When investing in stocks, this is not merely an exchange of stocks for money, but also an expression of hope or a wish for the future, or even a manifestation of greed for wealth. Participating in a gamble despite knowing there may be losses is similarly a result of the acts of hope and greed that accompany the exchange of money.

Money, like language, is a sign and at the same time a medium of exchange. Accordingly, just as the exchange of language embeds speech acts, the exchange of money also embeds money acts. Money acts go beyond the simple exchange of goods and money, encompassing the effects on the actions of the parties involved. Money acts reflect and project power, greed, or hope between the parties involved. Thus, acts such as questioning, promising, commanding, and warning also accompany the exchange of money.

Money, which has gained strength through the sophistication of money acts, finally severs its ties with goods and expands its performative power within its own realm. Now, rather than being just money, under the name of finance, money exists as a device that produces, references, and represents itself. Finance establishes itself and grows by representing itself within the structure of finance, in relation not to real goods, but to its own framework. Financial derivatives and various financial engineering products no longer refer to the real world.

The 21st century, including the late 20th century, will be recorded as an era of self-referential finance driven by self-propelling growth. It is precisely in this regard that finance meets the simulacrum. Rather than representing real goods that fundamentally should be referenced, the characteristic of finance becomes a simulacrum—an illusion that copies itself or other copies, independent of goods (Christophe Schinckus, 2008).

Unlike the simulacrum that postmodernism gazes upon with awe, financial simulacra are accompanied by anxiety and suffering. It is precisely at this point that the problem of morality arises. The problem of morality is fundamentally rooted in the fetishism and idolatry of finance (David Hawkes, 2019). Magic refers to claiming efficacy not through scientific connectivity, but through procedures or formal connectivity. Magic signifies a symbolic efficacy that references itself rather than a rational relationship with reality. In this regard, finance becomes magic. Through magical fetishism and idolization, modern finance leads people to confuse the symbolic phenomena—images that exist only in their minds —with those that exist in reality. This results in a confusion between subject and object, and between reality and imagination.

In the financial market, we often hear the expression that the tail wags the body. However, a more accurate expression is that an illusion shakes the real. This is because finance is not the tail, but a symbol and an illusion. The harm of financial magic lies in the fact that illusion and symbolic actions have an excessive impact on reality. The moral flaw of finance is that it brings pain and despair to many people who diligently live their lives grounded in reality and the real things.

The magical influence of illusion on the real is amplified through the excessive redundancy of representation (David Hawkes, 2019). Modern financial innovation fractures into forms where finance is copied and referenced to give birth to new finance, much like living organisms reproduce through the replication of their genes. Through the endless repetition of self-reference, the gap of finance from the real which was its original reason for existence, grows uncontrollably. In financial markets, this phenomenon is labeled as a bubble or volatility, but its essence lies in excessive self-reference and replication. The more replication occurs, the further finance drifts from the real. Yet, the influence of this illusion on the real expands through Brownian motion as the distance from the real increases.

The fact that finance, an imaginary creation, replicates itself and reproduces like a living organism is precisely the harm of finance that Aristotle had warned against long ago. In his eyes, the most detestable phenomenon was that money, like a living being, gave birth to offspring in the form of interest. Modern finance, having been liberated from the prohibition on interest, has gone beyond simply producing interest as offspring; it now boasts prolific reproductive power, displaying large-scale propagation. Awed by this astonishing power of reproduction, people have come to worship and idolize finance, ultimately lowering themselves to submit under its dominion.

Accounting: Insurance And Talisman

Or, they may occasionally glance at the accounting ledger. However, they know that the ledger neither reveals the essence of the firm nor shows the future—it is merely past numbers. Therefore, those numbers no longer hold any real meaning. Yet, the reason they still need those numbers is because they serve as insurance, just in case.

The numbers in the accounting ledger allocate responsibility when necessary. Here lies the irony of accounting. While the financial market is a world of simulacra, where essence no longer matters, winners and losers are still divided in the game of speculation. Now, those once-meaningless numbers can offer a glimmer of hope to the losers. The defeated need to shift some of the blame for their failure onto someone else, even partially. After all, wouldn't it be too miserable if everything was solely due to one's own ignorance or fault? Thus, the accounting ledger exists not as a guide for investment, but as a supervisor or sheriff.

The numbers in accounting do not reveal the essence of a firm and merely reflect the past—they are lifeless. Yet, by recording the past, they are always ready to be resurrected as evidence in discourse and courts. The modern significance of accounting ledgers lies precisely in their legal evidentiary capacity. Legal evidence is not drawn from future possibilities, but from traces of the past.

Under advanced capitalism, neither intrinsic value nor accounting value exists as the sun illuminating the financial markets. Contrary to the hopes of many, they fail to reveal any fundamental value. Instead, they exist as evidence in discourse and courts, and as surveillance mechanisms in the Panopticon of financial market oversight. In the design of the Panopticon, the identity of the observer is unimportant, and it doesn't matter if an observer even exists. All that matters is simply the perception that someone is watching.

However, there is no need to rigidly connect the concept of legal evidentiary capacity solely to laws, trials, or prisons. Even if it doesn't lead to a courtroom, it would be meaningful to provide the losers at least with something to embrace their failure or serve as a shield. For this reason, accounting ledgers exist for many investors not as records of value, but as talismans. What is called intrinsic value is not true value either; rather it exists as a talisman to soothe anxious minds. Within the ritual of finance, the intrinsic value and accounting value of stocks serve as talismans to ward off misfortune or relieve feelings of resentment.

Financial Myths

In economics textbooks, it is often stated that stock prices should align with the intrinsic value of the stock, or that they will eventually align. In their minds, Plato is reincarnated. The Platonic idéa of true value may not be visible, yet it must exist, and the "eikon" is believed to perfectly mirror this idéa. For them, stock prices must be eikons. Eikons are constantly oriented towards the idéa and aim to represent it faithfully.

However, this notion results from an insufficient and inaccurate observation of the origins and movements of stock prices. Speculation in financial markets is not a game of truth. The outcome of winning and losing is not determined by which price aligns with an intrinsic, true value. Their idéa does not exist, and even if it did, it would not be visible. Given that the idéa remains unknowable in the end, claiming that the eikon faithfully represents it would be audacious. Moreover, arguing over it would be a meaningless endeavor.

However, a closer look at the textbooks reveals that the theory flows in the opposite direction. After defining stock prices as eikon, they then claim that stock prices must be representing the idéa. They must do so. If stock prices are not eikon, the very purpose of the stock market's existence evaporates. Likewise, the meaning of the corporate goal to maximize stock prices would also vanish. This is the cosmological order that sustains the financial market. Within the rituals of finance, the cosmological order must be maintained, and even if it collapses, it must be quickly restored.

Therefore, in the ritual of finance, stock prices—or more broadly, the prices of financial assets—must correspond to one of two narratives. First, they must be something to be "right". From this, we derive the equation that the market price is right. Market price is right not because it is found to be right, but because it must be right. Since it is self-justifying, it does not extend beyond itself. It simply rotates around itself.

Or, in cases where it may not be right in itself, it must be, at the very least, something that revolves in orbit around what is right or that fluctuates near it, whether it randomly leaps up and down or oscillates. Just as a planet revolves around the sun, it must orbit around what is right.

Hence, the claim that the financial market is efficient oscillates between these two narratives. Sometimes, they argue that a price is right in itself, and at other times, they console themselves by believing it at least revolves around what is right. This is the cosmic order imagined by financial rituals: prices either become stars, rotating on their own axis, or become planets, revolving around stars.

In ancient rituals, myths created new imaginations by drawing lines between stars selected from among the countless ones. These imaginations created mythological worlds and established order. Financial rituals, borrowing from astrophysics, have reconstructed the motion of celestial bodies into a new financial myth, aligning cosmic order with financial order. Just as the many stars in the cosmos rotate and revolve in a harmonious order to form the universe, so do the prices in financial markets rotate and revolve, maintaining the market's order. Up close, each movement may seem irregular and chaotic, but from a distance, the whole reveals itself as a beautiful and orderly universe. In financial rituals, all that is needed now are the sagas of mythical heroes and beautiful narratives of love, while any attempt to disrupt this cosmic order is not tolerated.

Thus, in the financial markets, numerous charismatic heroes and prophets have emerged, and finance has become filled with blessings and representations of love. The courageous foreign exchange investors who stand against a country's evil currency manipulation, the stock investors who succeed in long-term investments by penetrating the essence of a firm, or the activist shareholders who deliver a blow of justice to corrupt management—all of these figures become heroes who restore the cosmological order. Additionally, countless sages and prophets are born in the financial markets, reading charts and predicting the future. Just as ancient astrologers once read the stars to foresee the future, today's financial market astrologers navigate the charts that cross the dark night sky of the markets, searching for jewels that shine brighter than stars, embarking on adventurous journeys.

And that's not all. The financial industry is filled with heartwarming stories of success—tales of those who built businesses through difficult times with the help of the power of finance, stories of financial support for the poor and small business owners, microfinance, or inclusive finance among others. Just as the hero who overcomes adversity ultimately triumphs, so does the market triumph. Despite all hardships, finance becomes a beautiful practice of love in the end. The modern financial markets, full of heroes, prophets, and love, become a modern myth that gives people comfort and hope, just as the myths of the past did.

So in the financial markets, while the hero's adventure may exist, speculation should not. After all, how could the hero's adventure be considered speculation? The hero's adventure, though it may seem meaningless in itself, is always given meaning and justified. Heroes embark on their journeys not for themselves, but to save their country, their family, or to practice justice, sacrificing themselves in the process. The heroes of the financial markets are no different. Their actions must be driven not by personal greed, but by sacrifice for the advancement of the economy and finance.

However, myths cannot consist of only heroes. There must be monsters that present them with challenges. Fortunately, in the financial markets, monsters abound and are scattered across the landscape. Foreign exchange volatility, interest rate fluctuations, asset price instability, governance issues, or unexpected events and accidents—these are the monsters that constantly emerge, calling for heroes. In the modern financial markets, these monsters play the role of disruptors of the cosmic order, hindering the harmonious rotation and revolution of the celestial bodies. To restore the cosmic order, that is, to find the "right" price, the heroes fight through adversity, vanquish the monsters, and return triumphant to cheers and applause.

However, the hero's struggle is not only with the monsters that he need to overcome. The hero also suffers because of the foolish masses who fail to recognize him. The hero's feelings toward these masses are dual. While the hero faces difficulty due to the masses' ignorance, he also fights the monsters for the sake of these very people. Thus, on the one hand, the hero criticizes the masses, but on the other hand, he sympathizes with and pities them. In the financial market, the "ants" (small investors) represent these masses. This is why, in the financial world, ants are both mocked and pitied—they embody the foolish yet sympathetic crowd that the hero ultimately fights for.

Speculation is something that only the foolish masses do, but heroes never do. When people invest their retirement funds, rental deposits, or even borrow to invest, it is a foolish gamble they should not engage in. However, a hero's leveraged investment or short selling is a sacrifice to save foolish people or a heroic saga. Chart analysis and economic analysis are the work of heroes, not something the foolish masses should dare to attempt. The masses can only overcome adversity by relying on the hero. The emphasis on institutional investors and financial literacy in the financial markets is likely a call for the masses to escape their foolishness and rely on the hero.

When the hero finally returns after defeating the monster, the foolish masses will follow and believe in the hero. But the problem is that, amidst the chaos of this myth, the hero and the monster are indistinguishable. Only after everything is over will the winner be called the hero, and the loser, the monster. Thus, this myth always ends in a happy ending.

In this way, the financial market we understand today is a modern narrative which is a faded myth from the past dressed in the garb of capitalism and reappearing before us. The financial market is not something to be understood through scientific truth, but rather through mythic imagination. And ritual and myth only become true when people believe in them. Viewed from outside the ritual, with awakened eyes, they may be intriguing but are ultimately fictional narratives. However, if everyone believes the ritual to be true, then that belief makes the fiction come to life in reality. The power of financial rituals lies precisely in this: their performative ability to turn fiction into truth.

17. FINANCIAL ILLUSION

Gdp: Paranoia Of Measurement

Capitalism is a system of measurement. It measures value and price, and the means of measurement is called money. Max Weber's insight stood out when he identified rational calculation as a defining feature of capitalism. To calculate is to measure, and by measuring in the same unit, comparisons become possible. Measurement transforms two heterogeneous goods into something homogeneous. Thus, money stands at the center of capitalism.

Goods that have regained their homogeneity through measurement by money are exchanged freely without hesitation. The space where such goods are exchanged is called the market. While markets have existed since ancient times, it is only in the age of capitalism that the market becomes taken for granted, and the myth is created that everything is achieved through the market.

Capitalism is not satisfied with merely measuring the price of goods; it continually seeks to expand the scope of what can be measured. It is no longer just about pricing apples or shoes, but about assigning prices to abstract and invisible things. So prices were put on copyrights and patents, and so were firms. Eventually, it even aims to put prices on life and even on a nation.

How could one possibly put a proper price tag on life or a nation? Yet, the new religion armed with markets and money was prepared to assign a price to anything in the name of markets and money. Thus, they attached price tags to life, enabling its trade, and assigned a price to a nation, preaching that this is the value of the nation. This is how GDP (Gross Domestic Product) emerged, as the total price tag for a nation's yearly output.

By general definition, GDP refers to the total market value of goods and services produced within a nation over a specific period (typically one year) (Wikipedia). In other words, GDP is the monetary expression of the total value of market transactions within a nation during a year. Although Simon Kuznets, often considered the founder of GDP, warned against using it as a direct indicator of national welfare, GDP has nonetheless become regarded as one of the most critical components of welfare indicators. Nations are obsessed with GDP and the growth rate measured by the increase in GDP.

According to its definition, GDP measures only the value of goods traded in the market, meaning that any exchange or creation of value outside the market is excluded. For example, if two people clean their own homes, GDP does not increase. However, if they clean each other's home and exchange 10,000 won, GDP increases by 20,000 won. In the latter case, GDP has grown, but the result is essentially the same as in the former. This implies that GDP does not fully or accurately measure all economic activities. Furthermore, if people don't clean others' homes as thoroughly as they would their own, the welfare in the latter case might actually be worse than in the former, despite the GDP increase. This discrepancy highlights the fact that GDP growth and welfare can head in different directions. This is probably what Kuznets sought to caution against.

Of course, economics textbooks are not ignorant of the limitations of GDP measurement. They list the problems of GDP including the facts that GDP is not a measure of welfare or quality of life and that exchanges outside the market are excluded. As repeating the textbook discussions is unnecessary, let us turn our attention to a story less visible in those textbooks.

What, then, is GDP truly trying to measure? Above all, GDP grants a special status to market trades. As long as nations are ranked by GDP and the competence of those in power is evaluated by growth rates, market trades occupy the highest position. Given that market trades are exchanges based on self-interest, GDP is essentially measuring the total sum of a nation's self-interest. Since individual self-interest cannot always align with social welfare, Kuznets' warning is simply an obvious statement that social welfare cannot be measured by the total sum of self-interest.

Nevertheless, the fact that GDP remains the standard for comparison and assessment of competence reveals the cult-like belief in capitalism that elevates selfishness as the ultimate good. This belief is so deeply entrenched that alternative metrics, such as the UN's Human Development Index (HDI) or Bhutan's Gross National Happiness (GNH), are mentioned briefly before fading from our collective memory.

GDP measurement deifies market trades. Just like God, an absolute being, GDP records market trades as an absolute entity. Some trades may be harmful to society or may result from harmful actions. Yet, deification means that, without consideration for the quality of those trades, they are always recorded as an increase in GDP. Just as a negative or positive number is transformed into a positive number when given an absolute value, GDP is calculated as an absolute value.

In all of God's actions, there is a reason, and it is unthinkable to judge them as good or evil by human standards. Air pollution caused by industrial activities, treatments for damages caused by accidents, legal lawsuits stemming from the breakdown or conflict of capitalist trades and contracts, the various surveillance mechanisms in financial markets to monitor and discipline firms in which investors have placed their money, and the harms from speculative investments permitted to stimulate the capital market—all of these leads to an increase in GDP simply because they are legally traded in the market.

However, with a bit more thought, one can see that pollution, conflict, surveillance, and speculation are all dark maladies of capitalism. The capitalist system, while producing goods, also generates social maladies. Market trades emerged, ex post, to manage or cure these maladies. Although trades related to treatment might seem like value creation at the moment, the underlying maladies were something the economy had to produce first before treatment can occur. If GDP increases by healing each other through market trades only after hurting each other, then that GDP growth is working against true welfare.

The calculation of GDP, by recording all trades as positive absolute values regardless of whether they are of positive or negative value, increases the gap from true welfare. Recording all trades as absolute positive values—that is the deification of trades, making them absolute beings. For those who fail to see the true nature of this deification, an increase in GDP becomes something that is unquestionably good.

As the economy develops and industrial structures become more advanced, it leads to the idea that it is the service sector, not the manufacturing sector, that grows. At this point, people often think of the legal, accounting, financial, and healthcare markets as key service sectors. In developed economies, the significant contribution of these service sectors to GDP may make it seem as though the size of the service sectors is a marker of economic progress. However, the hidden truth behind this is that as capitalist economies developed, the harm they inevitably inflicted on society grew as well, and the service markets expanded to deal with the harm. Thus, these service sectors are, in a sense, also indirect measures of the maladies of capitalism.

Since GDP records all sources of trades—whether good or evil —as good, the growth of the service market is reflected as an increase in GDP. On the other hand, efforts to reduce harm may be recorded as evil because they can lead to fewer trades, thereby decreasing GDP. And despite Kuznets' warning, GDP is forced as a welfare indicator more than anything else, leading to the belief that the development of the service market enhances a nation's welfare. As a result, within the myth of capitalism, not only are good things but even evils recorded as contributing to welfare. Conversely, when government policies genuinely aim to improve welfare, they are recorded as going against welfare the moment they lead to a decrease in GDP.

The ability to blur the line between good and evil through the confusion of terminology—this is where the remarkable power of capitalism lies. By confusing and misusing terms, both good and evil become good within the market, while both are seen as evil outside the market. This is why capitalist economics is so impregnable.

Gdp: Totality

Another remarkable aspect of GDP lies in its totality. When GDP records market trades, it presents them as a simple sum of exchanged monetary values. Since money was originally created for arithmetic operations, this process seems natural. However, mathematicians as early as the 18th century discovered that human utility cannot be replaced by monetary calculations. These discoveries even form the foundation of modern economics. Yet, it is ironic that GDP, which is merely a monetary calculation, still reigns supreme as the king of economic measurement. Why, then, do so many economists who emphasize utility over money forget this fact and bow before the gleaming crown of GDP?

Consider the case of distributing 100 between two people. One method is to distribute 50 equally to each, and another is to give 1 to one person and 99 to the other. In terms of monetary sum, both scenarios result in the same total of 100, so the difference between them is not recognized. However, distributing equally is fairer than concentrating the majority on one person. While it's true that utility cannot be summed up, this does not mean it should be replaced by the summation of money. The fact that utility cannot be added together simply indicates that there are many factors to consider, not that the complexity should be reduced to a mere monetary total.

The worsening polarization as capitalism develops is not

unrelated to the deified concept of GDP. If GDP is the summation of trade amounts which represent someone's income, then the totality of GDP focuses solely on the aggregate sum of income. This, in turn, boldly disregards income inequality. As long as the total sum increases, it is regarded as the ultimate good, even if inequality worsens.

While the problems with the totality of GDP are well recognized, fixing them is not allowed. In fact, there's no need to modify GDP itself; what is necessary is to break free from its deification and place importance on alternative indicators. In the realm of economic measurement, there is no need for a single deity. However, those who deny the modification of GDP also reject the use of other indicators. GDP reigns as the only God, as if GDP is the only objective metric. They believe that other indicators should only serve as accessories, rather than being valued on their own merit.

The summation of money itself may be considered objective. However, what they forget is the purpose of the economy. Isn't the goal of the economy to improve people's lives? If we measure the extent to which life is improved by utility as modern economics does, then the ultimate aim of the economy is to increase utility. When expanding this concept from individuals to society, it involves harmoniously enhancing the diverse utilities of the members within the society. If the purpose is to improve something subjective like utility, then what accurate measurement could it be, even if the means of measurement are objective?

Accurate measurement refers to reducing the distance between two entities. Therefore, what requires objectivity is not the means themselves, but the relationship between the purpose and the means. Only those who move in sync with the fluctuating waves can minimize their distance from them. If one measures the distance by moving linearly regardless of the fluctuations of the waves, that measurement will merely be inaccurate and irrational. The fluctuating nature of utility cannot be adequately captured through a linear summation of money.

National Pension: National Hypnosis

When the illusion of finance extends to the National Pension of Korea, or a public pension with funded system in general, it casts a spell over an entire population. National Pension is understood as follows: it is a social insurance system in which citizens are forced to save money with the state, and the state promises to manage that money well and return it to them in retirement. This system is implemented in many states and is a crucial pillar of social insurance. Since it guarantees income when people no longer earn wages in their old age, it is a matter of everyone's concern, but on the other hand, it is also a matter of everyone's complaint.

The point where financial illusion exists lies in the very idea that the money collected by the state will be invested through financial means to generate returns and be given back later. Before discussing the financial illusion in detail, let us first examine the rationale behind the existence of the National Pension.

National Pension is generally understood as a mechanism of forced savings. In principle, individuals are best equipped to manage their own money. At the very least, when they manage it themselves, the responsibility is theirs, and there is no one else to blame. However, the National Pension involves the state intervening in this process. For forced savings to be justified, there must be an assumption that the state can invest and manage money better than individuals. Clearly, this is not entirely accurate. The state might manage money better than some individuals, but not necessarily better than others. There is no guarantee that, on average, the state can manage money better. Even if, on average, the state could manage money better, it would be unreasonable to force those who can manage their own money more effectively to save through the state.

Therefore, the basis for the existence of the National Pension should be mutual aid rather than forced savings. It is this very notion—that wealthier individuals assist those who are less capable or lack the means to manage investments effectively—that makes the National Pension a form of social insurance. The justification for the National Pension must lie in being a system of mutual aid, ensuring that people who might otherwise live in poverty during their old age can maintain at least a minimum standard of living.

The first illusion of people is viewing the National Pension as a form of personal savings. As a result, they begin calculating how much interest will be added to their contributions after 10 or 20 years. They disregard the mutual aid spirit of the pension system and focus solely on the difference between the amount they've contributed and the returns they'll eventually receive. What is unfortunate is that the government, which operates the National Pension, also seems captivated by this savings-based concept and continuously promotes it as such.

If the National Pension exists solely as a form of personal savings, it loses its justification for existence. There is no reason for the state to manage personal savings on behalf of its citizens. Furthermore, claiming that the private sector can invest more efficiently, doesn't the state end up entrusting people's money to private investment firms? The state does not invest on behalf of the people, but merely acts as an intermediate logistics warehouse through which investment funds flow. The state, which claims to invest on behalf of the people, paradoxically leaves the investment decisions in the hands of the people again, revealing self-contradiction. Even the officials overseeing the warehouse fail to grasp their true role. Even the civil servants managing this system seem unaware of their true role. The National Pension as a savings mechanism presents this self-contradictory illusion to all people.

The second financial illusion is more intriguing and more hidden compared to the first, making it less apparent. It is the very idea that the state invests money and generates returns. Typically, when people think of savings or investments, they envision investing a certain amount of capital into a bank or investment vehicles and earning interest or profits in return. The purpose of investment is singular—to generate returns and increase one's wealth. The higher the returns, the wealthier one becomes.

Thus, people become highly attentive to the investment returns of the National Pension Fund. The logic is simple: higher returns mean greater wealth. If the fund's return rate falls below other benchmarks, public criticism erupts. The National Pension also strives to increase its returns, which is why it entrusts investment management to the private sector. News media, which feeds on public attention, are busy criticizing or praising the government and publishing comments about the future welfare of people whenever the fund returns are released. If returns are poor, they report extensively on how much poorer people might become in the future.

This is where the financial illusion grows. Just as people believe they become wealthy when their personal investment returns are high, they think that if the National Pension Fund's investment returns are high, both they and the nation become wealthy. Since everyone is caught up in this illusion, a battle of wills arises among the public, the media, and the government every time the fund's investment returns are released.

Until they realize that finance is not real, they will continue to struggle in their illusions. Finance represents rights or claims over real assets. Those who hold stocks possess rights to a portion of the company's value that the stock represents. The essence of finance begins with the right to real assets. Although financial products like derivatives are created based on other financial products, tracing back to their origin, there must ultimately be a foundational real asset. Moreover, since derivatives are not directly tied to real assets, they become pure gambling instruments. This is why derivatives are often criticized as zero-sum speculation. While this is an interesting point, it is not the focus here, so let's delve further into the financial illusion surrounding National Pension.

If individuals invest and earn high returns, they become wealthier. The reason they become wealthier is that they have gained more rights to real assets. Because they hold the rights to real assets that could have gone to someone else, they get to enjoy greater wealth.

But if all individuals increased their returns by the same proportion, have I truly become wealthier? (For convenience of explanation, let us ignore the unequal distribution of money and financial assets. Ultimately, what we need is the wealth of the entire population.) The easiest way to understand this is through the example of inflation. Imagine the government suddenly doubles the money supply, causing the value of everyone's assets and returns from interest or stocks to double. Does that mean I've become wealthier? Wealth is determined by whether one's rights to real assets have increased, and since everyone's money has doubled, my claim to real assets hasn't changed at all. A smaller example could be a stock split. If a stock were split into 10 shares through a stock split, investors would have 10 times the number of shares than before. However, this does not mean that the investor's stake has increased. This is because everyone's stock count has increased tenfold.

The reason an individual can increase wealth through high financial investment returns is because it increases his claims to real assets. It is not simply because the returns are high, but because they are higher than others'. The only case in which everyone becomes wealthier by equally higher returns is when they are returns on real assets, not financial returns. When the value of real assets increases, an individual's wealth can increase although his relative claims remain the same. However, if the value of real assets has not changed, the individual's wealth can only increase by achieving higher financial returns than others and thereby increasing the share of real assets. At this point, since the total sum of shares is set to 100%, it becomes a zero-sum game.

The financial illusion of the National Pension lies in projecting the perspective of an individual's financial investment returns onto the entire nation. This can be seen as a "fallacy of composition". While individuals can increase their wealth by achieving higher financial returns, unfortunately, a nation cannot do the same. When the financial returns of entire population increase, it merely maintains the wealth of everyone at the same level. The same applies even when financial returns are low. The National Pension covers the entire population (even though, in reality, several public pensions coexist, this is not important to our discussion, so let's disregard it). Whether the National Pension invests in finance with high or low returns, it does not make the population richer or poorer as a result.

Let us rethink what the state should truly do. If the state genuinely cares about the welfare of its people in their old age, its task is to find ways to increase the returns on real assets. When Keynes said, "We cannot, as a community, provide for future consumption by financial expedients but only by current physical output"(Keynes, 2016: Ch.8, p104), he pointed out that the state cannot directly save or accumulate national wealth through financial means. Finance is a zero-sum game of claims on real assets. In a zero-sum game, the wealth of each participant may fluctuate, but the total value remains the same. Even if the state joins the game and increases its returns, it has no effect on the overall value.

In contrast, when the value of real assets increases, that value flows to someone, ultimately contributing to the wealth of the people. What the state should focus on is raising the returns on real assets, not financial returns. The state should not attempt to raise financial returns, as individuals do with good strategies in finance. The state's focus should be on real assets, not finance.

Thus, the idea of the National Pension that individuals save through the state, or that the state can invest individuals' money on their behalf to achieve high returns is merely an illusion, and we must now break free from that illusion. The National Pension Fund for financial investments was never necessary in the first place. Its justification existed only within the financial illusion.

From the outset, the idea that the state could save on behalf of its people must have been flawed. From that idea, the National Pension was inevitably compared to numerous private investors. This likely led to an obsession with raising returns through excessive stock and bond investments. Consequently, the more important mission of social insurance—protecting the weak and the poor and ensuring a minimum standard of living—was forgotten, and attention shifted to a meaningless financial return game. Both the government and the people were losing their rationality amid the financial illusion.

At best, finance is a mirror reflecting real assets. To improve one's appearance, it's not the mirror that needs changing, but the reflection—one must improve the actual self that is being reflected. The state should manage its funds not with the goal of generating returns through financial investments, but with the aim of increasing the value of real assets. However, if the National Pension Fund were used like general fiscal expenditures, the public would likely be displeased. Perhaps it would feel as though the money they entrusted was being given away to others. Even if this were truly in the best interest of the people, the sentiment would be hard to change. No matter how good the intentions, without trust, there is nothing that can be done.

Therefore, if trust cannot be restored, the next best option would be to eliminate the fund intended for financial investment altogether. The state's fundamental duty is not to invest people's money on their behalf through financial means, but to ensure a minimum standard of living for the weak and the poor. The way to do this is by collecting taxes from those with more resources and redistributing them to those in need. It is not through financial investments but through taxes and subsidies that the state should ensure fairness among its people. Under this principle, there is no need to focus solely on old-age welfare. Not all elderly are poor, and not all young people are wealthy. The National Pension has grown by promoting to people the illusion that the state is taking over individual financial savings, while neglecting its fundamental role. However, as long as we remain trapped in this financial illusion, the savings mechanism of the National Pension will only create greater conflicts as the fund grows.

Bankrupt Society

If an individual or a firm, as a debtor, fails to repay borrowed money, resulting in default or bankruptcy, we tend to think of the debtor's incompetence, laziness, or reckless management. This holds some truth. If one borrows excessively to spend or expand their business and fails, they fall into the pit of default.

In the past, the poor borrowed money to maintain their livelihood. However, today, not only the poor but also the wealthy borrow money to accumulate even greater wealth. Modern capitalist society encourages debt. As a result, in the past, a defaulting debtor was seen as a pitiable figure suffering from the pains of poverty and falling victim to the greed of creditors. But today, the defaulting debtor is often suspected of being greedy, and the creditor is sometimes seen as the one victimized by the debtor's greed. In the historical flow, capitalism's remarkable ability stands out in that it has reversed the long-held morality of debt.

Capitalism feeds on risk and debt. Both risk and debt approach from the future into the present. The operational principle of capitalism is a reverse-flowing energy movement that converts uncertain future wealth into certain present wealth. Those who know how to properly ride this reverse wave become winners, the rich, while those who cannot become losers, the poor.

The medium that converts future wealth into present wealth is, of course, money. In modern capitalism, money is issued as national debt and expands as it passes through the banking system, drawing in new debt. It is like a stream flowing through a valley, expanding its power as it flows and eventually forming a river. Capitalism is a constant flow of debt, sustained through the proliferation of debt.

However, debt is accompanied by interest, which becomes a

contradiction of debt and also a contradiction of capitalism, as seen below. Yet, this contradiction is not easily visible to individuals. To individuals, interest is simply understood as the opportunity cost of profit, from which receiving interest seems natural. But what holds true for individuals does not necessarily apply to society as a whole. A fallacy of composition also exists when it comes to the perception of interest.

To understand the contradiction of debt, it may be necessary to invoke Aristotle's view that money is sterile. Interest is often referred to as the offspring of money, but sterile money cannot produce offspring on its own. Interest is not a natural growth of the principal but rather an addition of new money to the principal. It is at this point that the contradiction of debt arises.

In modern capitalism, money is debt, and debt comes with interest. However, since money cannot reproduce itself, it cannot generate interest on its own. To pay the interest attached to debt, new money must be added from outside the existing pool of money. If no new money is introduced and the current money supply remains the same, it becomes, in principle, impossible for all debtors in society to repay the interest on their debts (Roger Langrick, 2010). From an individual's perspective, it may be possible to pay off interest by temporarily incurring new debt or taking money from others. But for society as a whole, this is not a solution and will ultimately increase the need for additional money.

While interest may seem natural to individuals, it becomes unnatural and unfeasible for society as a whole. The solution to this problem, unless interest is prohibited, is to continue issuing new money. Only with the supply of new money can all existing debt be settled. However, since money is essentially debt, this means that debt must continuously increase. Thus, we live in an era of modern capitalism characterized by the constant increase of debt. This era of constantly increasing debt is the era of modern capitalism.

In reality, some borrowers may be unable to repay their debts due to laziness or reckless behavior. However, even if every individual in society is diligent and hardworking, if the supply of money is insufficient, some of them will still fail to repay their debts. This can be seen as individual misfortune. Yet, that misfortune is also an original sin that was conceived when capitalism was designed. The fact that individuals may be unable to repay debts regardless of their efforts or diligence is an unfortunate but inevitable consequence of the modern capitalism.

18. THE 2008 FINANCIAL CRISIS

In "Anna Karenina", Tolstoy wrote, "Happy families are all alike, but every unhappy family is unhappy in its own way." However, when it comes to unhappy nations, rather than having their own reasons, they often have countless reasons. The global financial crisis of 2008 was no different. The loose real estate and financial policies of governments of advanced countries, especially the U.S., combined with the greed and speculation of investors and the reckless financial engineering tied to the development of financial technologies, led to the greatest financial crisis since the Great Depression. This U.S.-led financial crisis spread worldwide through the global financial network, plunging the entire world into shock in a while. As a result, vulnerable European nations faced national bankruptcy crises, and the weakened global economy, before even having a chance to fully recover, was on the verge of collapsing again due to the invasion of COVID-19 in 2020.

There is no need to repeat the experts' or scholars' diagnoses of the causes, developments, consequences, or solutions to the financial crisis. Here, let us address the points where the financial crisis is connected to the essential nature of finance and the illusion surrounding it.

Home And Finance

It would be appropriate to view the 2008 financial crisis as having its origins in mortgage loans and the mortgage-backed securities (MBS) tied to them. A mortgage loan, as the term suggests, refers to a financial institution's, such as a bank's, lending money to a homebuyer with the house as collateral. Since such loans typically involve large sums of money, borrowers generally repay them over a long period, usually 20 to 30 years. In order to recover the lent money, the lending bank must endure that long waiting period.

However, uneasy with waiting for such an extended time, the bank may choose to sell the rights to receive those repayments to a third party in exchange for a certain price. One method of trading those rights is by turning them into securities and selling those securities on the market. That is what mortgage-backed securities are. As a result of this trade, the bank secures cash immediately, while the investor in the securities expects to earn returns over time through the repayments of the loan.

It would be natural to talk about mortgage-backed securities and the distortion of bank incentives related to them as the starting point of the financial crisis. However, isn't the mortgage-backed security one of the most successful financial innovations? If the most successful financial innovation has such problems, we could assume that other financial innovations may have similar or even more serious problems.

This idea behind such financial innovations is a result of the myths of capitalism and finance mentioned earlier, including the belief that the growth of financial markets leads to public welfare and the illusion of financial measurement. Events such as financial crises reveal that this illusion was truly an illusion.

The very idea that one can own a home by using it as collateral is based on the premise that private ownership and self-interest must extend to housing. A home is a fundamental prerequisite for survival and life. However, this basic premise has been masked by the illusion of individual ability and absorbed into the realm of self-interest. Home finance, through mortgage lending, serves as a convenient mechanism that allows people who lack the immediate wealth to own a home by leveraging their future. However, as this convenience transforms into the illusion that anyone can simply purchase and own a home in the market, it leads to a collective forgetting of the fact that a home is a fundamental necessity. If a home is both a basic prerequisite and something anyone can supposedly own, it no longer appears as an issue that requires attention. Although a home is a basic prerequisite, there is no need to worry about it, as long as anyone can own it.

Consider why there are so many homeless people in the United States, where mortgage-backed securities were first developed and most widely used. Mortgage financing has produced homelessness by blocking fundamental questions about the meaning of home through the illusion of homeownership. While mortgage financing can provide a current residence, it requires the borrower's future to be mortgaged. What was actually being mortgaged was not the home, but the future itself. Since the future is the territory of the ghost of risk, those who are hated by the ghost become homeless as their future evaporates into nothingness. Mortgage financing instills the illusion that anyone can own a home. But the underlying truth is that with the home being captured in the territory of self-interested ownership, anyone can now have his home taken away.

When the self-interested market captured home within its territory, banks and investors finally began to generate profits through mortgage-backed securities. The idea that home could be a basic right gradually faded and homes became a source of speculative profit as they became just another product. Mortgage-backed securities seem to have succeeded in transforming home into finance, beyond viewing it as a mere commodity. Homes were no longer solid but had turned into liquid, flowing among people. Since anyone can and should own a home, even well-intentioned individuals were naturally drawn into the ranks of speculators. The state, hiding behind mortgage financing, aided and abetted this process, and the heat of speculation drove the market to its boiling point, producing bubbles.

Contrary to popular belief, the 2008 financial crisis did not arise simply because good systems like mortgage loans and mortgage-backed securities were misused by government missteps, reckless lending by banks and investors, or speculation by individuals. Of course, these factors are not unrelated to the crisis. However, they are merely visible links in the chain, and it is more accurate to view them as effects rather than causes. The more fundamental cause lies in the truth hidden in the belief that mortgage-based finance is a good system.

The financial market is a gamble, and in gambling, there is competition with winners and losers. When homes entered the realm of markets and finance through mortgage-backed financing, the stakes of the gamble grew fiercer, dividing winners and losers more sharply. The winners would gain great profit, but the losers would lose their homes and be left adrift. This was not a gamble for momentary entertainment, but a gamble where lives and futures were put at stake. The true cause of the 2008 financial crisis lies in the fact that society accepted this kind of gamble without any awareness of problem.

Polanyi described the commodification of land as a fundamental characteristic of capitalism. Under financial capitalism, an advanced form of capitalism, real estate—including land—has become more than just a commodity; it has become finance itself. If commodification implies an object of trade driven by self-interest, financialization implies an object of speculation. The heat generated by the energy of speculation is incomparably higher than that of simple trade. If trade in goods produces a slight warmth, financial speculation can produce a hot heat capable of melting a solid at any time. The 2008 financial crisis was a period when the entire world felt the intensity of that heat.

Credit Default Swap: Insurance Illusion

Financial products derived from mortgage loans gradually

merge with other financial products, transforming into even larger financial instruments. Typically, this is hailed as financial innovation or financial engineering, viewed as a novel and brilliant invention. However, once we recognize that finance is liquid, we see that this process is no different from one stream meeting another, merging and eventually flowing together as a river. We don't call the merging of two streams into a river an "innovation." Thus, what we term "financial engineering" is not engineering, but rather geography, an inherent part of the flow and circulation of nature.

Even in casino gambling, insurance is traded. Gambling is inherently a pursuit of risk, but insurance is sometimes traded to reduce unnecessary risks. When financial products derived from mortgage loans merged and blended to the point where the risk in finance could no longer be traced, this was not embarrassing, but in fact natural. Looking at a flowing river, we cannot trace which water droplet originated from which mountain valley.

Amidst the swirling waters, investors sought to calm their anxieties by purchasing insurance known as credit default swaps (CDS). They viewed CDS as insurance because it promised to cover losses if their invested bonds defaulted. Yet, the one selling this insurance was just another speculator, equally incapable of tracing the origins of risk in the turbulent financial flow. An anxious speculator might have taken comfort by making another trade in the name of insurance, but his anxiety simply became another's speculative opportunity. No one truly had the ability to foresee or bear the risks of the future.

The trade of insurance that failed to accurately measure risk and price was simply another name for gambling. Speculators wanted to believe they were purchasing true insurance, yet the CDS they bought were, in fact, not insurance at all. Other speculators, sensing this, treated CDS as a speculative instrument instead. Although CDS was called "insurance" and the naïve may have believed it, for both buyers and sellers, it was merely a means of speculation. The financial product called insurance, providing meaningless reassurance for some and becoming a new object of speculation for others, was poised to stir up fresh turmoil in the midst of the chaos in the financial markets.

Thus, homes dissolved into droplets, and the water that began flowing from the mountain joined countless tributaries, swelling as it moved through valleys, and flowed with great force into the river. Yet, with the sudden surge of water, the river could no longer hold its banks, churning wildly until it finally burst forth like a waterfall. This is the very essence of the 2008 financial crisis.

In fact, the financial crisis was not intended to cause confusion and chaos in the financial markets; it was a force meant to clear up already chaotic markets. However, policymakers in various countries were unable to see this essential truth. Instead, in an attempt to quell the visible turmoil, they ended up amplifying the very causes of chaos. Rather than cleaning up the financial markets, they chose to supply new funds to the speculators who had caused the crisis, effectively encouraging them to continue their gambling.

Some people sensed the oddity of this movement, but most had no choice but to support it willingly. Those who were unable to escape from the illusions and myths of finance believed they were improving their own situations while handing over their money as gambling stakes to wealthy speculators.

As economist Hyman Minsky observed, financial crises come hand in hand with crises of debt. Capitalism is built on the desire for wealth accumulation and real consumption, and this desire is amplified through debt. Financial crises originate from the bubbles of desire and debt, yet the governments of various countries, in response to such crises, tend to expand debt further to stoke the embers of desire. Thus, one bubble becomes enveloped by another bubble. While the true resolution of a financial crisis lies in the moderation of desire and debt, capitalism, built upon desire, actually exacerbates both desire and debt, calling this a solution (Seog, 2020a, c).

Desire And Debt

The truth that the financial crisis reveals before us is that capitalism is an economy of desire and debt. Desire is represented in two forms: consumption and wealth. Consumption represents desire through the consumption of real goods or conspicuous consumption. In fact, the representation of desire through consumption is not unique to capitalism; it has likely persisted throughout human history. What differentiates capitalism is probably the unprecedented expansion in the types and methods of consumption. This is because capitalism is an economy based on the market, and it requires the maximization of consumer desire to legitimize the existence of market. Thus, an endless variety of goods is introduced to the world and also disappears in the name of consumer satisfaction or competition. The concept of necessary consumption no longer holds meaning. The virtue of capitalist consumption lies not in the consumption that fulfills basic needs, but in the consumption that satisfies and perpetuates desire.

A defining feature of the capitalist manifestation of desire is its representation through wealth. While wealth can certainly be accumulated as a means to secure future consumption, the desire for wealth does not stop there. Capitalism's distinctive characteristic lies in its drive to represent desire through the accumulation of money itself, beyond merely serving as a means for consumption. Why, then, does one seek to accumulate wealth endlessly beyond what one could possibly consume in a lifetime?

The desire for wealth is expressed through financial means, contrasting with the expression of consumer desire through real goods. This distinction is precisely why finance becomes the hegemonic industry in capitalism. Physical consumption is inherently limited. Although some individuals may pursue excessive consumption driven by a conspicuous desire, it is fundamentally impossible to infinitely increase consumption desire.

Since monetary wealth can be accumulated without limit, or at least it appears so, finance, standing guard over this seemingly boundless realm, gains hegemony. To generate endless wealth within this infinite domain, finance must continuously create new finance. New finance appears before us as if it is a magic wand, under names like financial innovation, financial engineering, fintech, or insurtech, aligned with the trends of the times. This is why finance has come to dominate as capitalism has advanced. Only finance is the magic that can continuously infuse capitalism with life by fulfilling the endless desire for wealth.

Let us pause to consider the social implications of wealth generated through finance. While finance, detached from real things, may offer new wealth to individuals, it is a zero-sum game on a societal level. More precisely, it incurs a loss equivalent to the social effort invested in this zero-sum game. Because finance itself is not a real thing, it does not in principle become wealth or produce wealth. When Adam Smith asserted that a nation's wealth does not depend on its stockpiled gold, he pointed out that finance itself does not constitute national wealth. The same applies to Keynes when he stated that a community cannot provide for future consumption by financial expedients. Finance can only affect the wealth of society to the extent that it is indirectly reflected in real things. This is where individual and societal wealth diverge: while finance may satisfy individual desires for wealth, it cannot do the same for society as a whole. In society, finance is simply a method of distributing wealth but cannot become wealth in itself. Yet capitalism derives its vitality not from societal well-being, but from individual desires for wealth. As a result, capitalism becomes a system that inherently generates conflict between individuals and society.

How does the desire for wealth operate through finance? Money and finance are signs given to our hands, with future wealth as collateral. Thus, finance, no matter what it is called, is always debt. What money and finance truly are is debt, a golden sign that originates from the future and moves backward through time to stand before us. This financial desire, represented before our eyes, may indeed serve as wealth for some, but it is offset by the debt borne by others. Consequently, on a societal scale, it becomes zero-sum.

This debt, grounded in an uncertain future, strives to capture anything that can offer even the slightest certainty. It seeks to seize present assets as collateral, monitor borrowers' deposit balances, or use laws and regulations to pressure debtors. A financial crisis refers to an event that signals the breakdown of these mechanisms of collateral, surveillance, and pressure. It is an event that declares that individuals' desire for wealth has collapsed on its own, blocked by the wall of future and uncertainty. While individual desires for wealth may be limitless, they fail to transcend the boundaries of time. Thus, a financial crisis is an event where human hopes to conquer the future crumble into despair.

The solution to the financial crisis should be to extend relief to those who have suffered real losses, not to speculators who have suffered losses through empty financial speculation. Since financial wealth is not the wealth of society, the goal should be not to protect financial speculators, but to protect society from financial speculation. A more fundamental and ultimate resolution begins with freeing ourselves from the illusion that the hollow wealth accumulated in the present, with the future as collateral, constitutes the real wealth of society.

19. COVID-19 AND LIFE

Covid-19

The coronavirus (COVID-19), which began spreading at the end of 2019, struck the world in 2020, bringing it to a standstill. This novel coronavirus infection was declared a global pandemic by the World Health Organization (WHO) in March 2020. With its tremendous transmissibility, it has resulted in numerous infections and deaths worldwide.

The crown-shaped COVID-19 virus is an RNA-based virus, making it highly reactive with other substances and prone to mutations. When COVID-19 invades human cells and reproduces through chemical reactions and combinations, it can cause inflammation in the lungs or heart and, in severe cases, lead to death.

COVID-19 unveiled a new world and era for global economies and finance, one that had never been experienced before. This new world is played out as a symphony of three variations on life. The first life is about breath; the second life is about living or the economy. Here, living can be divided into the real side, dealing with the connectivity of the supply chain, trade, and consumption, and the financial side, involving interest rates and liquidity. The third life concerns information, the alter ego that could be called a soul.

Breath

Individual life has never been less than precious, but when life is viewed through the lens of population or groups, it becomes objectified as something to be managed or governed rather than as something noble. Death within a group is expressed as a mortality rate, a figure that remains merely an object of management without any implication to nobility or morality. While an individual's life is precious, at the same time, everyone ultimately dies. These two divergent perspectives lead, on the one hand, to efforts to preserve life and, on the other hand, to the treatment of life as just an input value in calculations.

In our response to COVID-19, we find ourselves conflicted due to this divergence of perspectives. As the number of infections and deaths rises, the rate of numerical change begins to appear smaller. Individual lives fade from view, leaving only the rate of increase as the focus. As deaths accumulate, the growth rate of deaths naturally diminishes. Even when many lives are lost, society becomes increasingly stable, and this state is eventually accepted as normal. This is the "new normal", a new state of life. The new normal is not about total values, but about increments. When the increment stabilizes it is entered as the new normal. A new normal is created not by the return of abnormality to its original state, but by the dulling of our senses.

By training ourselves to become desensitized to the deaths of others, we adapt to a new life. Television and mass media report daily on the numbers of infections and deaths not only domestically but worldwide, expressing sorrow over the losses. All we can do is take comfort in having recorded fewer deaths than others, but infections and fatalities continue to emerge everywhere, at any moment.

Broadcasts continually enumerate statistics and measures, seemingly competing with each other in their concern for health and life. They always emphasize the sanctity of life, focusing on stories of life such as vaccines, treatments, prevention guidelines, and recoveries alongside mourning the dead. Yet, whether intentional or not, what these broadcasts truly imprint upon us is the message to accept death as normal. As more and more people pass away, death increasingly becomes an ordinary and universal part of daily life.

Thus, the new normal begins when we accept the contradictions of the two vectors: the dignification of individual life and the normalization of death within society. Perhaps our ancestors faced a similar reality. They, too, likely felt the many contradictions in the weave of life and death, fortune and misfortune. The method they chose would have been simply to accept the contradictions by compromising with them.

Furthermore, it would be even better if they could craft narratives to explain these contradictions. Thus, myths and folktales were born, and religions were created. Without compromise with contradictions, it may have been difficult to overcome the mental breakdown in confusion. Without some form of reconciliation with contradictions, overcoming the mental fragmentation amid confusion would have been challenging. Now, COVID-19 calls upon us to forge the myths and religions of the 21st century. For the new normal to function, we need a narrative that can overcome contradictions and divisions. In this way, COVID-19 has confronted us with the awareness of life and its inherent contradictions.

Living: Economy And Connectivity

Another question that COVID-19 presents to us is the contradiction between life as breath and life as living. While the former is life in terms of surviving from infection, while the latter is life in terms of making a living. If the former represents life in terms of health, the latter represents life in terms of the economy. This contradiction between the two forms of life is the contradiction between health and the economy.

Capitalism is an economic system where the life as living depends on others. In fact, in capitalism, life as breath also relies on others, namely the healthcare system and medical personnel. Capitalism is a system that depends on others for maintaining life as both breath and living.

The development of capitalism has been driven either by the magnitude of the force that brings more and more people closer together, or by the direction of the force that propels them faster toward each other. Urban concentration and advances in transportation are the driving forces of industrial capitalism. The narrative of the Industrial Revolution began with the steam engine, not merely because it was a new power source, but because it symbolized a new vector of force. The ability to gather and disperse while maintaining directionality is the essence of capitalism. In this way, capitalism is expressed as a vector of force.

By bringing people together in one place or enabling rapid movement, firms could generate higher profits, and consumers gained access to a wider variety of better products. The statement that capitalism has developed is, in fact, a roundabout way of saying that it has progressed in a direction that increases interdependence among people.

COVID-19 parasitizes precisely on this interdependent system. No, rather, it parasitizes on us who parasitizes on the system. COVID-19 seems to be jealous of people who depend on each other, demanding that they stay apart. It tells us not to gather or travel, but to remain in place, each in isolation. Thus, the impact of COVID-19 has hit first the sectors of the economy that thrive on gathering and movement. The driving force of capitalism, having operated without rest for so long, is now being told to pause its energy, even if only temporarily.

Yet, this pause left many people struggling to survive. For those who were already barely holding on, even a brief pause didn't offer rest—it drained them of their remaining energy. Many found even a short pause unbearable, and when the economic vector pointed to a standstill, they were forced to choose between breath and living. In economic history, COVID-19 might be depicted as a brief pause. However, within that picture, the countless people who perished at the crossroads of choice will be painted with transparent colors, rendering them invisible.

To respond to COVID-19, capitalism needs to transform. Would it be enough if products could gather and move even if people didn't do so? Although certain industries may rely on people gathering to form a market, other industries that can replace such markets may thrive instead. The strong network which interconnects tightly among people and the economy is shifting to the more efficient weak network which connects loosely around a few hubs. And isn't there already a virtual network of connections online and in mobile spaces? In this way, COVID-19 guides us naturally into a new yet already emerging world.

Living: Liquidity And Interest

Each of the COVID-19 viruses may be tiny, but their mobility resembles the liquidity of liquid. They slide and flow here and there, ultimately striving to fill any empty space. Although humans call it infection, from the virus's perspective, it is simply flowing as a means of its own survival. This is why COVID-19 resembles especially finance within capitalism.

Just as finance flows along networks, giving life or death to people and firms, COVID-19 is the same. Just as finance holds our lifeline, so does COVID-19. Healthy people or firms may not have problems surviving even if finance tightens around them; the same goes for COVID-19. A cold may give a healthy person a bit of rest, but for someone already tired and weak, it can be fatal.

Thus, COVID-19 is a mirror image of finance. It is no coincidence that the main tool governments around the world use to respond to COVID-19 is finance. Finance is a replicated copy of the virus. Before we are brought down by COVID-19, we must inject finance to keep us alive. Isn't a vaccine, after all, also a replica? It is hoped that finance can play the role of a vaccine in the body.

Apart from this intimacy between the virus and finance, COVID-19 raises a fundamental question about finance. In so-called advanced capitalist countries, liquidity has been released in immeasurable amounts, and central banks have rushed to announce zero or even negative interest rates. While some of this was triggered by the 2008 financial crisis, many people, including experts, reluctantly accept that zero interest rates are inevitable.

However, few understand that a zero interest rate is more than just a number and fundamentally undermines the foundations of modern capitalism. Capitalism is an economy of debt, and debt is based on interest. Governments around the world, pressured by the urgency of consumption, are only trying to restore the relationship between interest rates and consumption. They do not realize that their actions are shaking the very foundations of capitalism.

As previously discussed, economics teaches that the interest rate is an opportunity cost. The borrower must compensate the lender with interest for the profit the lender could have made by using the money elsewhere instead of lending it out; this is opportunity cost. When a lender loans money to a borrower, the lender's tangible and intangible costs are calculated as interest. For the borrower to repay this interest, which represents opportunity cost, they must invest in a more efficient place. By the borrower earning a higher return than the lender's cost, finance is used efficiently. In this way, finance becomes the bloodstream of the capitalist economy, driving economic development and prosperity. If the interest rate as an opportunity cost is zero, it means there are no profitable investment opportunities for a borrower to make a return by borrowing money. From the perspective of opportunity cost, it means that the capitalist economy can no longer advance.

A key moment in the development of capitalism alongside modernity lies precisely in the liberation of interest rates. Didn't capitalism finally flourish when the prohibition of interest in medieval Europe was dismantled along with the Reformation and Enlightenment?

Many were once cynical about regions where interest is still prohibited. Yet these same people do not scoff at zero, or even negative, interest rates set by central banks. They comfort themselves by saying that there are valid reasons and that it is unavoidable. However, they fail to consider that such reasons might have existed not only now and here but also then and perhaps there.

In fact, when you think about it, there is no absolute reason for central banks to set interest rates at zero. It's simply a policy decision to fulfill their mission of stimulating the economy. That mission, too, is merely a self-imposed goal, not something inherently necessary. It's only been about a century since central banks were given the authority to officially set interest rates. This isn't to say that central banks shouldn't do such work, but rather that the mission of central banks is merely a self-imposed duty within the particular context of the capitalist system. Just as zero interest rates are seen as legitimate within our current culture and environment, so too was the prohibition of interest in the past.

To reiterate the previous point, another intriguing aspect that COVID-19 quietly reveals is that, ultimately, interest is not an opportunity cost. What opportunity loss does the central bank's benchmark rate replace? Central banks do not consider interest rates as an opportunity cost; they simply set the rate based on what they judge to be suitable. While they may take economic stagnation or stimulation, inflation or deflation, into account, the interest rate is fundamentally the result of arbitrary judgment. The interest rate set by central bank decision-makers is based on their own predictions about the future and is determined in an arbitrary manner according to their self-defined methods.

If the central bank's interest rate is arbitrary, can we also say that the other interest rates, which are determined by adding a premium based on that rate, are not arbitrary? Perhaps one could argue this way. Since the idea of opportunity cost is involved in calculating the premium, might we not call the interest rate an opportunity cost? Even if we accept such an argument, it is merely an individual perspective. While the interest rate may appear to individuals as an opportunity cost, the interest rate for society as a whole is an arbitrary and unilateral constraint rather than an opportunity cost.

As far as finance is concerned, COVID-19 itself has become a liquid, flowing between connecting nodes while simultaneously reinfusing the forgotten religious fervor of medieval Europe and Islam into modern capitalism. In this way, the finance of COVID-19 infiltrates capitalism, much like a virus with its pointed head piercing into a cell to infect us.

The attitudes of various countries in responding to COVID-19 have been revealing the contradictions of capitalism without our awareness, showing its illogicality and irrationality. It demonstrates that capitalism is merely a cultural phenomenon and a promise, not an inevitable result of rationality. In this way, capitalism becomes a "sad tropic" (Claude Lévi-Strauss, 1998).

Soul: Information And Alter Ego

In response to COVID-19, firms and individuals have begun to find appeal in so-called contactless interaction. While online and mobile contactless functions were already abundant, COVID-19 seems to have shown the necessity and advantages of these functions more clearly. Therefore, although it is not a difficult prediction, many are focusing on contactless as the field that will drive the post-COVID-19 economy.

COVID-19 is believed to accelerate the already emerging information age—often referred to as the digital age or the Fourth Industrial Revolution. While the information age may be easily discussed as a strategy for addressing COVID-19, in truth, information itself is perhaps the most virus-like entity. Just as a virus replicates, edits, and transfers itself, so does information.

Information is another life phenomenon. Just as life replicates and grows through cell division, information exists precisely to perform this function. Like living organisms that produce alter egos through cloning, information also produces alter egos. In the information age, our identities and lives are replicated and fragmented, traversing networks in virtual spaces, manifesting in various forms across different realms.

In virtual space, data is a sequence of numbers created by 0s and 1s. When life is infused into this data, it becomes information. New life is born when a simple number sequence is given special meaning on a network. Since information embodies the spirit or soul of various entities and individuals, it can create life through this force. As information travels across networks, an individual's soul is likewise transferred, as if accompanying the information itself. It is much like the Maori's "hau", which resides within the gift and transfers along with it (Marcel Mauss, 2000).

In virtual space, information is "dividuals", which are souls and alter egos of individuals. Like Hong Gil-dong's self-replication technique, whether they want it or not, individuals replicate their souls into information, revealing themselves in multiple places. This means that information in virtual spaces should be understood, not merely through the concept of property or ownership, but rather through the concept of life and existence. This is because the alter ego with a soul is life. This may explain why information issues in virtual spaces often turn into issues of life dignity determining life and death rather than ownership. For some, information may be nothing more than a means of making money, but for others, it is an alter ego that contains one's soul.

COVID-19, on the one hand, threatens our physical lives, but on the other hand, it demands that we produce new lives through the soul replication and alter ego. This pattern of life replication precisely mirrors the survival tactics of the virus itself. This is because viruses continuously flow through the world's networks by replicating, twisting, and metastasizing their own souls. The repetition of creation and destruction of information, as combinations of 0s and 1s, in virtual space is also a copy of the virus's ability to traverse the border between life and non-life. By mimicking the virus, we can survive, whether in real or virtual space. COVID-19 compels us to copy its survival strategies.

Lessons From Covid-19

To understand the world that will change due to COVID-19, one must comprehensively grasp the three variations of life —breath, living, and soul. Breath and living intertwine and sometimes conflict with each other. The replication of the soul through its alter egos must breathe within new systems of connection and become a way of living. A hidden lesson of COVID-19, as observed above, is that it reminds us that we are still living in the medieval and mythical eras from which we once believed ourselves to be long disconnected.

Another hidden lesson from COVID-19 lies in its exposure of the fundamental vulnerabilities in the "organic solidarity" of a society based on division of labor and capitalist markets (Durkheim, 2014). The interdependence formed by domestic and international divisions of labor collapsed in the face of the COVID- 19 pandemic. Solidarity which has been reluctantly held based on the circulation of money lost its luster in the face of the slogan "every man for himself." The organic solidarity rooted in markets was ultimately built on self-interest. Under the strain of the crisis, the self-interest had no choice but to follow the path of individual survival. Consequently, states locked their doors and blamed one another, while individuals, firms, and industries entered a period of fragmentation and isolation. The solidarity lacking the fundamental insurance spirit of risk sharing melted away like snow in spring when it was most needed. Only community itself was left to bear the weight of the insurance spirit. And each state was forced to reveal, stripped bare, whether it was genuinely striving to embody true solidarity.

20. CONCLUSION

Modern economics and business studies, grounded in the capitalist system, discuss individuals, markets, and firms, along with the nature and roles of governments and institutions. This book is an essay-style exploration intended to question and reflect on the fundamental assumptions and principles underlying economics and business studies. The central themes include risk, money, and trades—the core components of capitalism—and also cover institutions that embody these components, such as insurance, markets, firms, and finance. It further addresses the 2008 financial crisis and the COVID-19 pandemic.

To understand the modern economy, what we need is imagination. This isn't for absurd fantasies but rather to grasp that the rationality and scientific rigor supposedly underpinning economics are not solid at all. With this in mind, we turn to myth, magic, sorcery and ritual to reinterpret capitalism. In addition, firms and finance can be understood in the forms of matter—gas, liquid, and solid. We already use these metaphors everywhere. These matters transform, move, interact, and even conflict, reviving the forgotten alchemy of the Middle Ages in a modern context. Thus, while capitalism may be partially understood through science and rational calculation, it can be fundamentally understood only through the lenses of myth, ritual, and alchemy.

We began this text with a myth of beings that are half-human, half-divine. Although this myth is common and unremarkable, it serves as a foundational myth for understanding capitalism. Although firms are endowed with personhood by law, they are god-like beings that pursue immortality. Modern capitalism is a system in which these firms compete, pursuing and capturing the liquidity called profit. Yet, when the heat becomes excessive, it can ultimately melt the firms themselves and, further, dissolve the lives of the people who depend on them.

The myth of capitalism can be understood through risk, money, and trades. Risk, elusive and invisible, is a gas or ghost that approaches us as an ongoing, unseen presence. Capitalism demands that individuals and firms confront such a risk and extract profit from it. While humanity has always faced and battled risk, capitalism generates its own risks, laying even more before us. Now, risk becomes part of a competition game, where the winners are promised rewards in the form of liquidity.

Money is a means of exchanging goods in the market and a symbol that measures the value of goods. Given that language is a symbol for expressing and exchanging thoughts and meanings, money becomes the language of goods, and conversely, language becomes the money of meaning. Originally, money was a promise and invention of mankind to measure and trade other goods, but today's money becomes an object of trade and also measures itself. The fact that money measures and trades itself reveals a contradictory tautology, which defines a word with the same word. Yet this contradiction no longer feels like a contradiction; instead, it is praised as a process of innovation and value creation. This contradictory mechanism of pricing money with money and exchanging money for money is what we call finance.

In order to overcome its fundamental contradiction, finance must trade with itself not on the same time, but on different times. Thus, finance is always a trade between the present and the future, a mechanism that translates an uncertain future into a certain present. In this sense, finance is inherently inseparable from risk. By exchanging time, finance also becomes a mechanism for exchanging risk. Risk is always something of the future, and the future always comes with risk, making risk and time inseparable. Capitalism was able to begin when such risk and time were unnaturally separated.

Capitalism is an economy that views trades as inherent to human nature and orbits around markets and trades. Anthropologists have clarified that, at its core, the exchange of goods is essentially a gift, not a trade. But they also observe that a gift is not much different from a trade in another respect. From the opposite angle, a trade is not much different from a gift either. Just as a gift resembles a trade as an exchange that requires a return, a trade also resembles a gift as an unequal exchange. Thus, in the modern economy, the distinction between gift and trade becomes more blurred. While gifts are perceived as bribes and fairness demands equivalent trades, the exchange of goods within a firm and the social security system actively accept the gift mechanism. Capitalism, therefore, appears to be an era of markets and trades, yet it is equally an era where trades and gifts continuously invade and overlap each other's territories.

Understanding risk requires understanding insurance. Insurance originally encompasses all the various ways humanity deals with risk, yet today, we first think of insurance products traded in the market. This is where the misunderstanding about insurance stems from. The fundamental spirit of insurance is to mutually help people in risk and to achieve solidarity. This spirit starts with compassion for others and ultimately moves in a direction beneficial to oneself. However, in the insurance market, the direction of the vector is reversed. It starts from individual's own benefit and flows toward helping others. Since this reversal of direction is only possible by undermining the insurance spirit, the insurance market clashes with the insurance spirit. While the insurance spirit is collective and altruistic, the insurance market is individualistic and self-interested. Thus, the insurance market becomes a space of conflict among self-interested individuals, rather than a place of social solidarity.

The contradiction in the insurance market reveals that it is a true symbol of capitalism. The inclusion of fundamentally anti-capitalist insurance into the market indicates that no product is beyond the reach of commodification. Another axis through which the insurance market becomes a symbol of capitalism lies in the trading of risk itself. Risk and time were inherently inseparable in nature, but capitalism succeeded in forcibly separating risk and time through the insurance and financial markets. Now, risk and time are separated into different axes and measured independently. Even when these two are combined, they are expressed as an arithmetic sum so that they can be easily separated again at any time. The insurance market and the financial market stand as both the symbols and bloodlines of capitalism, bearing the contradictions of the spirit of insurance, the contradiction of the separation of risk and time, and the contradiction of money's trading with itself.

The insurance market becomes a symbol of capitalism also through its connection with the spirit of capitalism as modernity. If modernity is characterized by transformation of episteme from the superficial similarities to fundamental identity and difference, then the episteme of identity and difference aligns closely with the risk classification of insurance. The discovery of actuarial science starting with gambling probability, the classification of risks through it, and the development of the insurance market also represent the episteme of identity and difference. The insurance market operates by continually classifying risks and further by producing and consuming risks. This episteme of risk classification not only propels the insurance market forward but also underpins modern governmentality by placing risk governance for population at its core. Insurance exists with us in a complex and contradictory form, symbolizing capitalism through the insurance market and risk contracts on the one hand, and representing socialism through social insurance and safety nets on the other.

Another direction of conflict inherent in insurance lies in the nature of insurance itself, which is fundamentally an exchange between the present and the future. Insurance is a promise of the future from the present. Yet, the promise of the future itself also creates additional risks and uncertainties. Ideally, promises should be truthful and always fulfilled, but in reality, falsehoods, errors, and imperfections arise. This is where information problems sch as moral hazard and adverse selection come into play. These informational challenges reveal that insurance, which aims to mitigate risk through the promise of future, ironically ends up producing new risks. Herein lies another contradiction: insurance, while reducing risk on one hand, creates it on the other. If an information problem exists, it would be good to resolve it. Yet the approach taken to resolve these problems is crucial. Whose perspective dictates the solution? If the approach undermines the fundamental spirit of insurance, the solution itself can produce new conflicts. Thus, rather than merely solving information problems, embracing them can sometimes be a more desirable solution.

Insurance itself is information. Information, in the sense of a symbol containing meaning, is homologous to language and money. Since symbols embody promises, and insurance, as a promise of the future, is also a symbol, it becomes information. When insurance as information is exposed to incompleteness, problems like moral hazard and adverse selection arise. In reverse, information, as a promise carrying the future and uncertainty, also remains inseparable from risk and insurance. The so-called information revolution, or the Fourth Industrial Revolution, is no exception. The information revolution signifies a transformation in the quantity and speed of information, which are introducing various changes to our society. However, its depth and shadows are only fully revealed through the lens of risk and insurance. Because the goal of the revolution in quantity and speed of information is ultimately to produce and classify risks, the information revolution becomes an insurance revolution. The information revolution becomes a gesture for the entire economic and industrial spheres to share the privileges of classification and discrimination that the insurance market has long enjoyed along with capitalism.

If insurance revolves around risk, finance revolves around time. Along the axis of time, money exchanges with money, giving birth to and generating more money. This process is akin to liquids merging and expanding in force. In this sense, money becomes a living thing that reproduces itself, multiplying its kin. Initially a lifeless solid, money defies natural laws to become a liquid and then a living thing. This unnaturalness of money becoming a living thing was always an object of suspicion in ancient and medieval times. Eventually, when the wariness peaked in Western Asia and Europe, interest became the devil and a target for execution.

Eventually, in the age of merchants, the waves of the Reformation liberated interest from the devil, redefining it as a fair reward for effort or compensation for the lender's lost opportunity. Finance was now poised to shed its demonic image and take on the visage of an angel. When the Scientific Revolution sought to find naturalness not in life force but in matter and extension, money and interest became natural in themselves. Whether living or non-living, the exchange of force and motion are all natural. Since interest is a by-product of monetary movements, this is also natural. Thus, after passing through the observation of force and motion, capitalism effectively endowed money with vitality. This vitality of money was no longer perceived as something unnatural.

Liquids, now endowed with the status of self-replicating living beings, have become independent from real goods that were the original purpose of money. Interest is no longer compensation for lost real opportunities. Stock prices have detached from the value of shares, and various derivatives maintain their vitality by referencing and replicating other financial instruments rather than any real assets. Deviating from its essence, finance has become a simulacrum, an illusion that replicates and references itself.

Now, attempts to connect finance with real values become a futile effort to give legitimacy to finance. At the same time, however, they also function to cloak finance in a moral guise and obscure its fetishistic deification, thereby maintaining its hegemony. Finance, as a living thing armed with morality, becomes wealth when it stays still and generates wealth when it circulates. Yet the basis for this becoming and generating of wealth arises from self-measured and self-judged indicators. This is why, even amidst financial crises or bubbles, finance is again proposed as the solution. The very reason explains why the damage from the bubble is passed on to the public who have nothing to do with speculation.

Just as a species of living beings thrives, the thriving of the species called finance seeks to expand kinship through self-reference and replication, thereby extending its power. In this way, it becomes disconnected from the real, which is its original reason for being, and enjoys power within a fragile protective shield of its own surface tension, ruling the world. Thus, modern finance is a magical ritual. Since everything is rationally connected and effective in the ritual, it is impossible to distinguish illusion from essence as long as one believes in the ritual and myth. Within the myth of modern finance, a new hero is born each day, breaking out of the egg of adversity. This hero slays monsters for the feeble masses, ultimately saving the world of finance and returning home in triumph.

Like insurance, finance too is a language and a symbol. The point where finance differs from language is that while language acquires meaning through difference, money and finance acquire meaning through identity. Money gains its reason for existence by placing different goods on the same measurement, thus becoming a common divisor. Just as language entails speech acts, finance, as the exchange of money, involves money acts. Finance goes beyond simple exchanges of money, commanding actions from the parties involved. Projecting the forces of power, greed, or hope between the parties, finance becomes a surface where these forces collide, and at the same time also becomes a promise, a command, or a warning. It is this high performativity of money that underlies modern finance's ability to become a space of simulacra. Finance has shown the confidence that it can now act on its own and sustain itself independently, even if severed from the real world.

Capitalism could emerge, as time and risk moved towards each other again after they were separated in finance and insurance. Capitalism then created the creature known as the corporation. The corporation came down to earth as a half-human, half-god being who had to plan for long-term journeys through time, perpetually seeking profit amidst risk. Originally solid, the corporation must extract the liquid of profit from the gases of risk and opportunity. The corporation becomes an alchemist who crosses solid, liquid, and gas. Therefore, it cannot be understood solely in terms of transaction costs or information problems, which, while closely related, are merely outward manifestations. The corporation must be viewed through the lens of myth, ritual, and desire to be truly understood. It is like a god in myth, a wizard in ritual, and an alchemist fueled by burning desire.

The firm began before capitalism as a cooperative organization for people to satisfy their thirst for liquid. However, under capitalism, the firm had to face infinitely extended time and significant risk. Thus, the firm had to become an immortal, god-like being and also transform itself into an insurance machine. Only after becoming a god and an insurance machine could the capitalist firm serve as a machine for producing or moving goods. What breathes life into the firm and sustains it is, above all, the desire for profit and the ability to extract liquid from gas to fulfill that desire. In this way, the firm becomes a machine possessed by the paranoia of desire, where desire moves upward and command moves downward in a straight line.

The tool for measuring all these flows and profits is a liquid called money. As a result, it is liquid, not gas or solid, that holds hegemony over the firm. The firm, originally solid at its core and self-identified as such, is evaluated solely by its contribution to liquid. When the language of liquid became the common language and the grammar of liquid was codified, liquid could seize symbolic power and move to the center of social power. Thus, when a firm asserts its solid nature, it begins to be criticized for inefficiency or immorality. Polluting the liquid becomes equivalent to polluting society. Herein lies the firm's contradiction and conflict. The contradiction between solid, which must stand on the ground and endure gravity, and liquid, which can flow across the surface at any time, is unavoidable. Debates over firm value, corporate governance, or social value ultimately reduce to the firm's material nature—specifically, the inescapable contradiction between liquid and solid.

Everyone in modern times wants to accumulate wealth. The ways for modern people to accumulate wealth is either through the magic of adhering to desire and riding on the illusion of speculation and finance, or through the corporate alchemy of extracting the liquid of profit from the gas of risk and opportunity. Although modernity appears to be an era dominated by rationality and science, it may be that humanity's methods of accumulating wealth still depend on magic and alchemy. Capitalism has simply unfolded to us new myths, rituals, and alchemy, different from those of the past. In these myths and rituals, the future intersects and interferes with the present, and time with risk. Solid, liquid, and gas also intersect and interfere with one another. In their struggle, liquid currently appears to prevail over solid and gas. In this way, modern capitalism is an era in which liquid holds hegemony and forces its perspective upon us.

BIBLIOGRAPHY

Arrow, Kenneth (1963), Uncertainty and the Welfare Economics of Medical Care, American Economic Review 53 (5): 941–973.

Arrow, Kenneth (1968), The Economics of Moral Hazard: Further Comment, American Economy Review, 58: 537-539.

Austin, John L. (1962), How to do things with words, (Oxford University Press: Oxford).

Baker, Tom (1996), On the Genealogy of Moral Hazard, Texas Law Review 75 (2): 237-292.

Baudrillard, Jean (2012) [1981], Simulacres et Simulation, in Korean translated by Tae-hwan Ha (Minumsa: Korea).

Bourdieu, Pierre (2020) [2001], Language and Symbolic Power [Langage et Pouvoir Symbolique], in Korean translated by Kim Hyeon-kyung (Nanam: Korea).

Bowen, Howard R., (1953) *Social responsibilities of the businessman,* (Harper & Row: New York, NY).

Brealy, Richard A. and Stewart C. Myers (2003), Principles of Corporate Finance, International Edition, 7th ed (McGraw-Hill: New York, NY).

Carroll, Archie B. (1979). A three-dimensional conceptual model of corporate social performance. Academy of Management Review 4: 497–505.

Carroll, Archie B. (2016), Carroll's pyramid of CSR: taking another look, International Journal of Corporate Social Responsibility, Article Number 3.

Choi, Won-Oh (2019), [Social Doctrine of the Church Fathers] (31) The Sin of Usury, *Catholic Peace Newspaper* No.1525 (2019.07.28), https://www.cpbc.co.kr/CMS/newspaper/

view_body.php?cid=758489&path=201907.

Coase, Ronald H. (1937), The Nature of the Firm, Economica 4(16): 386-405.

Coase, Ronald H. (1960), The Problem of Social Cost, Journal of Law and Economics 3 (1): 1-44. https://doi.org/10.1111/j.1468-0335.1937.tb00002.x.

Dahlsrud, Alexander (2006). How corporate social responsibility is defined: an analysis of 37 definitions. Corporate Social Responsibility and Environmental Management 15: 1–13.

Deleuze, Gilles (1992), Postscript on the Societies of Control, *October* 59: 3-7.

Deleuze, Gilles and Felix Guattari (2003) [1980], A Thousand Plateaus [Capitalisme et Schizophrénie 2. Mille Plateaux], in Korean translated by Jae-in Kim (Saemulgyeol: Korea).

Deleuze, Gilles and Felix Guattari (2014) [1972], Anti-Oedipus [Capitalisme et schizophrénie. L'anti-Œdipe], in Korean translated by Kim Jae-in (Minumsa: Korea).

Douglas, Mary (2001)[1966], Purity and Danger (Taylor & Francis e-Library)

Douglas, Mary and Aaron Wildavsky (1983), Risk and Culture: An Essay on the Selection of Technical and Environmental Dangers (University of California Press: Berkeley and Los Angeles).

Durkheim, Emile (2014) [1893], The Division of Labor in Society (Free Press: New York, NY)

Ewald, François (1991), Insurance and risks, in Burchell, Gordon, Miller (eds), The Foucault Effect: Studies in Governmentality (U of Chicago Press: Chicago): 197-210.

Ewald, François (1999), The Return of the Crafty Genius: An Outline of a Philosophy of Precaution, Connecticut Insurance Law Journal 6: 47-79.

Fama, Eugene. F. and Michael C. Jensen (1983). Separation of Ownership and Control. Journal of Law and Economics, 26 (2): 301-325.

Ferguson, Niall (2008), The Ascent of Money: A Financial

History of the World (Penguin Books: New York, NY).

Foss, Nicolai J. (1993), Tests of the firm: contractual and competence perspectives, Journal of Evolutionary Economics 3: 127-144.

Foucault, Michel (1991), Governmentality, in Burchell, Gordon, Miller (eds), *The Foucault Effect: Studies in Governmentality* (U of Chicago Press: Chicago, IL): 87-104.

Foucault, Michel (2012a) [1966], Words and Things [Les mots et les choses: une archeologie des sciences humaines], in Korean translated by Kyuhyun Lee, (Minumsa: Korea)

Foucault, Michel (2012b) [2004], Birth of life management politics [Naissance de la biopolitique], in Korean translated by Autrement (Nanjang: Korea)

Freeman, R. Edward (1984), Strategic Management: A Stakeholder Approach (Harpercollins: New York, NY).

Freud, Sigmund (1961) [1920], Beyond the Pleasure Principle, translated by James Strachey (W. W. Norton & Company: New York, NY)

Friedman, Milton (1970), The Social Responsibility of Business is to Increase its Profits, New York Times Magazine (1970.9.13), http://umich.edu/~thecore/doc/Friedman.pdf.

Friedman, Milton (2007) [1962], Capitalism and Freedom, translated by Sim Jun-bo and Byeon Dong-yeol, (Cheongeoram Media) [University of Chicago Press: Chicago, IL]

Geisst, Charles R. (2013), Beggar Thy Neighbor: A History of Usury and Debt, (University of Pennsylvania Press: Philadelphia, PA)

Girard, René (2007) [1982], The Scapegoat [Le bouc émissaire], in Korean translated by Kim, Jin-sik (Minumsa: Korea).

Graeber, David (2011), Debt: The First 5000 Years, (Melville House: Brooklyn, NY).

Hart, Keith (2000), The Memory Bank: Money in an Unequal World, (Profile Books: London, UK).

Hawkes, David (2019), Against Finance Derivatives: Towards an ethics of Representation, Journal of Interdisciplinary Economics 31 (2): 165–182.

Hollander, Jacob H. (1903), The Residual Claimant Theory, Quarterly Journal of Economics 17 (2): 261-279.

Jang, Deok-Jo (2017), *Corporate Law*, 3rd Edition, in Korean, (Bobmunsa: Korea).

Jensen, Michael C. (2001), Value Maximization, Stakeholder Theory, and the Corporate Objective Function, Journal of Applied Corporate Finance 14 (3): 8-21.

Jensen, Michael C. and William H. Meckling (1976), Theory of the Firm: Managerial Behavior, Agency Costs and Ownership Structure, Journal of Financial Economics 3 (4): 305-360.

Knight, Frank H. (2009) [1921] Risk, Uncertainty, and Profit (Signalman Publishing: Orland, FL).

Keynes, John M. (2016) [1936], Employment, Interest and The General Theory of Employment, Interest and Money, in Korean translated by Cho, Soon (Bibong Publishing: Korea).

Kim, Geon-Sik, Hyuk-Jun Noh, Jun Park, Ok-Ryeol Song, Soo-Hyun Ahn, Young-Shin Yoon, and Moon-Hee Choi (2018), *Shinchegye Hoesabup* [New Systematic Corporate Law], 7th edition (Park Young Sa: Korea).

Langrick, Roger (2010), A Monetary System for the New Millennium, http://www.worldtrans.org/whole/monetarysystem.html.

Levi-Strauss, Claude (1998) [1955], Tristes Tropiques, in Korean translated by Park, Ok-jul (Hangilsa: Korea).

Levitt, Theodore (1958), The dangers of social responsibility, Harvard business review 36 (September- October): 41–50.

Luhmann, Niklas (1993), Risk: A Sociological Theory (de Gruyter: Berlin, Germany).

Marx, Karl (1867, 1885, 1894), Capital: A Critique of Political Economy [Das Kapital: Kritik der politischen Ökonomie], translated by Samuel Moore and Edward Aveling, http://en.wikisource.org/wiki/Das_Kapital.

Mauss, Marcel (2000) [1925], The Gift: The Form and Reason for Exchange in Archaic Societies, English translated by WD Halls (1990), (Routledge: London, UK).

Merriam-Webster, https://www.merriam-webster.com/.

Nietzsche, Friedrich (2002) [1887], *Genealogy of Morals [Zur Genealogie der Moral]*, (from Nietzsche's Complete Works 14: Beyond the Good Covenant & Genealogy of Morals), in Korean translated by Kim, Jeong-hyeon (Chaeksesang: Korea).

Oxford English Dictionary, https://www.oed.com/.

Park, Jeong-Sik, Jong-Won Park, and Jaeho Cho (2015), *Hyundai Jaemugwanri* [Modern Financial Management], 8th edition, (Dasan Publishing: Korea).

Parkes, D. C., and M. P. Wellman. 2015. Economic Reasoning and Artificial Intelligence, *Science* 349 (6245) (July 16): 267–272. doi:10.1126/science.aaa8403. http://dx.doi.org/10.1126/science.aaa8403 .

Pauly, Mark V. (1968), The Economics of Moral Hazard: Comment, American Economic Review, 58: 531-537.

Plato (2013), *Politeia*, (Plato's Complete Works 4), in Korean translated by Cheon, Byeong-Hee (Soop Publishing).

Polanyi, Karl (2001) [1944], The Great Transformation: The Political and Economics Origins of Our Time, (Beacon Press: Boston, MA).

Rowell, David and Luke B. Connelly (2012), A History of the Term Moral Hazard, Journal of Risk and Insurance 79 (4): 1051-1075.

Saussure, Ferdinand de (1959) [1916], Course in General Linguistics, Eds. by Charles Bally and Albert Sechehaye, translated by Wade Baskin (Philosophical Library: New York, NY).

Schinckus, Christophe (2008), The Financial Simulacrum: The Consequences of the Symbolization and the Computerization of the Financial Market, *Journal of Socio-Economics* 37: 1076–1089.

Searle, John (1965), Chapter 2. What is a Speech Act?, *Philosophy in America*, Maurice Black (ed.), (Allen and Unwin: London, UK): 221-239.

Searle, John (1969), *Speech Acts: An Essay in the Philosophy of Language*, (Cambridge University Press: Cambridge).

Seog, S. Hun (2014), *Gyeongyounghak Mueosle Malhaeya*

Haneunga [What Should Business Studies Say], (Wisdom House: Korea)

Seog, S. Hun (2018a), Firm Value: Its Fairness and the Confusion of Language, *Review of Fair Economy* 3 (4) (2018.12), #1: 1-18.

Seog, S. Hun (2018b), Risk and Insurance Demand in a Two-Time Setting, Working Paper.

Seog, S. Hun (2020a), After COVID-19: Risks, Debt and Desire, *Seoul National University Entrepreneurship Center Newsletter* (2020.06.22), https://snubiz1.tistory.com/31, http://ect.snu.ac.kr/.

Seog, S. Hun (2020b), Information Revolution and Insurance Ethos, Working Paper.

Seog, S. Hun (2020c), *Risky Risk* (Seoul National University Press: Korea).

Slovic, Paul (1987), Perception of Risk, Science 236: 280-285.

Slovic, Paul, Melissa L. Finucane, Ellen Peters, and Donald G. MacGregor (2004), Risk as Analysis and Risk as Feelings: Some Thoughts about Affect, Reason, Risk, and Rationality, Risk Analysis 24 (2): 311-322.

Smith, Adam (2001) [1776], The Wealth of Nations [An Inquiry into the Nature and Causes of the Wealth of Nations], (A Penn State Electronic Classics Series Publication).

Smith, Karl (2012), From Dividual and Individual Selves to Porous Subjects, Australian Journal of Anthropology 23: 50-64.

Steinmetz, Greg (2015), The Richest Man Who Ever Lived: The Life and Times of Jacob Fugger (Simon & Schuster: New York, NY).

Stiglitz, Joseph E. (1993), Economics, (W. W. Norton and Company: New York, NY)

Weber, Max (1930) [1904-5], The Protestant Ethics and the Spirit of Capitalism, English translated by Talcott Parsons, (Routledge London: UK).

Weber, Max (2019) [1919], Politics as a profession [Politik als Beruf], in Korean translated by Jeon, Seong-woo (Nanam: Korea).

www.ingramcontent.com/pod-product-compliance
Lightning Source LLC
Chambersburg PA
CBHW071536200326
41519CB00021BB/6509

* 9 7 9 8 9 9 4 6 5 4 5 1 4 *